CHARIOTS OF MAHABHARATA

UNTOLD STORY OF MAHABHARATA

Himanshu Rai

Invincible Publishers

First published in India in 2017 by Invincible Publishers

ISBN: 978-93-86148-48-3

Invincible Publishers
G - 120, Sushant Lok III, Sector 57, Gurgaon-122002

Opposite Kasturba Ashram, Radaur Distt Yamuna Nagar, Haryana- 135133

Dedicated To

1 billion, 660 million, and 20 thousand men, who perished in a war of Mahabharata, to save Dharma.

Special thanks
Love you always

To my dear wife Sona and son Rhythm. Sharing our life along this journey together is a blessing beyond words.

You both kept patience and listened to the story of my novel. Your support kept me motivated and inspired me even on the darkest days.

Thank you both for always being with me.

Acknowledgement

No words can thank the man behind what I am today: My Father Late Shri Prafulla Kumar Rai.

Thanks to Invincible Publishers for believing in me and helping me shape my story into a beautiful piece. I big thank you to Ajay Setia for guiding me from time-to-time. Thanks to Cheena for editing my script and giving me your valuable suggestions.

Sneha, you designed it so well. Thank you.

Thanks to my relatives, friends and my telecom colleagues for their never-ending support.

I express my deep sense of gratitude to my mother Meera Rai, for inspiring me to keep writing.

Prologue

Mohoriti recognized him and, suddenly, it was a total blackout in front of his eyes. His body temperature started rising. He started feeling a burning sensation all over his body. He closed his eyes and saw an entire hut burning with his sons, Maaru, Duru, Indriya and Tejaswa, present inside. He could see Pandavas and Kauravs burning to fumes and converting to ashes. His eyes turned red and he could smell the bodies burning. He was sweating blood. He could feel the souls of dead soldiers gathering in that hut. He could also feel the dead bodies and the body parts of the slaughtered soldiers piling up there.

He scorned his existence. It seemed to him as if he was standing in a pool of blood and was drowning slowly into it. He felt like he had entered hell. Among all these dark pictures filled with fire, smoke and dead bodies, he saw a bright, white light behind Shree Krishna, who was standing at the centre.

Shree Krishna smiled while looking at him and said, "What are you waiting for Mohoriti? These dead peoples' souls and bodies are waiting for Antyesti. Please help them burn to ashes. It's the time for purification."

Mohoriti kept on looking at that dark picture and could not hear the sounds of the external world. He picked up the woods, which he was carrying on his back, and started arranging them around the blind king, Drithrastrya. He seemed to be in a subconscious stage. He was working as if he was following some orders. Drithrastrya kept on asking him, “Who are you? What are you doing?”, but Mohoriti continued arranging the wood around him.

Drithrastrya shouted and shook him, but didn’t receive any answer from him. Mohoriti’s state of mind was not under his control. Drithrastrya shouted at him, “Stop! What are you doing? Kunti, Gandhari, Vidhura, where are you all; stop this man! Something is not correct here!” He tried to hit Mohoriti with a wood log, which came handy to him, but still could not stop him.

Mohoriti, then, picked a firelight placed at the corner of the room in order to perform Antyesti. Drithrastrya understood what was coming with the approaching heat of the firelight and he started running around out fast, hitting himself to the wood poles and the wood logs placed all over him. He fell on the ground as a result of his efforts. He stood up again and tried to run, but this time Mohoriti held him. He seized Drithrastrya and squeezed him with all his strength, thereby crushing his arms. In the end, he placed the firelight on the wood logs he placed in the hut.

Chapter-1
Curse to Mohoma

Period: 1000 BCE

It was getting dark. Cold wind rustled the leaves of the tall trees covering each side of the River Ganga, spreading the fragrance of freesia, phlox, sweet peas, scented daffodils, rosemary herb, lavender, tuberose and rose flowers all across the forest.

Clouds turned dark and struck with each other, creating thunder and lightning. The sky was getting dark with crimson dusk in twilight setting in.

From the long, high green grasses came running a beautiful golden deer with long brown horns, smelling of *kasturi* or musk. Behind it came a chariot pulled by four big black horses, all galloping simultaneously. The deer sprinted from the bushes, running for his life and trying to evade the chase from the chariot.

A nine feet tall and handsome king, Shantanu, with his foot set firm on the chariot, had his arrow fit against the bowstring and target set at the golden deer, which was running hither and thither in front of him.

Shantanu was a Kuru king of Hastinapura. He was a descendant of the Bharata race of the Lunar dynasty. He was the youngest son of

King Pratipa of Hastinapura and had been born in Pratipa's old age. The eldest son, Devapi, was suffering from leprosy and had relinquished his inheritance to become a hermit. The middle son, Bahlika, abandoned his paternal kingdom and started living with his maternal uncle in Balkh and inherited the kingdom there from him. Shantanu became the king of Hastinapura by default.

The golden deer started running towards the bank of the River Ganga and was constantly being followed by the chariot of King Shantanu. While the deer was running with all his might, the tides from the River Ganga kept sweeping against his feet, as if trying to stop him for the King Shantanu.

Following the chariot of King Shantanu was another chariot of his courtier, Mohoma. Mohoma was very close to King Shantanu and was more of a friend than a courtier. He was the person who guided King Shantanu on his day-to-day decisions and actions.

Mohoma was riding in his chariot behind the king's, both his horses trying to keep up with him. Mohoma was ready with a sword in his hand, while minding the control of the chariot. Behind him were other soldiers, who were covering up to protect their king.

King Shantanu's eyes constantly followed the golden deer, which was running and jumping. He pulled the bowstring on which an arrow was already set and, now, after observing for some time, he relaxed his fingers to release the arrow. The arrow moved with the speed of light and before the golden deer could jump again, it pierced his left leg. The deer took a long jump and fell on the ground. The king's chariot reached close to the deer and the charioteer pulled the ropes to stop the horses. The horses raised their front legs up in the air to stop.

King Shantanu didn't step out from his chariot. He took off the case carrying his bow and arrows and kept it aside. Mohoma's chariot also reached the site. He immediately stepped down from his chariot and treaded towards King Shantanu.

Mohoma bowed before King Shantanu and spoke politely, "King! Congratulations for your precise aim; it was amazing to see you hunt such a fast animal. I request you to proceed toward the palace along with the soldiers while I search and seize the deer and bring to you for your dinner tonight."

Wind started blowing fiercely now and it was quite dark. Mohoma kept looking at King Shantanu moving away till he disappeared slowly behind the tall trees. He turned back and asked one of the soldiers to search for the deer, which fell somewhere on the long green grass at the side of the River Ganga.

Mohoma walked few steps and reached the bank of the river and started feeling the fresh air and the smell of flowers on this victory.

Suddenly, one of the soldiers came running to him and said, "Sir, you need to come and see this deer, it's glowing like white moonlight; please come along with me."

Mohoma turned towards him and asked him the whereabouts of the deer's body. He started following the soldier along the long green grass. As he reached closer, he saw bright light coming from the grasses, emitting a white ray in to the dark background.

Mohoma was an intelligent person. While he was removing the grass beside the deer, his eyes fell on that of the deer, which were still blinking. He asked his soldiers to get back to the chariot and wait for him there.

He waited till all the soldiers went away and, then, moved his hands to touch the deer. As he touched it, the light emitting it brightened manifolds. Mohoma took a step back and covered his eyes with his hand. Within a few seconds, from that light appeared a beautiful lady. Mohoma moved his hand from his face and looked at her with awe standing still on the ground. She stood in front of him, staring with her eyes wide open. He had never seen such a beautiful lady before. He thought she might be a goddess. He joined his hands and bowed before her.

"Who are you, Devi?" he asked in astonishment.

"I am a celestial nymph, Devapima, from the court of Lord Indra."

He bowed his head again hearing her words as she continued.

"About two hundred years ago, I made a mistake and laughed at Lord Indra and he cursed me to be born as a mortal. I begged him to send me on earth as a deer and he agreed. He had pity on me and even told me that one day, a king will come and hunt me down and that day, I will be released from the curse and will be taken back to the heaven."

She continued to speak while Mohoma quietly listened, "Your king unknowingly attempted at breaking my curse by trying to hunt me down but you interrupted him and asked him to go back to the palace without having me killed completely. Due of this, I will, now, have to again take birth as a deer and will have to wait for another two hundred years when your fourth generation would come and hunt me down."

Mohoma got frightened and pleaded with her, "Devi, I was doing my duty towards my king; please consider my request and do not curse me."

Devapima continued hearing him plead and said, "It is because of you that I will have to suffer for another two hundred years. Mohoma, you followed your king; your punishment is that yours and your family's life will always be affected by the move of your king and his family till the time I don't go back to the heaven having being hunted by your fourth generation. I will continue to suffer for next two hundred years but I am giving you a chance to create your own destiny, as you were doing your duty. I will tell you something about your king's past and something about his future as well. Now, you'll have to create your own destiny with that."

"In his previous birth, Shantanu was a powerful king named Mahabhisha of the Ikshvaku dynasty. Mahabhisha possessed many virtuous qualities and after performing a thousand Ashvamedha Yagnas (horse sacrifices) and a hundred Rajasuya Yagnas (to qualify as an emperor), he was also able to attain heaven after his death. Once, he got an opportunity to visit the court of Brahma where all the Devas along with Ganga were present. While the celestials were worshipping Brahma, wind blew and stripped Ganga off her clothes revealing her body. Everybody present ingloriously bowed their heads, except for Mahabhisha, who continued gazing at her body. Upon seeing this act, Brahma lost his temper and cursed him to be born as a mortal, when Ganga would cause much emotional pain to him. Mahabhisha then begged Brahma to let him be born as the son of Kuru king, Pratipa, and got his wish granted.

The Kuru king, Pratipa, was once meditating in order to seek atonement for the crime he had committed by seizing the throne of Hastinapur. At that time, Ganga appeared as a beautiful woman, approached the king and sat on his right thigh. He stopped meditating and asked her what she wanted. Ganga requested him to become her husband. Pratipa, however, refused since he had taken a vow not to lust after women; also, she had sat on his right thigh, which according to the traditions is the space meant for his daughter or daughter-in-law while the left thigh was for the wife. He, then, proposed to her to get married to his son and she agreed.

A child was born to Pratipa and his wife in their old age. He was named Shantanu, as when he was born, his father had controlled his passions by ascetic penances.

Ganga would come back for him; that is only what I can reveal. I hope this helps in making your life.

While Mohoma kept looking at her, she vanished with her light in the darkness of a forest near Hastinapur.

Mohoma was not able to understand what had happened. He felt miserable and stupefied for some time and was also worried about the curse.

He stood up and looked at the sky which was turning even darker and the clouds were striking to produce thunders. He moved towards his chariot and asked his charioteer to take him to the palace.

The charioteer pulled the rope, started moving towards the palace and soon increased the speed of the galloping horses.

The big doors of the palace opened on the arrival of Mohoma. His chariot moved inside; he stepped down and went ahead to meet King Shantanu.

On his way, one of the maids stopped him and said, "Sir, King Shantanu has asked you to meet him in the war room immediately."

Kings usually moved to the war room when some security concern was raised against the land or when they wanted to discuss some invasion.

Mohoma understood that there must be some problem with their neighboring states. He made his way towards the war room, which had long wide corridors with big ancient statues of Kuru dynasty on both the sides.

After every ten steps, there were firelights installed on the strong stone walls making the atmosphere bizarre and yellow, with guards standing at every corner. He even thought of informing the king about the golden deer.

As he reached outside the war room, guards opened the door for him. Before he could speak anything, the king stated, "Mohoma, we have a situation here."

"Yes, my lord?" He asked.

"We have received information that Trigarta Kingdom, which is to our north, is moving with his army towards Hastinapur and we need to work out a plan to stop them." He continued, "Trigarta kingdom has always been our friend; I wonder what made them do this. I don't want a war with them."

There were two different Trigarta kingdoms: one at the west, close to the Sivi Kingdom, and the other at the north of the Kuru Kingdom. The territory of Trigarta kingdom was spread around the three rivers of Sutlej, Beas, and Ravi.

Mohoma listened to him and, then, replied "My Lord, as per the information I'd received a few months ago, rivers Sutlej and Beas had flooded the Trigarta Kingdom and there was dire scarcity of food. We need to check first whether they coming to attack or seek some help."

"Good, Mohoma! You may be correct. Please reach out to them immediately and let me know their intentions. Go there as a peacemaker." King Shantanu commanded Mohoma.

By merely adopting a virtuous behavior, Shantanu could easily conquer the entire world without having to use any weapons and this was his best quality.

Mohoma lived in a house outside the palace with his parents. Before moving to Trigarta Kingdom, he asked for permission from king to visit his home so that he could carry along some necessities. King Shantanu allowed him.

Mohoma boarded his chariot and asked his charioteer to take him to Vanasaki's house. Vanasaki was the woman whom he loved a lot and was also planning to marry soon. He wanted to meet her before he left for his venture.

Vanasaki was a fisherman's daughter and Mohoma had fallen in love with her at the first sight and, also, desired to marry her. On asking for the permission to marry her, her father had agreed on a condition that Vanasaki continues living in the same town to support her old father, who was physically challenged.

Mohoma respected Vanasaki's father's thoughts and agreed to his condition as he was deeply in love with Vanasaki and did not want to lose her. Vanasaki also reciprocated the same feelings for Mohoma.

Mohoma reached the bank of River Ganga where Vanasaki was waiting for him.

Mohoma's chariot reached the bank of the river, where he saw her carrying lantern in her hand. She was looking beautiful in the reflection of the yellow light. She'd covered her head with the hem of her white sari.

Mohoma stepped down from his chariot and moved towards her. As he reached closer, she hung the lantern on the tree behind her and ran into his arms

Without speaking a word, she expressed her love to Mohoma. He, too, took her in his embrace.

"I am moving tonight to Trigarta", he said while still hugging her.

Hearing this, she freed herself from his embrace and asked him, "When will you be back?"

"I cannot say, but I'll try to come soon to marry you." Mohoma replied.

They spent some time together and, also, made love that night. Then, he stood up to leave as he had to set out early the next day. Mohoma was worried about the curse pronounced to him but he buried that deep in his heart.

He, then, bade adieu to Vanasaki and steered his chariot towards Trigarta.

The next day, he reached the border of Hastinapur where Trigarta's army was waiting to attack.

Mohoma's chariot had a white flag hoisted at its top to convey that he was here for peace talks.

He asked his charioteer to stop at a distance as he wanted to analyze the strength of Trigarta army. He could see hundreds of elephants (Gaja), numerous chariots (Ratha), hundreds of horses (Ashwa) and five soldiers on foot (Padhata) and, then, he saw a lot of men accompanied by women and kids.

He understood that he was correct in guessing the reason behind their arrival here. The people of Trigarta had taken this step for the survival of their progeny.

He asked his charioteer to move towards the camp of Trigarta and the charioteer followed his orders.

On seeing him nearing them, Trigarta army took their position to attack, but understood the message conveyed by the white flag.

His chariot moved fast between the wide valleys to reach the valley floor where Trigarta army was stationed. The valley was between tall hills covered with tall, green pine trees, which made it appear dark green in color.

Mohoma was a tall man with wide shoulders and long beard. His long hair was reaching beyond his shoulders. He stepped down without his weapons, his intention being to be friendly and not to show them Hastinapur's strength.

Mohoma took long steps and reached where the guard was standing. He asked him to give a message to the king of Trigarta that the peacemaker from Hastinapur was here to have a word.

The guard moved inside one of the camps, while Mohoma waited outside and tried to analyze the strength of Trigarta. The guard came out and asked Mohoma to come along with him to which he agreed.

Mohoma entered the camp and saw Kshemankara sitting on his throne. Kshemankara was a tall and handsome king with a powerful physique. In his camp, Kshemankara was having a bowl full of almonds, cashews and other dry fruits.

"Welcome, Mohoma!" spoke Kshemankara while picking up one handful of almonds.

Mohoma joined his hand and said, "Kowtow" and continued, "I am here to know the reason why Trigarta army is moving towards Hastinapur. Trigarta and Hastinapur have always shared a friendly relation with each other; then, what made you take this step? We can talk and find a solution to any issues you might be facing."

Kshemankara stood up from his throne and stepped towards Mohoma. He was taller than Mohoma. He kept one of his hands on Mohoma's shoulders and replied, "I understand what you're saying, Mohoma, and I am still a friend of Shantanu. Our progeny was suffering since long because of the floods and our dear friend from Hastinapur never came to help us."

He took a pause and turned towards Mohoma, "so, we thought

of notifying you."

Mohoma replied, "My Lord, I will take your message to the king of Hastinapur and I am sure he will not miss a single chance to stand with you and your progeny in your difficult times. Let me take your message and come back to you with what our king has to say. I hope you will understand and accept my proposal."

Kshemankara looked at him and held both his shoulders and added, "I will wait for the next two suns and, then, my armies will be commanded to proceed."

Mohoma bowed before him and asked to take a leave. His charioteer began moving his chariot towards Hastinapur.

Hastinapur and Trigarta had a very long relation. The father of Kshemankara was a very good friend of King Pratipa, the father of King Shantanu. Shantanu and Kshemankara had spent many beautiful days together during their childhood and were there for each other in need.

Mohoma returned to Hastinapur the next day and asked for a permission to meet King Shantanu. Mohoma briefed him on the complete situation.

After listening and understanding the complete picture, King Shantanu asked his courtier to get ready to move to meet Kshemankara. His courtier immediately took the orders and made the arrangements. King Shantanu did not waste any time and moved with his caravan in the night itself, so that they could reach on time.

His caravan was accompanied by hundred horses, fifty elephants, hundred soldiers and twenty courtiers. Besides, he carried stock of food and fruits for the progeny of Trigarta.

Kshemankara gave time for two suns while Shantanu had made it after the first sun itself; his caravan had run without stopping to reach as fast as possible.

As his caravan reached the floor of valley where Trigarta army was stationed, Kshemankara came out of camp and stood in front of the chariot of King Shantanu to greet him. King Shantanu stepped out from his chariot and before Kshemankara could utter a word, said to him, "I am sorry my friend for provoking you to take this step. The complete empire of Hastinapur and Kuru dynasty is here for Trigarta."

Kshemankara stepped forward and took Shantanu in his arms.

"Thank you, my friend! We, Trigarta people, are obliged to you and we are sorry for asking for help in such a way."

They both placed their free hands on each other's shoulders and moved inside the camp.

After discussing for some time about the situation with Kshemankara, Shantanu addressed his courtier and the progeny of Trigarta, "Progeny of Trigarta and my courtiers! Kuru and Trigarta share friendly relations from our forefather's times and it's our responsibility to continue and maintain the same. Kuru dynasty has always been there and will always be for Trigarta dynasty. I would like to declare hereby that till the next full moon, Hastinapur will be supplying food, fruits and other daily necessities to Trigarta without any fail. The people of Trigarta are our people and we will take care of you as our own. Mohoma, one of my courtiers, will be residing in Trigarta to manage the complete plan and will stay there till my next order. We are friends with the people of Trigarta and we will do our best to bring you out from this situation. We'll perform Indra Yagna to please Lord Indra so that he can help us to come out from this problem soon."

King Shantanu completed addressing the audience but his words shattered the life plans of Mohoma. Mohoma had planned to get married to Vanasaki after his return, but as per the king's order, he needed to stay in Trigarta till he hears next from the king. His plans were all shattered. He looked at Vyom to imagine how he would continue living without Vanasaki in Trigarta.

He requested the king to allow him to visit Hastinapur once, so that he could make some important arrangements for his family and, then, return to Trigarta. The king agreed and allowed him to go but, also, asked him to take the full control of the situation and keep him updated.

Mohoma thanked the king and started planning his travel back to Hastinapur.

He reached Hastinapur and planned to meet Vanasaki's father to discuss arranging his marriage with Vanasaki without any delay.

Mohoma's chariot reached Vanasaki's, house, which was on the bank of River Ganga. Her house was built of stone and mud and was decorated with beautiful paintings of flowers and with peacock feathers. Belonging to a fisherman, the house had a lot of pictures depicting water bodies. Vanasaki's house was beautiful just like her and was surrounded by tall trees and long grasses. The deer and the squirrels roaming around made the house look even more picturesque.

As she saw Mohoma's chariot reach outside her house, she ran inside and informed her father. Before Mohoma stepped out of the chariot, Vanasaki's father came out of the house, greeted him and welcomed him inside.

Mohoma, hailing from an upper caste, always had the upper hand. Mohoma also joined his hands and bowed before Vanasaki's father with respect.

He took his seat, which was made of tree root. He said, "Father, I think it's the right time that I and Vanasaki get married."

Vanasaki's father looked at him awe as Mohoma continued, "You may start the preparations for the wedding; I will leave again for Trigarta tomorrow and will be back after the next full moon. You have sufficient time for making the arrangements. We will get married on the third day after the next full moon."

Vanasaki's father did not speak a word. Instead, he went inside the kitchen and returned after few minutes with sweets made of fish and flower juice.

"Son, this is amazing news! I assure you, your Vanasaki will be ready for you on the third day after the next full moon." Vanasaki's father told Mohoma.

Mohoma smiled and picked a sweet and turned around to see if Vanasaki was hearing from the inside. He could hear the sound of her ornaments from behind the door.

He joined his hands before leaving and moved towards his chariot. Mohoma finally moved to Trigarta on his duty.

Mohoma started coordinating on the daily help being received from Hastinapur and managed the distribution. Meanwhile, he also spent his nights thinking about Vanasaki. The day when he would return to Hastinapur and marry Vanasaki was approaching fast.

Chapter-2
The Ganga Effect

Once, Shantanu came across a beautiful lady on the bank of the River Ganga and fell in love with her at the first sight. She was Goddess Ganga. Shantanu immediately asked her to marry him and she agreed, too, but on a condition that he would not question her on her actions, whatever they may be. Shantanu agreed to this and married her.

Mohoma came to know about his king's marriage, but could not make it to the wedding because of his involvement in Trigarta. He was happy for his king and was, also, waiting to go back home as the time to return was nearing. He decided to write a letter to King Shantanu asking for his permission to return.

Soon Mohoma's messenger moved to Hastinapur with a message but Shantanu was totally lost in love with Ganga and did not find time to look at the message and revert. Mohoma's messenger returned without any answer.

Mohoma got upset and decided to send a message again after a few days. Time was passing fast and his marriage was nearing.

One of his close friends visited Trigarta and informed him that Vanasaki's father had made all the arrangements and everyone in Vanasaki's family was waiting for his return. Mohoma decided to send another message to the king. Alas! The messenger returned this time, too, without any confirmation from the king and told that the king was busy with Ganga and doesn't meet anyone or receive any messages.

Shantanu was lost in the beauty of Ganga and was not bothered about the things happening around.

Even the king's other courtiers also felt the distance from the king during this time and saw the situations turning chaotic.

Mohoma sent messages to the king regularly but didn't receive any reply. He was worried about his marriage as there was very little time left for his marriage.

Just before the day of Mohoma's marriage, his friend visited Trigarta once again to know his status. He told Mohoma that Vanasaki was worried and has been crying most of the time. She also sent a message to Mohoma that she was pregnant but she had hidden this news from everyone. She was worried if people in society would come to know about her pregnancy before marriage, she would be abandoned and might also get killed. She asked Mohoma to reach for the marriage on time at any cost.

Also, Vanasaki's father was worried and angry with Mohoma and he had declared that if Mohoma would not be available on the scheduled day of marriage, he would marry his daughter to his friend's son, Majhara, in Matsya.

Mohoma was worried about the message he'd received but was, also, happy to hear that Vanasaki was pregnant and would be giving birth to his child. He wrote a final letter to his king and waited for a reply.

Finally, it was the day of his marriage but he had not received any reply from King Shantanu. Lastly, he was shattered on hearing the news that Vanasaki was getting married to Majhara.

Vanasaki wrote a letter to Mohoma before she got married and told him that she didn't want to get wedded to Majhara but couldn't go against her father's wish. She didn't disclose that she was pregnant and will never disclose in future, too.

She moved to Matsya after her marriage, while Mohoma continued to wait for his king's order to return.

Mohoma's life was shattered and he cursed his king that he would also experience the same pain for love.

After some days passed, he got news from Hastinapur that the king's wife, Ganga, was expecting a baby and the king was very happy. He had asked Mohoma to be back in Hastinapur and look after the arrangements.

Mohoma received the message and was not at all excited. He had lost the love and desires of his life. He reached Hastinapur, obeying the orders.

He started performing his daily duties; however, every night he went to the bank of River Ganga to remember Vanasaki whom he would miss forever now.

One night, when he was getting nostalgic sitting on the bank of the river, he heard clinking sound of bangles and a few ornaments. He turned around to check who was coming. He saw Ritikawali, a friend of Vanasaki and a person who knew Mohoma since a long time. She came near Mohoma and spoke, "I see you every night here missing Vanasaki; she is gone now and will never come back."

Mohoma kept looking at the river waves.

While wind was blowing slowly carrying the fragrance of flowers with it , Ritikawali came closer to Mohoma and touched his shoulder.

Her touch brought a new height in the waves in Mohoma's heart; he turned back to her and looked into her deep, black eyes. She was looking beautiful wearing ornaments made up of elephant teeth and flowers.

She was looking like a goddess in the moonlight.

She came a little closer to him and showed him her love. Mohoma held her hand and asked if she would marry him and her eyes answered everything.

While she turned back to move, she told Mohoma that Vanasaki had given birth to the twins named, Chintan and Mahantam.

Mohoma got very happy to know that his children have been born but, on the other hand, he was upset, too, that he would not be able to give his name to them.

He decided to move on and married Ritikawali.

Meanwhile, Ganga gave birth to a son, but she drowned him in River Ganga soon after his birth. Shantanu could not ask her the reason because of his promise, but he was heartbroken having lost his son.

Mohoma met his king and asked him if he was able to know why the queen had drowned their son but Shantanu, who was caged in his promise, had no answer to it.

He replied to Mohoma, "It's destiny; that's all I can say."

Mohoma was worried for his king and his progeny as his personal problems were affecting Hastinapur's development and happiness.

Once, Ritikawali was alone in the forest, searching for wood to make food. It was a dense forest inhabiting many wild animals. She carried a bow and arrows for her protection. Walking in middle of the dark forest with tall trees all around, she could hear the sounds made by the wild animals; but, she, being the daughter of a brave warrior, was not afraid of anyone. Suddenly, she saw a calf caught by a crocodile at the corner of the river. The cow was standing at some distance.

The crocodile was big enough and his strong claws held the calf with all their strength. The calf was trying to free itself with all its might and crying loudly with pain and fear.

Ritikawali could not resist herself on this sight and immediately pulled out her bow and arrow and aimed at the crocodile.

The bow pierced the crocodile's stomach and it let the calf free. The calf ran towards its mother and she started licking the wounds of her child. As Ritikawali reached closer, the cow transformed into a goddess.

Ritikawali immediately bowed before her. Goddess asked her to look at her and said, "I am a goddess from the court of Lord Vishnu. I wanted to test you on the grounds of mercy. I am impressed by your caring and concerned attitude towards animals. I bless you that you will give birth to twenty sons, who will all be as brave as you, strong like the skin of crocodile and their presence will be marked in the future."

Ritikawali thanked the goddess and, following this, the goddess disappeared.

Ritikawali was happy to get the blessings from the goddess and, that night, she told this story to Mohoma, who was also very happy after hearing this.

In the next seven years, Ritikawali gave birth to twenty sons and her eldest son was named 'Mohoriti', alliteration from the names, Mohoma and Ritikawali.

Also, in these seven years, Ganga gave birth to seven sons, but she drowned each one of them in the river.

Shantanu was in deep pain after losing his sons one by one and had lost interest in his progeny and kingdom. He somehow regretted the promise he had made to Ganga but he still loved her.

During these seven years, many adjoining kingdoms tried to invade Hastinapur considering the loss in the focus of king Shantanu but Mohoma always led the army and controlled the situation. He never let the flag of Hastinapur go down.

Most of the wars were won by his diplomacy and not by actual fighting.

One day, he went to meet King Shantanu and upon seeing him worried, he asked "King, I am no one to ask you but looking at your condition, you need to think over, as your progeny is losing trust in their king. Adjoining kingdoms are regularly trying to take benefit of your absence."

Shantanu was left with no expression on his face. He said, "Friend, I still have no answer to your question as I am stuck between my love, Ganga, and my children".

"But you need to get the answers; it's about your successor now." Mohoma replied.

Shantanu listened to him but didn't reply.

After some months, Ganga gave birth to their eighth son and, as usual, took him to drown in the river. This time, devastated Shantanu could not refrain himself and confronted her.

Finally, she told Shantanu about Brahma's curse given to Mahabhisha, her antecedent from the previous birth. She also told him that her eight children were eight Vasus who were cursed by Vashistha to be born on earth as mortal humans; however, when they pacified him, Vashistha limited his curse and told them that they would be freed from this curse after their birth as humans.

She told him that she released seven of them from this earth by drowning in river but because of him, Vasu Dyaus is left now. He is cursed to live a long life with no wife or children.

She explained further, "Vasus was once led by Vasu Prithu to enjoy in the forest. The wife of Vasu Dyaus spotted a cow and found it very attractive. She persuaded her husband Dyaus to steal it for her. Dyaus, along with his brothers, stole that cow, which was owned by a sage, Vashistha . Vashistha had ascetic power and he had learned that Vasus had stolen his cow. He cursed them to be born on earth as mortals. But then, when Vasus pleaded before him for mercy, he responded that seven of the Vasus will be free from the curse soon after their births, but because Dyaus was the major culprit, he would have to pay the full penalty."

Ganga was requested to be born as their mother and freed them and that is why she had come to earth to give them birth. This was destiny; Ganga, also, informed Shantanu that she is taking Dyaus with her to heaven and will train him properly to become worthy of Shantanu's throne and the status of Hastinapur.

Shantanu was happy to have saved his son but was, also, sad as he was left with no one.

He fell on his knees and started weeping as Ganga took Dyaus in her arms, moved in the middle of the river and vanished. Shantanu could not control his feelings and burst out loud, making him audible till far distance. Mohoma, who was at some distance, ran towards his king and tried to control and console him. He managed to get his king on his feet and took him back to the palace.

The next few days, Shantanu was in deep pain and had restricted himself to a boudoir, while Mohoma was managing his progeny along with the other courtiers.

At the same time, Krivi tribe, which was spread from the bank of river Indus to a part of Panchal, was monitoring closely the political ups and downs in Hastinapur. Krivi tribe was a part of Panchal but was struggling to build its own existence. Krivi found this as an opportunity for them to extend their tribe to the kingdom.

Krivi tribe decided to invade Hastinapur and began moving with their small army towards them. Their army was very small but was in possession of a special poison, which could kill their rival soldiers within seconds.

They knew that Panchal would never agree for this invasion; so, they decided to move without the support of Panchal.

Soon, this information reached Hastinapur and Mohoma.

Mohoma informed Shantanu, but Shantanu showed no interest and concern.

Mohoma discussed this with the other courtiers and army chief of Hastinapur and prepared a plan. They decided to fight a war with Krivi. They were sure to defeat the small army of Krivi which stood nowhere in front of Hastinapur.

Mohoma asked the commander to get the army ready for the war.

In the next two days, Hastinapur's army was on the border facing Krivi army. Mohoma led the war along with the commander.

It was a bright sunny day. Both the armies stood a few miles away from each other in the lush green field. The flags of both the armies were visible from a distance. Krivi was a small army but was replete with confidence.

Hastinapur's army was huge and was accompanied by numerous elephants, horses, tigers and soldiers. Mohoma inspected the condition and was ready to defeat Krivi. With the blow of a conch shell, both the armies got ready and started moving slowly towards each other. Then, they stopped suddenly because of a command from their commander. King Shantanu had appeared from nowhere on a six-horse chariot carrying a flag. Shantanu had finally moved out from his boudoir and was back in action standing with his army to defeat the opponent.

Mohoma, having looked at his king, immediately stepped out from his chariot to move towards the king and show his happiness.

"Today, Krivi Tribe will be erased from the face of this earth." Shantanu roared in rage.

Krivi army stopped their movement looking at the big army of Panchal approaching from behind. Panchal army had appeared to show their loyalty towards their contemporary, Kuru, and make strong, friendly relations with them.

Panchal king commanded to blow the conch shell and, soon, Hastinapur and Panchal burst on Krivi army. Within a few moments, it was blood and bodies without heads lying on the earth. Krivi army was badly defeated having no existence left thereafter.

The area near Indus River which was a part of the Krivi tribe became a part of the Panchal Kingdom and they decided to protect and take care of Krivi tribes under their reign.

Shantanu decided to move on from his past and work for his progeny. He was happy with Mohoma and the support he had received from him while he was recovering from his pain.

In the next few years, Mohoma became an important courtier in King Shantanu's court and handled many important portfolios.

Mohoma noticed that Shantanu was very close to him and as Shantanu had no heir, Mohoma could take a chance to introduce his eldest son, Mohoriti, as Shantanu's successor.

Mohoma introduced Mohoriti to the king and asked him to be a part of the army drills. He also asked him to feature himself as a strong contender for the throne.

Mohoma's intentions were not bad, but he wanted a successor for Hastinapur and he could only see his son as the most eligible person to tackle this situation.

Shantanu appreciated the bravery and fighting skills of Mohoriti and, soon, even Mohoriti became very close to Shantanu. Shantanu always took Mohoriti along with him on forest tours before he had quit hunting when Ganga left him alone.

Once, when Shantanu, along with Mohoriti and Mohoma, was on tour to explore the forest surroundings of Hastinapur, he saw a strange thing. More than fifty trees had holes in their trunks at the same height and of the same diameter. They were so perfectly aligned that if you looked from one hole, you could see through the other side from the last tree's hole.

It seemed as if someone extremely skilled in archery had practiced on these trees. Shantanu got excited and desired to meet this expert, but as per the information from the tribes in the forest, it was done by a boy who had just disappeared.

One day, when Shantanu was walking along the bank of the River Ganga, he saw that the river had become shallow. He started walking along the river to find the cause. He, then, came across a handsome young boy who had checked the river's flow with his celestial weapon, but before Shantanu could ask him anything, he disappeared out of sight using his supernatural powers.

Shantanu bowed before Ganga and asked her to give him the answer about this mysterious boy. Ganga, thus, appeared in front of Shantanu and revealed to him that the boy was actually his son,

Devavrata, and that he was taught the knowledge of the holy scriptures by the sage Vashistha and the art of warfare by Lord Parshurama.

Shantanu was overjoyed on hearing and seeing his son. Ganga, then, asked Shantanu to take his son to Hastinapur. Shantanu took him to Hastinapur and declared him as his successor.

On hearing this, Mohoma's plans of making Mohoriti the successor of the throne were devastated. Although he was happy to see Devavrata back in Shantanu's life, but, somewhere in his mind, he felt defeated.

He, then, started comparing his son, Mohoriti, with Devavrata and found Devavrata better than his son in all the skills. He, then, asked his son, Mohoriti, to leave for Himalayas and practice austerity of Lord Parshurama, so that he could also gain the skills like that of Devavrata.

For the next four years, Mohoriti practiced austerity in tough conditions of extreme cold to make the Lord Parshuram happy and gain his blessings.

One fine day, when Mohoriti was lost in deep meditation, a beautiful lady came running towards him shouting for help, but he continued to close his eyes to be focused. She kept on asking for his help and pleaded in front of him. Finally, Mohoriti opened his eyes and saw a beautiful lady standing in front of him. She was beautiful like an angel with big, dark eyes, bejeweled with flowers and was sitting on her knees asking for help.

"What happened, lady?" he asked with strong voice.

"Sorry for disturbing you, but I need your help," she continued.

"I was taking bath in the nearby pond when some *rakshasas* came there and started abusing me. They are man-eaters and want to make me their food." she cried.

Mohoriti heard her words and, then, took his sword in his hand and moved towards the pond. Mohoriti was a tall man with wide shoulders. He was a perfect warrior. He stood on the top of the rock which oversaw snow spread all over.

He saw ten-fifteen *rakshasas* standing around the pond. While he was standing, his shadow fell on the *rakshasas*, forcing them to look at the might shadow cast on them. He was a perfect blend of light, snow and water and his large broad shadow reached till the other end of the pond.

Rakshasas looked at him and jumped to get him. He, too, jumped in the air and in his first move, cut the head of one of the *rakshasas* and threw it in the air.

Analyzing the power of Mohoriti, the *rakshasas* were completely shaken, but they still attacked on him with all their might.

Mohoriti jumped from one *rakshasa* to another, with so much aggression that the snow there started melting. There was so much power generated in each his hit that the snow around started melting, resulting in an increase in the water level.

When he held his sword and swung it towards them, his muscles got clenched and appeared like clouds shining with lightening.

Within a few minutes, the pond was red with blood and Mohoriti stood holding his blood-soaked sword in his hand.

As he turned towards the lady, he realized that the *rakshasas'* bodies were vanishing. He turned back again to check and it was all silent like before with no blood or bodies. He turned towards the lady and saw Lord Parshuram standing in front of him.

He kneeled down with his sword dug deep in earth and joined his hands.

"Get up, my boy," Parshuram asked Mohoriti.

Mohoriti stood up with his hands still joined to express his reverence.

"I am very happy with your austerity and fighting skills. Tell me what you wish from me."

"I want supreme power in my muscles to fight any war and live till I wish to die." Mohoriti requested.

"This wish will take you way ahead in your life and will also change the fate of your coming generation. You will fight till the end of your life with full power with all *astra-shastra*. Bless you!" said Parshuram and disappeared in the rocks.

Mohoriti was blessed and was, now, ready to take tough challenges to prove himself worthy for the throne. He moved back to Hastinapur and Mohoma was very happy to see his son blessed.

Chapter-3
Mohoriti, the warrior

Once upon a time, Mohoriti was traveling to the land of Lavanasura, named 'Madhuvan'. The name was kept after the thick woods present there. He saw a fisherman struggling in river Yamuna and expecting help. The fisherman's boat was inverted with some of the fishermen stuck within.

Mohoriti heard their voices and rushed to the bank. He saw high waves in the river and a boat stuck in the tide inverted. He also noticed a few fishermen trying to help and shouting from the corner.

He immediately got down from his horse and rushed to help them. He jumped straight in the river and swam to the bed of the river and back to the boat. He saw four-five fishermen stuck in the boat under water.

He swam upwards and held the boat's edges with his hands from both the sides and pushed the boat upwards turning it around. Fishermen, standing at the corner, were amazed to see Mohoriti's bravery and efforts.

He rescued all the trapped fishermen from the river and emerged standing straight in the high tides.

All the fishermen were happy and thanked him for saving

their lives.

One of the fishermen, named Dusharaj, came forward and thanked Mohoriti for saving his and his people's lives.

He asked, "Who are you, brave man, and where are you going?"

"I am Mohoriti, son of Mohoma, from Hastinapur and I am heading towards Madhuvan."

"You saved our lives and we would like to thank you. We request you to have food with us," Dusharaj insisted.

Mohoriti accepted the offer and joined them to their village.

While Mohoriti sat in Dusharaj's house, other fishermen stood around expressing their gratitude.

Mohoriti smelled a musky fragrance all the time while having food. After some time, one beautiful girl came out. Dusharaj introduced her as his daughter, Satyavati, and explained to Mohoriti that the musky smell was coming from her body.

"You are very beautiful and your smell is something that anyone could fall for." Mohoriti said to Satyavati.

Dusharaj narrated Mohoriti the reason behind her fragrance, "She is not my biological daughter. Once, I caught a fish from Yamuna and when I slit it, I found two babies inside its stomach. I was shocked to see this and immediately rushed to the saint near Yamuna. After meditating, he told me that one day the king of Chedi was on a hunting expedition when he had a nocturnal ejaculation while thinking about his wife. He sent his semen to his wife via an eagle but it dropped it in the river Yamuna while fighting with other eagles. This semen was, then, swallowed by the cursed celestial nymph, Adrika, who was living as a fish, and she got pregnant. After listening to the saint's words, I took both the children to the king but he accepted the boy child and asked me to take away the girl. I accepted her as my daughter and she, being the daughter of a fish, holds the fragrance in all her body.

Mohoriti heard the complete story about Satyavati and was impressed by her beauty and smell. Somewhere in his heart, he started loving her.

He decided to revisit their village and met Satyavati again so that he could take the matter of marrying her further.

After some days, King Shantanu was travelling near the bank of river Yamuna when he smelled a sweet scent coming from some other direction. He started following the same and saw Satyavati sitting on a boat.

He reached to her and asked her name. Shantanu saw her and fell in love with her and desired to have her.

He reached out to her father, Dusharaj, and asked for his consent.

On listening to the king's proposal, Dusharaj rejected.

When the king asked the reason, he told him that a few years ago, the marriage of one of his cousins' daughter, Vanasaki, was arranged with his courtier, Mohoma, but the marriage could not happen and he was responsible for that. As a result, she had to marry someone else even though she never wished to marry anyone other than Mohoma. This incident created an impression of irresponsibility on the part of the king and Dusharaj was worried for her daughter's future. On listening to this, Shantanu assured him that he would take full responsibility of her daughter and would never let her suffer for anything.

However, Dusharaj was adamant and he placed a condition that Satyavati's son would inherit the throne of Hastinapur.

Shantanu was angry with this condition as his eldest son, Devavrata, was the legal heir to the throne. He left his palace without agreeing on this.

Shantanu was still in deep love with Satyavati and was not able to forget her. He again restricted himself to the boudoir.

One evening, Mohoma was having dinner with his twenty sons. Then, Mohoriti asked his father, "I heard the king is in deep pain and is not meeting anyone. Do you have any idea why?"

Mohoma told Mohoriti about Shantanu's love towards Satyavati.

Listening to this, Mohoriti was broken, as he wanted Satyavati as his wife. He told his father upfront, "I had met Satyavati before the king and I love her a lot. I will marry her and will not let the king take her over."

Mohoma was shocked to learn about Mohoriti's feelings and asked him to bury his feelings deep in his heart. He also suggested that if somehow the king drops his plan to marry her, he can go ahead and marry Satyavati.

However, Mohoriti was not ready to listen and decided to

move to Madhuvan immediately to get his love.

At the same time, Devavrata came to know about this and for the sake of his father's happiness and Hastinapur, he decided to go to Madhuvan to talk to Dusharaj.

Devavrata was riding fast on his horse against the wind and Mohoriti was also racing to reach to get his love.

When Mohoriti reached Madhuvan, he saw Devavrata already reached and standing in front of Dusharaj.

"What is the problem you're facing with getting your daughter married to our king?" asked Devavrata.

Dusharaj looked at him and answered upfront, "It's you, Yuvraj," and continued, "you are great and extraordinary and no one else can be like you. You are the son of a goddess and you have the correct knowledge given to you by God. For me, too, you are God. No one can stand in front of you. Then, in such a case, what is the future of my daughter's children? They can never reach the throne. I'd put a condition before your father that Hastinapur's throne must be given to Satyavati's children in future. If he agrees to this, then I agree too."

Devavrata heard the condition and assured Dusharaj that he would never stake any claim to the throne, implying that the child born to Shantanu and Satyavati would become the ruler after Shantanu.

To this, Satyavati's father retorted that even if Devavrata gives up his claim to the throne, he would still be eligible for it. Under those conditions, Devavrata, being the eldest son of the king, will have the first right to claim the throne.

Mohoriti was watching all this from a distance but did not wish to interrupt as he was sure that there is no solution to this problem. However, he mistook the will power of Devavrata and what happened then changed the future of Hastinapur and the complete Kuru kingdom.

Devavrata took two steps back and took his sword out and placed the same above his shoulder in order to take the *Bhishma Pratigya*. This *pratigya* was a vow of lifelong celibacy and of service to whoever sat on the throne of Hastinapur. Thus, he had pledged to sacrifice his 'crown-prince' title and deny himself the pleasures of conjugal love. He declared that he will remain unmarried for his entire life and will serve the throne of Hastinapur.

Bhishma took another vow that he would always see his father's image in the claimant of the king's throne and would, thus, serve him faithfully and with full integrity.

He said that it's his decision and his father Shantanu must never be blamed for this.

King Shantanu also reached Madhuvan as soon as he heard that Devavrata had rushed towards Madhuvan but even he could not stop Devavrata from the taking the vow.

He cried and told Devavrata that he should not have done this but Devavrata was clear in his thoughts and told his father that it's his wish and he would be responsible for anything that happens with Shantanu in the future and will always take care of Hastinapur.

Shantanu, then, granted him the boon of *Ichcha Mrityu*, according to which he could choose the time of his own death, thereby, making him immortal till he decides to die.

The moment he uttered those words, gods and angels appeared from the sky, started showering flowers on Devavrata and cried "BHISHMA! BHISHMA!"

Having not expected such a sudden turn in the events, Mohoriti got furious. He was devastated and full of agony. He rode back on his horse towards Hastinapur.

He entered the arena and began practicing weaponry in rage when Mohoma came there.

"Save your energy; you'd need it in ruling the throne of Hastinapur." Mohoma told him placing his hands on Mohoriti's shoulder.

Mohoriti turned his face towards his father to look at him.

Mohoma continued, "Yes, my son, Devavrata has taken a vow that he will never take over the throne; what if someone kills the king before he has other children?"

Mohoriti could not understand and looked at his father anticipating clarification.

Mohoma smiled and said, "Now, it's the time for us to plan and kill Shantanu in order to take over his throne. Devavrata has taken a vow that he will always treat the successor as his father and will safeguard him. So, if you take over the throne of Hastinapur, Devavrata will be safely guarding you instead of taking revenge." Mohoriti now understood what his father wanted to say. He now needed to build a plan to kill Shantanu.

He called all his other nineteen brothers to discuss and devise a plan. The other nineteen brothers were equally adept in various arms and ammunition and were also a part of the Hastinapur's army.

They planned to gather other people, who were dependable and trustworthy, from the army. Their plan was to organize an exposition in the arena where various warriors would come forward to showcase their power and before anyone will be able to understand, Mohoriti would kill Shantanu and, thus, capture Shantanu's throne.

It's better to revolt and seize the throne than to live like a slave to Kuru, Mohoma contemplated.

The day of the expo approached and all the people of the kingdom got seated in the bleachers; the king, along with his newly married wife, was seated at the center, along with his courtiers sitting adjacent to him.

This was a yearly drill when warriors of Hastinapur would come forward and showcase their skills to boost their moral to fight for their country.

This year, even Devavrata had participated in order to showcase his skills and, so, Mohoriti was also occupied with the preparations.

The king stood up and addressed his progeny. He introduced his wife, the queen of Hastinapur, and his son, Devavrata to everyone. He, then, asked his courtier to start the drill.

As the gate opened, there entered a giant, furious elephant and the challenge was to chain it. Then, the second gate was opened and Devavrata, who was also known as Bhishma, entered and on his entry, everyone cheered him by calling him Bhishma.

Bhishma was tall and had wide shoulders and was one of the most handsome young men of his time. When he walked, it appeared as if the Himalaya itself was making its way in the arena. He appeared full of confidence.

He went straight in front of the king and bowed before him. The king blessed him and asked him to proceed.

Bhishma, then, turned around and moved straight towards the mad elephant, which was running wildly in the arena. Bhishma stood in front of it and looked straight in its eyes without batting an eyelid. The next moment, the elephant relaxed on its own and, then, sat on the ground by himself. This was sheer magic to have controlled an elephant without even touching it. However, the challenge was not over yet, as when Bhishma picked the chain up to shackle the elephant, another gate opened and from there entered five big, wild tigers.

Bhishma stood at the center of the arena holding the chain in his hand and observing the movement of the tigers, which were rushing into arena furiously for they hadn't been fed since many days.

They immediately pounced on Bhishma in order to make him their prey. Bhishma twirled the heavy chain in his hand and spun it in the air thereby throwing the tigers away. Elephant, which was sitting till now, stood up and attacked on Bhishma from behind with his trunk, throwing him a distance away.

The arena was filled with nothing but silence as the tigers started running towards Bhishma and the elephant, too, began going wild. One of the tigers pounced at him when Bhishma caught hold of its neck and twisted it to choke the tiger to death.

He, then, stood up again and ran towards the tigers. He caught hold of one of the tigers' neck in his armpit and twisted it thereby killing the tiger.

Everyone present in the arena was excited and was continuously cheering for their Yuvraj.

Mohoriti was observing Bhishma's powers very carefully.

Bhishma, then, jumped on other tigers and, within a few minutes, dragged them all to death. He, then, jumped towards the elephant, climbed onto him without putting in much effort and stood on his back. He bumped its head with his leg and, soon, the elephant was under his control.

He rode the elephant while everyone waved at him and chanted his name as loudly as possible. The king stood up to honor his son, but saw the arena gate opening once again. This time, it was a huge, tall, wide-shouldered man with dark beard, Mohoriti, carrying a mace in his hand.

Excited to see more, the progeny continued to shout even louder.

Bhishma wiped mud from his mouth and picked up his mace to begin *Dwand Yuddh.*

Mohoriti ran towards Bhishma holding the mace with both

his hands in an attempt to hit him straight on his face, but Bhishma moved aside and hit Mohoriti instead with his mace.

Mohoriti came back with another strike, which made Bhishma alert. Mohoriti was hitting hard and Bhishma defended every strike perfectly.

Two of the bravest warriors of the era, both blessed by Parshurama, were fighting against each other.

Both were hitting each other as hard as if they've been looking for an opportunity to kill each other. Everyone went silent looking at the aggressive fight. Mohoriti was never less than Bhishma and was giving him an equal competition.

The fight continued for a really long time, resulting nowhere and, therefore, Shantanu had to stop the fight.

One of the courtiers stood up and hit the drum signaling them to stop the fight. Hearing the sound, Bhishma stopped fighting and put his mace down, but Mohoriti took this as an advantage and hit Bhishma on his back with his mace, making Bhishma fall to the ground.

Without wasting any time, he signaled his well wishers to run towards Shantanu, while his other nineteen brothers pulled out their swords and attacked on the soldiers posted for security and protection.

Suddenly, the chaos started and everyone present in the arena started shouting and running haywire. Shantanu also pulled his sword out having sensed danger and betrayal. The fight began between the two groups and taking benefit of the chaos, Mohoriti rushed towards the throne to kill Shantanu. He jumped from the arena towards Shantanu and hit him hard with his mace but Shantanu blocked his blow with his mace and hit him back.

Bhishma, who was in the arena, pulled his sword out and rushed like the wind towards his father. He attacked his father's enemies and jumped to reach on top of the arena where Mohoriti was trying to hurt Shantanu.

Mohoma, too, pulled out his sword and tried to stop Bhishma by blocking his path to reach Shantanu.

However, Mohoma's powers stood nowhere in front of Bhishma's; he pulled him by his neck and he fell down. Bhishma, then, swung his sword and hit it on Mohoma's neck, thereby splitting it from the torso.

Having looked at his father, Mohoriti was shattered and it struck to him that he should run away as their plan had failed.

Mohoriti attacked both, Shantanu and Bhishma. Soon, he found an escape and rushed out of the arena leaving behind his nineteen brothers, who were still fighting for the throne.

Soon, Hastinapur's army captured all the people involved in the revolt and King Shantanu commanded to have all the captured accused beheaded in the same arena. He also asked his army to conduct a search operation for Mohoriti.

All the people involved in the uprising, including the nineteen sons of Mohoma, were beheaded in front of the entire kingdom and Ritikawali was arrested and sent to prison.

Mohoriti escaped and ran towards Sindhu River to a place called Sovir while Hastinapur's army was looking for him.

On his way, he hid himself in a forest in front of Abhira Kingdom. The kingdom of Abhira was ruled by Sivadatta, who was friends with Kurus. Hiding himself in any town in Abhira would not be safe for him, so Mohoriti decided to hide in the dark forest and waited for a correct opportunity to take revenge for his father and brothers.

He trode on the path deeper into the forest and started living like a saint there. He went into deep meditation. He needed time to plan the revenge and he knew his revenge was not an impulsive act.

He believed he and his father have been neglected despite doing a lot for Hastinapur. Mohoriti spent his whole life in service of the kingdom and he was one of most worthy claimants of the throne. He was also the first person to meet Satyavati, but could not marry her because of Shantanu.

He, also, believed that his mother, Ritikawali, might have gotten arrested, even though she was innocent and knew nothing about the revolt.

Mohoriti, being a brave and worthy warrior, had chosen the wrong path in agony.

One day, when he was busy meditating under a tree, he heard a beautiful voice of a female who was humming. He opened his eyes and followed the voice and saw a beautiful lady taking bath in a waterfall moving between the rocks.

He found her attractive and watched her for a long time.

Soon, the lady realized that someone was hiding in the bushes and dressed up to come out and check on him. She saw Mohoriti and frowned at him.

"Devi, I have never seen such a beautiful lady in my life; I find your voice very enchanting. I came out of my meditation and could not resist myself from admiring you."

She felt shy and turned her back. Mohoriti could not control his emotions and came near her.

"Devi, who are you and what are you doing in this wild forest?"

She turned back to him and replied, "This forest is my home and these wild animals are my family. I live here."

Mohoriti smiled and asked her name to which she replied as, 'Padmashala'.

"Will you marry me so that we both could make this forest a place of love and fortune?" Mohoriti proposed to her.

Padmashala was from the Rakshasa community and was not in her original complexion then. She, too, was attracted to Mohoriti and his wide, toned body and, therefore, she decided to keep her identity as a secret.

Padmashala was the daughter of Drumila, who was also the biological father of Kamsa, the ruler of Vrishni and Putna.

Padmashala agreed to his proposal and, soon, they got married and this marriage was witnessed by the forest and the animals.

On their wedding night during coitus, excited Padmashala lost her self-control and got into her actual, demonic form. However, Mohoriti was so attracted to her that he didn't protest about it and made love.

Padmashala feared that upon seeing her real identity, Mohoriti would disown her but it was not so. Mohoriti accepted her and continued to be her loyal husband.

In reality, Mohoriti was more focused towards his revenge and he knew if he has children from Padmashala, he would be able to have strong and highly skilled sons, who could help him take his revenge some day.

After nine months, Padmashala gave birth to two sons, named Duru and Maaru. Mohoriti was very happy to hold his sons in his hands.

He picked them and said, "You both will follow the path

shown to you by your father and defeat Bhishma in his life one day."

Their birth was witnessed by Padmashala's cousin sister, Putana. She was a *Yatudhana*, an evil spirit, and had terrorized the entire region.

Mohoriti was a proud father now and aimed to train his children to reach the throne of Hastinapur.

Time moved fast and there in Hastinapur, Satyavati gave birth to two sons of Shantanu, named Chitrāngada and Vichitravirya.

Bhishma, being their half-brother, took their responsibility as a father and decided to train them for the throne.

Everything was running perfect in Hastinapur till Shantanu started encountering sudden health problems. Bhishma and Satyavati were worried about him and gave him all possible remedies to get his health back in shape.

One day, Shantanu called Bhishma to him. Bhishma stood next to him, when Shantanu said, "Son, it's my time to leave you all. Your ancestors have built this throne with their wisdom and you need to carry the responsibility forward. Before I die, I want to see Chitrāngada as the king of Hastinapur. This is my order and must be immediately put into action."

Bhishma took the orders and planned the coronation of his brother, Chitrāngada. It was decided that the ruling king would be Chitrāngada but all the decisions would be made by Bhishma, since Chitrāngada was too young to rule.

As his coronation completed, Hastinapur went into deep woe due to the demise of their King Shantanu.

Chitrāngada had some issues with his attitude and because of which, his pride made Hastinapur face many border issues. Bhishma tried to guide him but Chitrāngada overlooked his guidance and committed a few terrible mistakes which made the Gandharva King angry.

Mohoriti also got to hear about the conflicts between Chitrāngada and Gandharva kingdom and he wanted to take this opportunity for his revenge.

He moved to Gandharva along with his elder son, Duru, who was young and adept in fighting and weaponry. He left Maaru with his mother.

Mohoriti reached Hastinapur and there, showed his interest in joining their army having kept his identity hidden. He was tested to be fit, where he showed his excellent capabilities in aggressive fighting and got selected along with Duru.

"So, what is our plan, father?" Duru asked Mohoriti one night while sitting in their camp.

Mohoriti looked at him while keeping his sword back.

"Soon, a war will start and we will get a chance to get closer to Bhishma and eventually take over him"

"I will try to attack and engage him while you'd also attack on him at that moment. This will be a surprise blow for Bhishma, as he would not be expecting any soldier with such exceptional skills to attack him." Duru explained.

"You are correct, my son, and this will lead us to the throne of Hastinapur." Mohoriti added.

On the other hand, Bhishma walked into Chitrāngada's cabin and told him he wanted to talk.

"Yes, *Pitamah*, what happened?" Chitrāngada asked. *Pitamah* was addressed to someone who was equivalent to father.

"I think your decision is wrong for the people of Hastinapur." Bhishma stated.

Chitrāngada turned towards Bhishma and asked, "Why? What is wrong with attacking Gandharva?"

"Gandharva kingdom is our friend and has been bound by a peace treaty with us since the time of our great grandfather and we must respect that." Bhishma retorted.

"The treaty was constituted by our great grandfather and I feel it's not correct and needs to be put an end to." Chitrāngada replied proudly and continued, "You only think about relations but we also need to think about expansion of our empire. We have our states till Takshila and Sindhu and if we are able to capture Gandharva, we will get straight access to trade with Parsik and open fresh avenues for growth of Hastinapur."

"But attacking on Gandharva will affect our relations with many other adjoining kingdoms, which might get threatened by us and might also revolt." Bhishma explained to him in detail but Chitrāngada paid no attention and instead asked Bhishma to follow his instructions.

Bhishma did not want to agree but he had to follow Chitrāngada's orders. Chitrāngada asked him to be in Hastinapur while he will be moving with the army for the war and, also, told him that he'll be called as per the need.

Chitrāngada started moving towards Gandharva for the attack along with his best army men and on the other side, Gandharva was all set to face any challenges.

On the battle day, both the armies were in front of each other and all the peace talks conducted had failed. Mohoriti, along with his son, was ready to take over Hastinapur but was devastated upon hearing the news that Bhishma was not present in the war.

However, he decided to stick to his plan and take over Chitrāngada in place of Bhishma.

Soon, both the armies impinged on the warzone and the bloodshed began. Mohoriti, being immortal, was moving like fire towards the Hastinapur army.

His sword had already ripped more than hundred heads off and everything was moving as per his plan.

He saw Chitrāngada at some distance attacking using his exceptional archery. He gestured Duru to move towards him and contemplated to move on the other side to take over Chitrāngada.

The war was being fought with all the might when Duru reached Chitrāngada and started throwing spears at him. This move of Duru made Chitrāngada attack back. Duru was an energetic boy; he kept changing his position frequently so as to keep Chitrāngada busy. Chitrāngada was continuously firing arrows at him and in the meantime, Mohoriti reached on other side to attack Chitrāngada.

Now was time for Mohoriti to attack Chitrāngada. He rushed towards him with full power but before he could reach him, one arrow hit straight at Chitrāngada, piercing through his chest.

It was shot by the king of Gandharva. Chitrāngada immediately fell off his chariot and died. Gandharva marked its victory over Hastinapur and took charge of the entire kingdom of Hastinapur.

Mohoriti had failed in his plan once again, but was happy to see the son of Shantanu lying on the earth dead.

Later, Bhishma came to know about this and rushed towards Gandharva. He met the king of Gandharva and signed the peace treaty once again and got his army released. He was in pain seeing his brother dead but he called it his destiny and, also, a lesson for others that the advices of the elders are not mere words but hold meaning as well.

After a few days of political ups and downs, Hastinapur's army was back in form.

Chapter-4
Effect of Amba

Mohoriti was back to Padmashala with his son, Duru. He was worried that he has not landed anywhere on his plan.

One morning, Padmashala got a message that her sister, Putna, was killed by a child named Krishna in Gokul. She was upset on hearing this news.

Mohoriti was with her in her bad times. He loved her a lot in spite of her being a Rakshasi.

"I need to go and sought revenge on that child for killing my sister," she told Mohoriti furiously.

Mohoriti looked at her and put his hands on her head and replied, "You must go. We must take revenge for our family if anyone does injustice to them."

"Yes, it's an injustice! That child needs to be killed; else, he will kill our brother, Kansa, too. Protecting oneself is never a sin."

Mohoriti looked in her eyes and saw the fire of revenge. He told her that he, too, will be heading towards his next destination for his revenge along with his sons.

"Being with you was a milestone and not a destination. I have to move on now. Someday, I know, we will meet again having finished our allotted jobs."

She kept looking at him and the spoke with teary eyes, "Hope we meet again."

Mohoriti did not want to get any more emotional. He stood up immediately and called his sons.

"Yes, father, why did you call us?" asked Maaru.

"It's the time for us to move on. Touch your mother's feet and take blessings from her. We need to reach and conquer."

Maaru, being close to his to mother, hugged her and sought her blessings. Even Duru touched her feet before leaving.

She blessed them to be victorious and Mohoriti and his two sons took over their horses and began moving towards Gandhar.

It was a long way to go and their horses had begun galloping in pace. By the night, they reached Kamyak forest and decided to stay there overnight. Kamyak forest was one of the most dangerous forests and was near to the Kuru kingdom. These forests had various tribes, which had to take up numerous battles for food and water, inhabiting them.

Major tribes inhabiting Kamyak were Matsya and Muru and they both had fought multiple battles for retaining their possession of the forest. The night at Kamyak could never be safe for all three of them.

Therefore, Mohoriti and his two sons decided they will take turns sleeping while guarding each other. Mohoriti wanted to reach Gandhar and work for them as he considered Gandhar a capable kingdom, which could challenge Hastinapur.

Maaru was given the duty to guard Mohoriti and Duru while they would take rest till the moon would be the highest in the sky. It was a tiring day for them and, therefore, within a few seconds, both of them went into deep sleep.

It was dark in the forest and the sounds of wild animals could be heard from all around. Maaru kept watching owls and snakes crawling around and many a times, he also tried to keep them away with from his father and brother.

Later in the night when moon was about to reach the highest

in the sky, Maaru heard the footsteps of a group of people walking towards them while whispering amongst themselves. This made him attentive and he immediately woke his father and Duru up.

They all became attentive and pulled out their swords in order to defend themselves if any of the tribes had thought them to be intruders. They hid themselves in the bushes and waited for the tribe to be visible.

Soon, they saw a group of ascetics along with a lady, who looked as if she had cried a lot, and sensed some trouble. Her hairs were messed up. Tears were still flowing from her eyes and ascetics were trying to console her.

Looking at them, Mohoriti kept his sword back and came in front, with his hands joined and head bowed in honor, followed by his sons.

The ascetics stopped looking at them and said, "Be blessed, but who are you and what are you doing in this dark forest this night."

Mohoriti adjusted his sword and replied to them politely, "My sons and I are travelling to Gandharva; we thought of taking rest tonight here in the forest."

He, then, looked at the lady with them and asked, "And who is she?"

Before the ascetics could reply, she started speaking in patronizing voice, "I am Amba, the eldest daughter of the king of Kashi."

"Oh! Please accept my kowtow. You seem to be in trouble; may I help you?" Mohoriti asked.

Hearing his words, she started crying again and sat on the trunk of an old tree.

There, a learned sage, Shaikhavatya, consoled Amba and asked her to tell them what had happened so that they could suggest her a solution.

She wiped her tears, while other ascetics seated themselves. She started describing the reason for her condition.

"I am the eldest daughter of the king of Kashi and my other two sisters are Ambika and Ambalika. Salva, the king of Saubala, and I were secretly in love and I promised him that I would place the garland around his neck during swayamvara. Somehow, Bhishma came to know of the ceremony. Despite not being invited, he came to the swayamvara to win me for his stepbrother, Vichitravirya.

On his arrival, Bhishma announced his intention to abduct the bride, challenging the assembled suitors to stop him. Bhishma forced us into his chariot and rode away. King Salva followed him and challenged for a duel. Bhishma overpowered and wounded Salva, but somehow spared his life.

He proceeded to Hastinapur and introduced us to Satyavati, who made arrangements for our marriage to Vichitravirya. I was not interested in this marriage as I was committed to Salva. I approached Bhishma. The council of the Brahmins had revealed that Salva and I are in love with each other, and I would choose him as my husband in the swayamvara.

Bhishma conceded that my reasoning was sound and decided to send me back to Saubala while my other two sisters would marry Vichitravirya.

I was very happy with the decision. All necessary arrangements were made to deploy me. Bhishma ensured that I would be escorted safely to Saubala Kingdom.

As I reached Saubala, I informed Salva that I came back for him, but he retorted that he no longer loved me as I was supposed to wed Vichitravirya, and was won by Bhishma.

He declared that I was rightfully won by Bhishma, who defeated and insulted him and the other kings present. He even accused me of happily leaving with him.

I pleaded to him to accept me, as I was still as pure as Ganga but he denied. I have no place to return now and, thus, I came to this forest.

Please suggest what I should do now?" she addressed everyone present there.

The ascetics discussed among themselves and suggested her to meet Parshuram and request him if he could ask Bhishma or Salva to accept her.

Amba agreed to their suggestion and decided to meet Parshurama.

"I have met Parshuram once to seek his blessings and I know where you can meet him." replied Mohoriti and continued shouting with anger, "Bhishma is a person who is responsible for spoiling the lives of many people on this earth and he must die now. If you would allow me, I could take you to Lord Parshuram."

"No, thank you brave man, I will go to him on my own, but why do you hate Bhishma so much?" She asked Mohoriti.

Mohoriti stood up and replied in agony, "He killed my father and nineteen brothers, and I am not going to spare him for this."

Suddenly, Sage Shaikhavatya interrupted, "I see the future. Amba would be responsible for Bhishma's death."

Mohoriti turned towards him and pulled his sword towards Amba, "I will kill Bhishma and if the future says it's you who'd be responsible, then I will change the future."

Amba stood up and came closer to his sword, "I am already a dead soul. So, it'd be better if we let destiny decide who will kill Bhishma."

Seeing the confidence of Amba, he lowered his sword.

Shaikhavatya placed his hand on Mohoriti's shoulder and asked him to calm down.

"Brave warrior, your fortune is linked to Bhishma and, in future, your generation will win all by losing everything. I suggest you to go to Panchal Kingdom and settle there."

Mohoriti joined his hands and thanked him for his wise words and suggestions.

"I will move to Panchal, as suggested by you, and will wait for my future to unfold there." Mohoriti added.

It was dawn by now and the darkness had blanketed the entire forest.

Mohoriti looked at the morning sun and kept gazing at it. He placed his sword back on his waist and asked the ascetics' permission to leave.

Having taken their blessings, he set out for Panchal with his sons.

After travelling the entire day, they reached Panchal at night. Panchal was one of the most powerful kingdoms situated on the Ganga-Yamuna doab. Panchal kingdom had Himalayas in their north, enriching them with beauty and safety. On the south, the kingdom extended to Charmanwati River which acted as a border between them and the Kuru kingdom.

Panchal and Kuru kingdom shared a common source of their roots from ancient King Puru. Where, on one hand, Panchal was prospering; on the other hand, Hastinapur was struggling for its survival.

In the past, Panchal and Kuru had multiple wars for their existence and, also, for water and land. Panchal had once invaded Kuru and exiled them to the bank of River Sindhu.

The Kurus and the Panchals were considered as the foremost among the ruling tribes, because they followed the Vedic religion in its dogmatic and purest form. Other tribes imitated the practices of these tribes and, thus, got accepted into the Vedic religion. Panchals were well known for understanding even the half-said words. They observed the duties enjoined in the Vedas along with the other respectable people, as they believed that the most pious among all the races are conversant with the eternal truths of religion.

Mohoriti reached the entrance gate which was huge, reflecting the empire's powerful image with depiction of its ancestors and stories from the past. He brought his horse to a halt and observed around for a while with Duru and Maaru following him.

Duru stepped down from his horse as per the instructions he received from Mohoriti and reached the gate which was closed with two guarding it on both sides.

When they requested the guards to open the gate, they, in turn, asked them to knock on the small window at the corner of the gate.

Firelights were installed on the corners of the gates and this lit the area around yellow; the blowing wind was making the light from them flicker. He knocked on the window, which was opened by another guard from inside the room.

"Yes, what happened?" he asked rudely from inside the room.

"We are new to Panchal and want to get in." Duru replied.

The guard pulled out a dry palm leaf and a peacock feather dipped in ink made up of charcoal and asked his name along with others who accompanied him. Duru informed about their names and mentioned their purpose of visit as business.

The guard noted all the details and, then, opened the door. Mohoriti acknowledged the prosperous kingdom of Panchal while slowly entering from the huge gate on his horse.

Both the sides of the entry were well-built and were beautifully decorated with firelights installed on small cabins throughout. The guards were posted at equal distance from each other to effectively guard the kingdom. It was structured and maintained very well. They stepped down and started walking holding the lead ropes of the horses.

Maaru was tired. He asked his father, "What is our next destination, father?"

Mohoriti didn't answer him and kept walking. Soon, they entered the market. The people of Panchal looked rich and prosperous and were busy shopping.

They moved to some distance observing, and found a place where people were being served food and Sura.

Sura was a beverage brewed from rice meal, wheat, sugarcane, grapes and other fruits and was popular among the warriors and the peasants of Panchal and Kuru.

Mohoriti asked Maaru to tether their horses in the corner so that they could go inside to have food. It was quite noisy as everyone was shopping and selling things.

Mohoriti stepped inside the place and was being followed by his sons. He saw people having dinner and drinking Sura.

Mohoriti occupied an empty chair made of wood having a wooden plank on top for seating. Mohoriti was seeing all this for the first time. Sura and the food were kept on the table and people were relishing their meals.

"Father, this place looks amazing." Duru took the front seat and spoke in excitement.

Maaru, too, nodded.

Soon, a person came and served boiled rice and Sura to them. They glanced for once and began eating without looking at anyone as they were very hungry.

While eating, Mohoriti noticed a tall and muscular man entering the place and taking a seat. He looked like a warrior from the king's court as everyone respected him and offered him place to sit.

Mohoriti stood up in order to approach him, joined his hands and greeted him.

"I am from a far town and want to meet the king to deliver a message to him." Mohoriti said politely.

"What is the message; you may tell me and I shall convey the same to the king in the court." The man replied.

"Sorry, it's a secret and is meant to be revealed only to the king." Mohoriti explained.

"Come to the court tomorrow and I'll arrange your meeting." The man gave an arrogantly reply.

He thanked him and moved to his place. All three of them completed their dinners and moved out to find a place to stay over for the night. They tethered their horses in a lonely shed and decided to stay put that night.

The next morning, Mohoriti reached the court along with his sons to meet the king.

They entered the court and bowed before the king of Panchal.

"Long live the king!" He said.

"What is the message that you want to give?" the king asked in a stern voice.

"I met your daughter, Kashi Amba, in a dense forest. She was completely devastated and was angry with Bhishma. She asked me to meet and inform you that she will be the reason for Bhishma's death in this birth or the other."

He continued, "She even asked me to wait for her in Drupada till she returns."

After hearing this, he questioned, "Who are you, a warrior?"

With a spark in his eyes and his chest full, he replied, "I am an immortal Mohoriti."

King looked at him and, then, at his courtier. He ordered, "He will be a part of the Panchal kingdom from now. He is assigned the role of a trainer in our army."

Mohoriti and his sons thanked him and stood lowering their heads down.

Mohoriti started training the new boys, who joined the Panchal army, and his sons, too, joined the army.

On the other hand, Amba performed austerities and pleased Kartikeya, the god of war and Shiva's son. He granted her a garland of ever-fresh lotuses and declared that the person wearing it can destroy Bhishma. With this garland, Amba made one more attempt to seek help from various kings and princes to support her in this cause.

However, there was no response from anyone to help her as they did not want to be on the wrong side of Bhishma.

Finally, she reached Drupada and the king here also declined. Frustrated, she cast the garland off on a pillar outside Drupada's palace and went for austerities in the forest again.

While Amba killed herself, no one dared to touch the garland.

Duru, on the other hand, was happy to see the garland cast on the pillar and was planning to steal it for his father Mohoriti, so that he could seek his revenge.

Duru decided not to disclose his plans and surprise his father with this gift.

Mohoriti was very good in handling arms and his skills were doing wonders in the army. Meanwhile, he was also training his sons to be their best so that he could create his own team to conquer Kuru.

One evening, when Duru and Maaru where practicing sword fighting at the bank of the river, they saw two extremely beautiful women coming towards the river to fill water.

They both were so beautiful that both the brothers could not resist themselves from stopping the practice and admiring their beauty. When both the women were filling water in their vessels, Duru and Maaru decided to talk to them

"What are your names, beautiful ladies?" Duru addressed them.

They both blushed and one of them replied softly, "I am Raksha and she is my sister, Vishaka."

They both were twin sisters and daughters of one the known pandits of Panchal.

Duru could not hold himself and immediately held Raksha's hand and asked if she would marry him. Maaru interrupted and asked Vishaka if she would like to marry him.

They both smiled and ran towards the village but their smile was an answer in approval.

That night, both the brothers expressed their wish to Mohoriti and Mohoriti was pleased to hear the entire incident. Next day, he met the girls' father and finalized their marriage.

Duru decided to steal the garland for his father and hand it over to him in order to thank him for fulfilling his wish to marry Raksha.

Stealing the garland was not a big task as no one even dared to touch it, but Duru was a brave man. He succeeded in stealing Amba's garland that night and reached home carrying it in his hand.

When Mohoriti opened the door, he was shocked to see the garland in Duru's hand and without asking anything further, he picked up a stick that was kept outside to scare animals away and started beating Duru mercilessly.

"You must have not done this." Mohoriti yelled.

"This is Amba's garland. You can't betray a woman." Duru explained.

"Is this what I have taught you as a warrior?" Mohoriti furthered.

He continued beating Duru in anger. Duru, on the other hand, was silent and did not reply back to his father out of respect; however, he was devastated and heartbroken.

Mohoriti kept hitting him and Maaru, who came out hearing the sound, found himself unable to stop Mohoriti.

"You can't be my son; my son can't be such a coward. Please go away from my eyes and never return." Mohoriti continued yelling and beating Duru.

Mohoriti was an immortal warrior and was hurt upon seeing his son take such a cheap step to defeat his enemy.

Duru cried and having heard such harsh words from his father, climbed on his horse and rode away. While Mohoriti was in deep anger, Maaru was stunned.

Duru rode his horse to the same place from where he'd picked up the garland and placed it back. He felt he was insulted in front of many people. He recalled his father's words and decided not to return and, thus, moved on to Matsya.

Mohoriti was in deep pain after knowing that Duru has left, but he was firm on his words and did not regret any part of saying them. He was a warrior and stealing could never be in his blood.

Next day, Mohoriti went to meet the brides' father.

He joined his hands and apologized, "Panditji, I am sorry; Duru is no more my son and has already left Panchal."

Panditji was afraid if the society will accept Raksha after knowing that her groom left away before the wedding.

Mohoriti proposed to Panditji to get both his daughters married to his only son, Maaru. Left with no other choice, Panditji accepted the offer and soon got both his daughters, Raksha and Vishaka, married to Maaru as Maaru's twin wives.

Although Maaru was not in favor of this proposal initially, but he couldn't go against his father's wish. Though Maaru was virtuous and abstemious, he soon became lustful after his marriage being proud of his youth and beauty. Both Raksha and Vishaka were tall and had a complexion akin to molten gold. Their heads were covered with black, curly hair and their fingernails were long and red. Their hips were fat and round and their breasts, full and deep. Endued with every auspicious mark, the amiable young ladies considered themselves to be wedded to a husband who was worthy of them in every which way. They loved and respected Maaru.

However, even after four years of their marriage, both the ladies could not deliver a grandchild to Mohoriti and this became a matter of concern for him.

At the same time in Hastinapur, Vichitraveerya died of ill health before having any child, leaving his wives, Ambika and Ambalika, childless. Satyavati, Vichitraveerya's mother, was distressed as the kingdom was left with no heir to the throne. She asked Bhishma to marry the widows of Vichitravirya. Bhishma refused, reminding Satyavati of the promise he had made to her father and his vow of bachelorhood.

Considering this, Satyavati called her first son, Vyasa, who was truly a realized soul and a wise sage, to perform *niyoga* with her widowed daughters-in-law, Ambika and Ambalika.

Niyoga was tough and not everyone could perform it for there were strict rules to be followed to perform it. A *Brahmin* was called upon for this purpose, a person who was highly revered and who would do this for the sake of *Dharma* only. The *Brahmin* should neither claim the woman nor the resulting child as his own. The child would only be regarded as that of the husband of the woman and not of the *Brahmin*.

With the help of *Niyoga* by Vyasa, Ambika and Ambalika gave birth to two sons, Dhritarashtra and Pandu, respectively, but Dhritarashtra was blind and Pandu was weak and pale.

Soon, the rumors started floating in the adjoining kingdoms, too, that Hastinapur's throne is in deep trouble because of the blind and weak children of Vichitravirya who have taken birth by Niyoga conducted by Sage Vyasa.

When Mohoriti heard this, he also got excited. He wondered if even he could take the help of some wise sage to perform *Niyoga* for his daughters-in-law and complete his son's family. He decided to move in search of the sage towards the Himalayas.

After traveling for four days and five nights, he reached the lush valleys of Himalaya. He was tired and wanted to drink some water; so, he stopped by a lake. While he was drinking water, he heard some sound asking for help. He started looking around to know who the person was and saw one aged sage lying in a cave taking his last breath.

Mohoriti placed his belongings down and went straight into the cave and sat beside the sage placing his head on his thigh.

"May I help you, Maharaj?" He asked politely.

Sage did not answer anything but asked for water. He was very thirsty and was unable to stand up to get water. He was thirsty since months.

Mohoriti stood up and rushed towards the lake. He brought water in a mud bowl he'd picked from a corner inside the cave.

He placed the sage's head on his thigh again and poured water in his mouth. Since the sage was very thirsty, he gestured for more water. Mohoriti went back and brought some more water but it seemed as if the thirst of the sage had increased immensely; therefore, he brought some more water to quench his thirst.

After finishing each bowl, the sage would ask for more water and this continued for quite some time. Mohoriti had nothing but the bowl to get water in and, therefore, he was bound to go back to the lake every time.

Finally, after two days and two night of constant feeding, the sage opened his eyes and said, "Thank you warrior for your help."

Mohoriti stood up and joined his hands and asked if he need more water to drink.

"No, I have been thirsty from last fifty years and have been waiting for someone with pure thoughts and aim to feed me water. You are the one who quenched my thirst." The sage replied.

He continued while still lying, "I am thankful for your efforts and ready to grant you any wish you desire for."

Mohoriti was thankful; he said, "I was in search of a wise sage who could perform Niyoga with my daughters-in-law and help me get my grandsons."

Sage closed his eyes and replied, "I am three hundred years old and I do not have enough stamina to perform Niyoga."

He placed an apple in Mohoriti's palm and said, "You may take this fruit and give it to your daughters–in-law. With my blessings, she will gave birth to your heirs." He closed his eyes then and his soul left for heavenly abode.

Mohoriti touched his feet and moved back to his house with a smile of relief. While still on his way, he realized that the sage had given him only one fruit where as he had two daughters-in-law to feed.

He forgot to mention to the sage that he had two daughters-in-law and, thus, received only one fruit from him.

Once he reached home, he called Maaru and said, "Give this apple to your wives and they will be surely blessed with children."

Maaru took it and thanked his father for bringing blessings for the family.

He went to Raksha and gave that apple to her asking her to have it and share it with her sister, too.

Raksha and Vishaka were also happy to have received the blessings. They cut the apple into two and took one half each.

Days passed and both the wives of Maaru got pregnant. It was a happy phase in Mohoriti's life. He called his wife, Padmashala, to visit his place and help his daughters-in-laws during their delivery.

After ten long months, the day arrived when both the sisters were about to deliver babies. Padmashala was inside the maternity room helping both the women deliver. After sometime, she came out with two sons in both her arms but tears in her eyes.

"What happened, Padmashala?" Mohoriti asked anxiously while looking at the babies. He was shocked after seeing the two sons alive in her two arms, but both of them only having half the body parts.

The son in her right arm was having only the right side of the body whereas son in her left arm only had the left side of the body.

Maaru was also shocked. Mohoriti understood that since the blessing was divided among the ladies, so even the sons got divided.

Mohoriti was left devastated once again for not understanding the exact words from the sage and regretted what just happened.

"Padmashala, they both are of no use. It's better to take them both to the jungle and kill them." He took the tough decision while holding Maaru's shoulder.

Maaru, who kept looking at his sons with love and pain, had no words on what should be done.

Padmashala kept crying but she, too, couldn't see any other option. She took orders from Mohoriti and moved to the jungle carrying both the sons in her arms. Once she reached, she prepared herself to kill them but her conscience was not letting her do the same and, somehow, her love towards them was also stopping her. So, she decided to change her appearance back to Rakshasi and, then, complete the job.

She spelt out some mantras to change her avatar and, soon, she turned into a huge Rakshasi with wild looks and big teeth.

She looked at them with her big eyes and, then, raised both the children from the ground holding each in her hands.

She thought of putting them together for once to see how they looked before she finally killed them.

She brought her both palms together and joined the two halves of the body. Suddenly, a white light started emitting from the body and the brightness ultimately closed Padmashala's eyes.

When she opened her eyes again after a few seconds, she saw both the halves joined and a smiling baby in her hand. It was the happiest moment of her life. She immediately spelled a few mantras to take back the avatar of a human and kissed the baby. She rushed back to Mohoriti who was sitting in deep sorrow along with Maaru at home.

Padmashala explained Mohoriti about what had happened and Mohoriti thanked God for taking care of his grandson.

"Thank you for your divine blessings and bringing our son back to life. He was born in parts and was joined to be a complete body; so, his name will be Indriya and he will be known for his powers for coming generations." Mohoriti declared.

Chapter-5
Introduction of Kunti

Duru reached Matsya after separating from Mohoriti. Matsya Kingdom was located to the south of Kuru and west of the River Yamuna, which also separated it from the kingdom of the Panchals. The capital of Matsya was at Viratanagari, which was said to have been named after its founder, King Virata.

He joined the Matsya army and started living in Matsya as their loyal soldier. Duru was brave and very good looking.

Shirakhand, who was a warrior in Matysa army and a senior to Duru, announced among all the other warriors that he is arranging a swayamvara for his three daughters and the warriors were invited to showcase their talent so that the capable one could win them over.

The grandsons of Vanasaki, who was about to marry Mohoma, were also posted in the Matysa army and were good warriors.

Duru decided to take part in the swayamvara to win over all the three beautiful women.

Vanasaki married Majhara and gave birth to two sons, Chintan and Mahantam. Further, Chintan and Mahantam had two and three sons, respectively. The eldest son of Chintan was Charayu and the eldest son of Mahantam was Vinashala.

Charayu and Vinashala were also a part of the Matysa army and were about to take part in the swayamvara. They both were brave, strong and handsome warriors and held strong positions in the Matysa army.

Shirakhand admired them and hoped they would win over his daughters.

The day for the swayamvara had arrived and many warriors were waiting for the announcement of Shirakhand's challenge for everyone to impress his daughters.

Duru was seated in the front row when he saw all the three daughters of Shirakhand arriving with garlands made of roses in their hands.

Shirakhand stood up and made the announcement, "My daughters are very special to me and they will only present the garland to the warrior who can win them over with courage. You need to present your acts of courage to impress them and they will decide if it is worthy or not. So, without wasting any time, let's start the swayamvara."

Charayu went first. He pulled out his sword and twisted it with his teeth, showing an extraordinary example of strength and power.

Vinashala came next; he tied two big rocks to his hair and rotated them like small balls showcasing another example of strength and power.

Duru was the next in line. He came in front, looked at everyone seated and joined his hands before them first. He, then, went straight to the women. While moving towards them, he plucked three rose flowers on the way and asked all of them if they would marry him and placed the flowers in their hairs.

"What type of stunt is this?" asked one of the warriors standing in his place.

Duru turned towards him and said, "I dared to present flowers to the women in front of hundreds of expert warriors. What else could have been a bigger stunt than facing a threat from you all?"

Many other warriors stood up with naked swords in their hands, "This is wrong and you cannot be saved now." Many others started shouting at him.

"I believe he dared; now, let the women decide." Vinashala

interrupted.

Shirakhand, too, agreed on the same and asked his daughters if they wanted to choose him or they should move on to the next warrior.

Two of his daughters hung the garland around Duru's neck and accepted him as their husband while the youngest daughter moved towards Vinashala and placed the garland around his neck, for she was impressed by his manly thoughts of supporting the correct.

Soon, Duru became a father of three sons and one daughter.

In Drupada, Indriya was growing up fast and Mohoriti was foreseeing his future in Indriya. Since an early age, Mohoriti started training him in various arms and ammunitions. Time was flying fast and Indriya was growing like a tree.

Maaru started facing severe health issues and one day, his soul left for the divine world.

Mohoriti taught archery and religion to Indriya and, somewhere in Hastinapur, Bhishma taught Pandu and Dhritarashtra archery, politics, administration and religion. Pandu was an excellent archer and *Maharathi,* whereas Dhritarashtra was blind and powerful but could not succeed in archery.

Once, Mohoriti came back from the palace and asked Indriya to go to the king of Shurasena with an invitation from King Drupada for a yagna at the bank of Sarasvati River.

Indriya took his orders and immediately moved to Shurasena. He extended the invitation from Drupada to the king of Shurasena, who was pleased to get the invitation. The king of Shurasena requested Indriya to stay over in his palace for the night and enjoy the glory of his janpad and leave for Drupada in the morning.

Indriya thanked the king and accepted his offer.

Indriya was a young, energetic and powerful budding warrior and his presence could be easily felt. He enjoyed the hospitality of Shurasena that night and, then, went to his room to sleep.

He was given a big room with huge windows from where he could see the Yamuna River flowing with strong tides. The palace was surrounded with big and beautiful gardens from all the sides and fragrances of flowers spread all over, making the atmosphere pleasant.

While he was preparing to sleep, he heard the voices of young girls and he could not resist himself from peeping through his window.

He saw beautiful girls playing around in the garden.

It was Shurasena's daughter, Kunti, and her friend, Mili.

Indriya could not resist himself from meeting them and, thus, jumped out from the window to reach the garden. Somehow, his foot slipped and he fell in front of them.

"From where did you come, boy; directly from heaven?" asked Kunti.

"I think he is a thief. Let's call the guards!" Mili suggested.

Indriya stood up, dusted himself and said, "No, girls, I am not a thief. I am a guest of the king and looking at you both playing, I could not resist myself from joining you."

"Oh! So you want to play with us? Do you know who she is, the daughter of the king, Kunti." Mili added with arrogance, "If someone would see you with her, you'd definitely reach your destination but beheaded."

Kunti looked a little afraid and hesitant while Indriya smiled and replied, "She is the daughter of the king, but what about you? You are as beautiful as her."

Kunti and Mili smiled and ran towards their rooms.

Indriya got attracted towards Mili and wanted to be with her, but there was no way he could not enter their room.

However, he was a brave man and didn't want to leave any chance.

He followed them while hiding from the guards and, finally, reached the window of the room where Kunti and Mili were present.

"Now, you may come in, brave man." Kunti instructed.

Indriya smiled and jumped inside the room.

"So, what do you want?" asked Kunti while Mili hid behind the curtains.

"Your friend is very beautiful. Can't we three be friends and enjoy the time till I am here?" Indriya proposed.

"She is Mili, the daughter of my father's charioteer." Kunti informed.

"Mili, nice name! You may come out of the curtains; I have seen you hiding there." Indriya suddenly addressed Mili while smiling at her.

"Oh! So, who are you? Why are you following me like an

insect?" Mili retorted while coming out in the open.

"Aha, you are just so sweet." Indriya exclaimed.

"Alright, we can be friends but only for tonight, as I am leaving to Kuntibhoj tomorrow." Kunti interrupted.

"So, you are leaving but I can continue living with Mili, right?" Indriya asked.

Mili and Kunti laughed again.

"OK, do you know, we are going to perform a mantra. Will you be with us?" Mili asked.

"What is it all about?" Indriya asked with suspicion.

"A few days back, Sage Durvasa visited Kuntibhoj. Do you know Sage Durvasa? He is known for granting boons to those who please him, particularly when he is served well as an honored guest." Kunti explained.

"And our Kunti served him up to his expectations and catered to all his unreasonable requests, including demanding food at odd hours in the night." Mili interrupted.

"Eventually, Sage Durvasa was gratified. Before departing, he rewarded me by teaching me the Atharvaveda mantras, which would enable me to invoke any god of my choice to beget children by him." Kunti continued.

"Really?" Indriya was excited to hear this.

"So, are you planning to test its legitimacy?" he asked.

Mili replied in affirmation.

"So, what are you waiting for?" exclaimed Indriya.

Kunti asked Mili and Indriya to hide behind the pillars while she would recite the mantras.

Kunti was confused as to which God she should call. She thought for a while and, then, decided to invoke Lord Sun. She started chanting Atharvaveda mantras with her eyes closed.

She chanted the mantras repeatedly, while Indriya and Mili kept watching her from behind the pillars. While Kunti was reciting the mantras, Indriya looked into Mili's eyes and she looked back into his eyes silently; both could see deep love for each other hidden in their eyes.

Standing behind the pillar, Indriya spread his arms welcoming Mili for a hug. She peeped again from the side of the pillar and saw

Kunti still reciting the mantras with her eyes closed.

Mili hugged Indriya and felt complete coming into the strong arms of Indriya. Indriya, too, felt relaxed hugging his first love. They both savored the moment and kissed each other enjoying complete peace and pleasure.

Soon, they saw a bright, white light produced in the room. It was so bright that Indriya and Mili couldn't open their eyes to it, but they could very well hear.

"I am Lord Surya and I am happy by your chanting of Atharvaveda mantras to invoke me. I would like to bless you with your first son, Karna, who would be wearing armor (Kavacha) and a pair of earrings (Kundala) that will prove he's my son."

Kunti was afraid to know that the mantras actually worked and she pleaded before Lord Surya, "I am afraid of being an unwed mother and even he will be known as a bastard. I request you to please take him back. It's my fault that I tested the legitimacy of the Atharvaveda mantra without thinking first."

"No, I can't. You invoked me and, now, I cannot take my boon back. I bless you and your son." Lord Surya replied and, then, vanished in the sky.

Indriya and Mili could open their eyes when the bright, white light was gone. They saw Kunti holding a beautiful baby in her hands with tears in her eyes.

"Wow! So, it worked!" Excited Mili turned towards Kunti.

Kunti was looking at her child with tears in her eyes.

Indriya understood her concern and asked, "What happened, Kunti? Why are you not happy?"

She spoke softly, "I am happy but I am still not married; what will I tell to my parents and the society?"

"Hmm… that's a problem, but what's the way out?" asked Mili.

Mili took the baby in her hands and started caressing him.

Kunti glanced through the window and said, "Should I run away with my baby to another kingdom? Indriya, you can help me in this."

Indriya moved a step backward and replied, "I am sorry; if I'd do so, the soldiers employed by your father will definitely kill me. Also, will you be able to give a respectable life to this child even if we managed to survive?"

Kunti looked confused and muttered, "Then, what should I do?"

Mili suggested, "Why not dig a pit and keep this baby in it and leave it up to mother earth to take care of him."

"No no, he might get hurt and wild animals could also hurt him or rather eat him up." Indriya replied apprehensively.

He thought for while and suggested, "Why not keep him in a basket well-protected and set it afloat in the River Ganga? I have heard a story that Mother Ganga set her seven sons afloat in the river, but saved the eighth one and nurtured him; maybe, she would take care of him, too."

Kunti looked at him with hope in her eyes, "You may be correct. Mili, please get a basket ready while I'd take care of my son."

Mili handed over the baby to Kunti and she took him in her arms and started fondling him.

Mili started arranging the basket. Indriya accompanied her in setting it up filling in the things which could make the baby comfortable.

"How will you go to the bank of the River Ganga? If you'd take your chariot along, others might come to know about this." Indriya asked Kunti.

Kunti was confused. She wondered what should be done.

Indriya was thinking about a way when Mili interrupted, "Why don't you take her there; you are our friend now?"

"Good suggestion!" Indriya smiled and Kunti reciprocated the gesture.

He continued, "I will go to the stable and bring my horse to the garden area from the back; you both can join me there."

"Wait!" Kunti interrupted, "Mili, you stay in the room and sleep on my bed so that no one notices my absence."

Mili agreed and Indriya went to the stable to bring out his horse.

In some time, Indriya reached the decided place and saw Kunti already waiting there. Kunti accompanied him to the bank of the River Ganga.

She prayed to Mother Ganga to take care of her son and take him to the safest place where he could grow with love and care.

She, then, placed the basket in the river and waited till it vanished with the tides.

Indriya consoled Kunti and took her back to the palace.

Kunti was highly obliged with his help and told him that she is in his debt and she will be happy to help him in any which way he required in future.

On the other hand, Indriya promised her that he will be her friend forever and will never let her down.

After dropping her back, Indriya went to his room and took rest as he had to leave the next morning. He promised Mili to return to marry her once his archery training was over.

Mili accepted his offer and Indriya returned to Drupad.

Kunti returned to Kuntibhoj and started living there without informing anyone about Karna.

Chapter-6
Plan to kill Pandu

Indriya, after reaching Panchal, started his training with his grandfather, Mohoriti, with complete dedication and sincerity.

He was getting trained in archery and politics. Drupad also observed the efforts of Mohoriti in developing his soldiers and gave him the position of commander in his army.

Once, when Indriya was practicing with Mohoriti, he came to Indriya and asked him, “Why do you think I am training you with so much expertise?”

Indriya joining his hands before his grandfather and said, “You want me to be the best warrior ever.”

“Yes, but before that, you are born to take revenge for your family, our revenge on Hastinapur and on Bhishma.” Mohoriti intervened.

Indriya could not understand what his grandfather was trying to tell.

“I would like to tell you something about your ancestors as I consider this as the right time now.” continued Mohoriti while Indriya sat beside him.

“Your great grandfather, Mohoma, was very close to King

Shantanu of Hastinapur and was his best courtier but his life was shattered due to debauchery by Shantanu. I was supposed to claim the throne of Hastinapur when Shantanu brought his lost son, Bhishma. Bhishma killed my other nineteen brothers and Shantanu married the love of my life Satyavati."

Mohoriti gave him the details about what all happened and the reason behind it; he explained to him that having strength and skills do not matter, if you do not also have the throne.

"Hastinapur's current claimant of the throne, Pandu, is weak and pale and Dhritarashtra is blind, yet they are sitting on the throne because they are the heirs of the king. It hardly matters whether they are capable of running the kingdom and looking after their progeny or not."

"You are a strong, brave and clever warrior; you can also win the throne. Soon, the time will come when you'd have to think in that direction and win the throne of Hastinapur back for me." Mohoriti explained to Indriya.

Indriya marked his words and assured him that he would work harder and would take the revenge for his family and for the pride of his grandfather.

At the same time in Kuntibhoj, a swayamvara was arranged for Kunti and she chose to get married to the king of Hastinapur, Pandu.

King Pandu wanted to extend the boundaries of Hastinapur. After inheriting the throne, he went on various wars conquering or allying with many kingdoms to join in Hastinapur.

Finally, he reached Madra and found the huge army of Madra waiting to have a war with him.

As the war began, Pandu found the charioteer of King Shalya of Madra driving the chariot so fast that he wasn't even able to aim his arrows to reach him. He tried to chase him but failed every time.

Finally, King Shalya stopped in front of Pandu and offered him a peace treaty by saying, "It is waste to have a war and lose so many lives and property. I am offering you to marry my sister Madri and let the two kingdoms be friend forever."

He unleashed his charioteer's face to reveal her as his sister, Madri. Pandu could not reject his offer after seeing Madri at the very first glance and agreed to stop the war and get married to her.

At the same time in Panchal, Indriya was basking in the love and the memories of Mili.

One day, Indriya was with his friend, Nadra, by the waterfall. They were sitting at the highest point on the hill, enjoying the view of the fall while Indriya was lost in the memories of Mili.

"What happened, Indriya; you looked lost." asked Nadra, his friend.

Indriya ignored him and kept looking at the waterfall.

Nadra playfully asked, "So, which girl do you see bathing in the waterfall?"

"No way, Nadra, you are a fool!" replied Indriya.

"Remembering Mili, the daughter of the charioteer of Shurasena?" Nadra taunted.

Indriya looked at him and smiled, "I am missing her; would she be missing me too?"

"You are too afraid. If I were in your place, I would have gone to Shurasena by now and would have brought her along with me." Nadra tried to provoke Indriya.

Indriya knew what was correct and what was not. He believed in his love and was sure what he was doing was right for his future.

"I have plans which need to be completed before I marry her and I assure you, she will be mine one day" Indriya tried to calm him down.

Somewhere in Hastinapur, Pandu was hunting in a forest and was looking for a hunt from a distance, his vision partially obscured by plants and trees. He mistook Rishi Kindama and his wife, who were making love, for a deer and shot arrows at them, killing the Rishi. The dying sage spelled a curse on Pandu, since he had not only killed them in the midst of lovemaking but also showed no signs of remorse for his action. King Pandu argued with Sage Kindama by misquoting Sage Agastya's ruling on the rights of Kshatriyas on hunting. Sage Kindama, then, cursed Pandu that whenever he would approach his wives to make love, he would die.

Pandu was shattered to have been cursed and so were Kunti and Madri. The news of the curse had spread to other kingdoms, too, as Pandu was one king who was expanding his territory to a great extent in a very short duration.

"Indriya, it's time for our revenge." Mohoriti informed Indriya while having food at night.

Indriya, who was still eating his food, stopped and looked at his grandfather.

"Yes, Pandu, after getting cursed, has renounced his kingdom and has decided to live as an ascetic with his wives and this can be the best opportunity for us to kill him. This will be one of the biggest setbacks for Bhishma and will also help us taking over Hastinapur." Mohoriti explained.

"So, what must I be doing?" Indriya asked about his plan.

"You are brave; you are an expert. Go to the forest where Pandu is living with his wives and kill him once you find a good opportunity." Mohoriti disclosed his plan.

Indriya understood what was needed to be done and decided to move towards the forest the next day. Indriya carried food and water along with his weapons and set out on his horse in search of Pandu, not knowing that Kunti is married to Pandu.

On reaching the forest in the next few days, he started his search for Pandu in the deep forest. One day, he was walking with his horse in the forest to find some footprints or marks, which could lead him to Pandu, when he noticed a small hut next to the lake.

He immediately took his position behind the trees and started monitoring keenly. He pulled out his sword to avert any emergency situation of attack. After a few minutes, he saw five kids coming out of the hut playing with pots and holding wooden arms in hands. He kept on watching in suspicion if these kids were of Pandu. Then, after a few minutes, Pandu came out of the hut along with his wife, Madri.

"I will be back in a few hours and will bring some fruits for the children and wood to cook food with tonight." Pandu told Madri

She smiled and asked him to return soon.

Indriya was, now, sure that he was Pandu. Finally, after walking for many days and nights, he'd found his prey. Looking at the physique of Pandu, he became sure that he would defeat him easily. He started following him, hiding intermittently behind the bushes and the tree trunks.

After walking for some distance, Pandu reached a place where there were trees of guava and orange. He placed his bag made of hay aside and pulled a stick to pluck fruits for dinner.

Indriya found this instance as a good opportunity to attack and kill Pandu. He immediately pulled his sword and rushed towards him, but before he could reach him, he heard a voice of a lady. He placed his sword back and saw Kunti coming from some distance behind the trees. She was wearing a sari and was simply dressed unlike how he had seen her before as a princess.

He was shocked to see Kunti and random thoughts started running through his mind, "Is this Kunti, my friend? But what is she doing here?"

He tried to hide himself back but Kunti saw him and shouted at him, "Who is there hiding behind the trees?"

Hearing Kunti shout, Pandu got alert and pulled his sword to check if some danger prevailed.

Indriya decided it was better not to hide and he turned his face towards them.

Kunti immediately recognized him as he was the one who had helped her hide her sin. She was afraid if he was there to tell anything to Pandu.

"Who are you, young man? And what are you doing here?" asked Pandu, bringing his sword to the front.

Kunti moved her hand towards the sword and asked Pandu to keep it back "I know him; he is Indriya, my old friend."

"But what are you doing here, Indriya?" she asked him.

Indriya smiled at Kunti and joined his hand before Pandu, "I was going to a nearby kingdom; somehow, I forgot my way and came in this direction."

Kunti smiled and said, "How strange it is to meet old friends like this."

She turned towards Pandu and told him, "He came to my father's palace once as a messenger and we became friends then. You know my friend, Mili; she is still waiting for him and see here he is roaming around in these jungles."

Pandu smiled at him and welcomed him. "You may have come by mistake, but now you are our guest tonight. You have to join us for dinner."

Kunti introduced Pandu to Indriya as her husband and asked

him to join them.

Indriya smiled and took the offer. He had devised a plan now; he wanted to be with him and kill him once he had a good opportunity. However, he was worried about his friend Kunti, as she was Mili's friend and he loved Mili more than he did to himself.

He was worried that Mili might hate him if she'd come to know that he killed the husband of her dear friend and might not marry him. On the other hand, he was tied to the promise he had made to his grandfather.

Being a warrior, he must follow the promise made to his family head even if it leads to him missing the love of his life. He decided to take over Pandu tonight.

He moved along with Pandu and Kunti to their hut. Once they reached, the five children of Pandu greeted him with their hands joined and stood behind their father.

"They are my five angles, Yudhishthira, Bhima, Arjuna, Nakula and Sahadeva, and she's my second wife, Madri" Pandu introduced Indriya to his clan.

Indriya, too, joined his hands and greeted her.

"He is Indriya, an old friend of Kunti. He will be staying with us tonight and will leave in the morning." Pandu told Madri.

"An old friend of Kunti didi means he is a special guest to us. Be assured, we will serve him to our best." Madri replied, smiling at Kunti.

The children started playing with his arms and giggled at him. He, too, loved playing with the kids and enjoyed seeing Pandu smiling on the small tantrums of his kids.

"It would be tough for such a big king to live life as an ascetic in these forests, right?" asked Indriya to Pandu while having dinner sitting on the floor.

Pandu looked at him and said, "Life brings challenges and we, humans, are made to handle them. If I were in my palace, I would have perhaps missed my kids growing up with me like this. Today, I am enjoying my kids playing on my lap and my wives cooking food for me," he paused and, then, continued, "this is a different phase of life and I am enjoying it as these moments will be with me forever."

Indriya was touched hearing his words and somewhere in

his heart, he was not willing to kill Pandu but he was bound to do it.

Once they finished their dinner, Indriya's bed was placed outside the hut in the open and Pandu's bed was on the other side of the hut near the lake, along with his five sons.

It was late at night and everyone was fast asleep, but Indriya could not sleep and was awake counting stars. He was waiting for the correct time to kill Pandu, but he was also wondering if killing him without a proper fight would be the right thing to do.

After giving it a lot of thought, he stood up, pulled out his sword and started tiptoeing towards him. He moved slowly so that no one would wake up. Within a few seconds, he reached near Pandu and saw two of his sons sleeping on his right side and three on his left side all holding each other's hands.

He raised his sword and moved towards Pandu but, then, stopped and started thinking if it was correct to kill him while he was defenseless. Pandu was a great warrior and he could have defeated Indriya easily. The questions running in his mind made him put his sword back in its sheath. He joined his hands before him and murmured in his mind, "I will kill you one day for sure but not like a coward but like a brave soldier in a battlefield".

He moved back to his bed and fell asleep. The next morning, he took his leave and decided to move back to Panchal to Mohoriti and make a different plan where he could take his family's revenge but like a warrior.

Chapter-7
Land of Indriya

"Hope you killed Pandu, my warrior!" asked Mohoriti while Indriya stood in front of him.

"I tried my best, grandfather, but my teachings didn't allow me to kill someone who was weaponless".

Mohoriti yelled with anger, "So, you mean you left him alive?"

"Whatever happened in the past, happened for the good; whatever is happening right now is happening for the good; whatever will happen in the future, will also happen for the good. Do not weep for the past; do not worry for the future. Let's concentrate on our present life and allow our life to take us to the point where we can fight and win the battle." Indriya replied.

"Do not test my patience, Indriya; we are born to take revenge and our family will not live in peace until we complete our revenge." Mohoriti roared.

Indriya knelt down and said, "Grandfather, I am never against revenge but we are warriors and revenge needs to be taken in the battlefield, not by hiding in the bushes; this will make me a killer not a warrior."

"What did you bring with your birth that you have lost? What did you produce that is destroyed? You didn't bring anything along with yourself when you were born. Whatever you have is what you have received from your ancestors. Whatever you will give, you will give to your ancestors. Everyone came in this world empty-handed and shall go the same way. Everything belongs to our ancestors only and you must repay them for bringing you on this earth." Mohoriti explained him in anger.

"Grandfather, I am abiding by my promise and everyone who is or who will be coming to earth in the family of Mohoma is bound to take revenge for the injustice done to you and our ancestors. However, we must not forget that we are soldiers and warriors and our first duty is to do what is correct." Indriya tried to explain him.

Mohoriti listened to him and, then, asked, "What is in your mind; what you want to do?"

Indriya now stood up and replied, "We must have our own land. We must build our own army, which is skilled and experienced. Then, let's take up a war with Hastinapur."

"And you feel we can stand even for a day in front of the huge army of Hastinapur?" Mohoriti questioned.

"Army is never big or small. It's an illusion in the mind of the soldier. It may take time but our goal will be fixed and our aim will be constant." Indriya replied.

Indriya continued, "We will get ourselves ready and make small plans which would hit them big."

Mohoriti thought for a while and furthered, "Ok, then let us have our own land and our own people, who can all think same."

Mohoriti decided to meet Drupad and ask if he could have a small piece of land outside Panchal where he could set up his family and build a new tribe which could support Panchal as and when required and work under his shelter.

Soon, he reached to the king to put forward his proposal.

The king of Panchal, Drupad, was sitting on his throne when Mohoriti stood in front of him with his hands joined and requested, "Long live the king! I have been serving your army and training the army men to reach to the best of their caliber since long now. I am here today to request you for something which is unusual. You will ask me for the reasons and I'd answer you, too, but before that, I'd request you to listen to me first."

Drupad asked him to continue and tell what he wanted.

"I would be highly obliged if you may give me a small piece of land, any unused part of the earth in Panchal. I would like to build my own tribe and would train that tribe with special skills and knowledge; this tribe could work as extra specialized hands of Panchal."

"And why should I allow you? Why don't you make my complete army trained and specialized and remain here?" asked the king.

Mohoriti replied to him with his head bowed, "King, big trees have branches, which are still a part of the tree. They might grow in different directions and specialize in housing the nests of different birds but still they remain a part of the tree and give strength to the tree. Rivers can have many tributaries but they still are a part of the river."

Drupad listened to him and before he could say anything, one of the court member interrupted, "King, one of your old friends, Dronacharya, is here and wants to meet you."

Dronacharya was the son of Bharadwaja Muni. Once, Bharadwaja Muni went with his companions to the Ganga River to perform his ablutions. There, he beheld a beautiful nymph, named Ghritachi, who had come there to bathe. The sage was overcome with desire which caused him to produce a reproductive fluid. Bharadwaja Muni captured the fluid in a vessel called Drona, and Dronacharya himself sprang from the fluid preserved. Dronacharya spent his youth in poverty, but studied Dharma and military arts such as archery in which he gained expertise, along with the prince of Panchal, Drupada. It was during that time when Drupada and Dronacharya became close friends.

Hearing that Dronacharya was in his court, he asked Mohoriti to wait till he meets him. He asked his courtier to send Dronacharya to the court.

Dronacharya entered the court and was happy to see his childhood friend, Drupad, who was now the prince of Panchal.

"My dear friend, it was long back we'd met. Please come down from the throne; let's hug to feel the warmth of our friendship." Dronacharya smiled and greeted Drupad.

Drupad remained calm and remained seated on his throne.

"You are standing in front of the king of Panchal, you must speak with due respect." said one of the courtiers.

Dronacharya moved one more step closer, ignoring the courtier. He said, "What is he speaking, friend? He doesn't know that we were best friends at one time when his king was still a prince."

Drupad raised his left hand and gestured Dronacharya to stop.

This faded the smile on Dronacharya's face.

"Friendship is possible only between people of equal stature in life. As a child, it was possible for me to be friends with you because at that time, we were equal, but, now, I am the king of Panchal. Still, as I know you since childhood, I would like to give you a chance to request what you want as a Brahmin." Drupad replied in arrogance.

Dronacharya was hurt. He had come to him for the sake of his wife and son, desiring freedom from his poverty. Banking on a promise made by Drupad during their childhood, he had decided to approach him to ask for help, but his words had left him devastated.

"I had not expected such a response from a friend who'd promised me something in his childhood." murmured Dronacharya.

Drupad stood up from his throne, came near to him and replied while pointing towards Mohoriti, "Look at this man. He is working as a trainer in my army since many years. He is capable and deserving, yet he's standing in front of me with his hands joined, asking for a small piece of land. Why should I help someone who has just come to my court saying I have studied with him in my childhood?"

Dronacharya had no words to say standing in front of his arrogant friend, ye he tried, "He is standing in front of you joining his hand because he is your servant and I came to you with open arms thinking you are friend. Remember one thing Drupad, open arms can solve bigger problems than folded hands as you have wider grip to hold things, but you who are drenched in arrogance and wouldn't see now."

Drupad spoke in a much louder voice now, "I still respect that you are a Brahmin and I urge you to leave after taking what a Brahmin deserves."

Dronacharya, too, replied in a louder tone, "I am a Brahmin but I still have studied Dharma and military arts such as archery, in which I hold a greater expertise than any of your warriors and, one day, I will return to conquer you."

Drupad, now, looked at Mohoriti and ordered him, "I will give you twice the land that you have asked for but drag this Brahmin out of my court like beggars."

Mohoriti immediately took the orders and asked Dronacharya to leave the court and, also, pulled his sword out. Dronacharya looked at him and yelled, "Don't worry, warrior, you are a servant of this arrogant king. I am leaving, no need to take your sword out for this Brahmin."

Dronacharya left the court without turning back at Drupad. Once he left, Drupad turned towards Mohoriti and said, "Great, Mohoriti, I am impressed by your loyalty. Take the land in the north-east outskirts of Panchal towards Kuru, next to the River Yamuna. Stand at one point and run forming a circle without stopping, in order to claim that land."

Mohoriti smiled and thanked him by joining his hands before him in respect.

He took his leave and moved straight towards Indriya, who was waiting outside the palace to hear the good news.

"Let's build our own tribe now," Mohoriti informed Indriya with happiness.

Indriya smiled with pleasure, "Grandfather, our land will be called Mohoma and we will be known as the Mohoma tribe from now."

He touched his feet and Mohoriti took him in his arms and gave him blessings.

Chapter-8
Building Mohoma

This would be a new beginning, when Mohoriti would be thinking differently about the changes in the generation of his family.

It was a dark night and Indriya was unable to sleep because he was busy building various plans in his mind to create his own tribe. He was happy to consider his grandfather as the head of the tribe and he was busy planning how his life would be living with Mili in his own land.

Mohoriti was observing Indriya turning sides on his bed again and again. He understood there must be something which is not letting him sleep. He stood up and went close to Indriya.

"You want to tell me something, I guess." he asked.

Indriya stood up and sat next to him, "I think I am getting excited planning for Mohoma land."

Mohoriti was an old man now; he clearly understood all Indriya's facial expressions. He replied, "Are you telling me the truth or you have something more to say?"

Indriya, now, started sweating and feeling shy. While still looking down, he spoke softly, "I am fond of a girl."

Mohoriti smiled and said, "Continue, I can understand it's

your age to fall for girls; who is she?"

"She is the daughter, Mili, of the charioteer of Shurasena king." responded Indriya.

"Hmm, so, my brave warrior is feeling defeated in love now." Mohoriti teased him.

And, then, he continued, "So, what are you waiting for? Move to Shurasena tomorrow and bring her to the land of Mohoma!"

Indriya was overjoyed. He touched his grandfather's feet and asked for the permission to set out the next morning to meet Mili and see if they could get married.

Mohoriti gave him blessings and said, "May you be victorious!"

Next day, Indriya was all set early in the morning. He hadn't slept the whole night. He sought blessings from Mohoriti and his mothers and left for Shurasena. As he reached Shurasena, he went straight to Mili's house.

He put his proposal to marry Mili in front of her father. He was happy to hear the same and asked Indriya to call his family so that they could arrange the wedding ceremony in Shurasena. Mili was very excited and happy. Indriya sent the information to Mohoriti and he, too, reached Shurasena with Indriya's mothers carrying gifts and sweets.

It was a big wedding and Indriya and Mili looked great together.

After finishing all the rituals, they went back to Panchal. The family was happy as everything was moving in a perfect direction.

💧♍♏■♏ 👍♒♋■♑♏

It was a breezy morning with sun glowing brightly. Mohoriti and his family were getting ready to leave to the land of Mohoma. Some of the well-wishers, who wanted to join them in making Mohoma a new land to live and be a part of the Mohoma tribe, were also waiting outside their houses. It is human nature to look for change and find benefits in the new opportunities and most of the people were finding the opportunity of new land and convenience in the land of Mohoma.

Women gathered early in the morning with cooked sweet rice dipped with Madhu (Honey) and a drink made of water boiled with herbs and dry fruits, which they were serving to all gathered for the travel. Most of them had brought fruits and vegetables along with them and collected on one of the biggest chart standing at the corner of the house. This collection would help on the way for food and at times when construction on the land would be done.

Mili, being the newlywed bride, was not allowed to work. She was sitting in a corner with a few ladies observing her ornaments and beauty. She was looking extremely beautiful wearing beaded ornaments made of Tulsi wood and dry roses. The jewelry she was wearing was not only an adornment, but also a protection against evil forces, endowed with mystical qualities. In her hands, she was wearing the Navaratna or nine gems, each sacred to a planet. In her left arm, right below shoulder, she wore maniratna called the serpent stone, which is used as a talisman to protect the wearer. Her ornaments consisted of Rudraksha and Tulsi seeds and sandalwood beads giving out an enchanting fragrance from her body.

Indriya, along with Nadra, his friend, was getting the carts ready to move. He was smiling while his friends taunted him and was turning back and admiring Mili from a distance. She, too, was trying her best to admire him through her veil.

Soon, those ten to twelve families moved to the bullock carts and took their seats anticipating the start of the journey. Mohoriti climbed the cart with Indriya's mother and Mili. He was followed by the carts belonging to the other families and those loaded with goods and food. Indriya, along with his friends, walked in the front holding the lead rope of his horse.

The land of Mohoma was located to the west of Panchal towards the large Himalayan ranges. The soil of the land was rich and fertile for the cultivation of herbs and apple orchids, but the terrains here made it tough to explore and build.

Other tribes inhabiting the places adjacent to the land of Mohoma were Tangana and Tittira, which were famous for breeding fine horses, Dasheraka, Pishacha, Madaka and Kirata, which were known for breeding elephants, Koshala, a famous solar dynasty of the Ramayana era, Khasa and Kimpurusha.

Among all these tribe, Kimpurusha was the closest and was suspected to pose a threat to the establishment of the land of Mohoma.

Kimpurusha tribe was one among the exotic tribes. These exotic tribes lived in the inaccessible regions of the Himalayan Mountains and had limited interaction with the civilizations of the other tribes. Thus, they were reckoned to be super human beings or natural spirits.

Kimpurushas were described to be monkey-headed beings with tails like monkeys. Lord Hanuman was a Kimpurusha, who set Lanka on fire with his long, burning tail. In some stories, they were mentioned as horse-headed. They could be a tribe of horse-warriors like the Kambojas. They were known to be people with the nature akin to that of a lion. They usually did not bother others, but they also didn't like interference in their territory.

They all finally reached the destination, which will be called as the land of Mohoma.

"Welcome all to the land of Mohoma; we are now the Mohomians!" Mohoriti stated loud and clear and continued, "We will be known as warriors in the history. Lord Brahma has given us ample opportunities on his land to survive; we have water, fertile land and strength to build opportunities for us. Next few days, we will be working hard to construct our houses and demarcating land for farming for each family in Mohoma. Who will grow what will be decided for all, so that we can produce enough food for everybody. We will be using the currency of Panchal as our currency and the food will be available on barter basis.

Everyone living in Mohoma will share equal right to speak and keep his or her thoughts. Hope our thoughts and deeds will make Mohoma one of the best clans in Panchal."

Listening to his words, everyone started waving and cheering "Mohoma! Mohoma!"

They, then, started building their houses, for which they had done extensive planning to use big stones as well as clay stones. Mili took the responsibility of the architectural planning of the land along with a few more ladies in the camp. Their main responsibility was to design the positions of everyone's houses and allocate areas to them. The design of the houses was such that every house had ample space to live in, with open area in the front so that even the pets could comfortably reside in them.

Every house was connected to a tunnel which supplied water round the clock every day as the final end of it was connected to a tributary of Yamuna River. Outside every house there was built a big fireplace meant to keep wild animals away.

In the center of the village, a big open space was allocated for gatherings and discussions, along with a fire area which could be lit every night to keep animals away.

They had designed a quadrangle watch tower to be put up outside the village in order to keep a watch on the enemy. Also, raised podiums were constructed at equal distances for attacking and hiding in case of any danger.

Young men used to go to the nearby forest to cut wood from the trees, which would be used to build houses. Mohoriti, along with a few men, decided to build an archery house and cantonment area setup and, also, finalized the positions for the watchtowers.

They worked day and night to build their land and in a few days, they started seeing the results with their beautiful houses getting ready with finishing touches of carvings and paintings of ancestors and gods. Amidst all this, Mohoriti was tensed by the strength of the young population in the tribe. He considered this as a threat for the safety and the security of the land. Soon, he needed to build his small army but he needed men for that.

One night, Indriya came to Mohoriti while he was busy building the archery house.

"Grandfather, there is a news for you." He said.

"What happened; is everything fine?" Mohoriti said, while still working.

"King Pandu died in the forest due to some curse and her queen, Madri, committed sati with him".

Mohoriti stopped what he was doing and said, "That's a bad news. We missed one more Kuru to kill." He paused and, then, asked Indriya, "Who is the king now, Bhishma?"

"No, Bhishma rejected to be king as per his pledge; so, now Dhritarashtra will be the king now."

At the same time, Nadra came running towards them. He was almost losing his breath while shouting Indriya's name again and again.

His loud sound alerted them, "What happened Nadra; why are you shouting?" asked Indriya.

He tried to catch his breath and informed them something.

He was trying to show something while pointing his finger to the north of the village. Mohoriti asked him to sit and hold his breath and, then, tell what had happened.

Indriya gave him water to drink.

"What happened, Nadra; please let us know?" Indriya asked.

He held his breath and tried to tell them, "I was working at the watchtower and I saw someone hiding behind the trees and monitoring our movement. To check who was there, I came down and move towards the tree and saw two super humans, one with the head of a monkey and the body of a human and the other with the head of a lion and the body of a human. They disappeared seeing me with the blink of an eye."

Mohoriti stood up and looked towards the north, "They have observed our presence and they are monitoring us".

"Who is monitoring us, grandfather?" Indriya furthered.

"Kimpurushas; they are here from the time of Lord Ram. They are highly skilled half-monkey and half-human. Kimpurushas is the tribe and this is the trait by which they are recognized. I hope they do not attack us; they don't like intruders and we are close to them. Also, on the contrary, we are very less in number. If they attack, it would be tough for us to resist them."

"So, what is the solution?" asked Indriya.

"There is no solution, except to not interfere with them and avoid going towards north as much as possible, at least till we are ready to face them." Mohoriti answered.

Indriya listened to him quietly and, then, replied to him, "We need to increase our tribe's strength; it is the right time to call back *Bade Pitashri* (Uncle) Duru and his family."

Mohoriti heard and turned towards him in anger, "Never take his name; he can't come back to us."

"Pitamah, you need to understand the situation now. What happened years back was not anyone's fault; he did what he thought was correct and you did what you thought was correct."

"He did wrong!" replied Mohoriti in anger.

"We are not the ones to judge who did wrong and who did right. Let's do our work and leave this decision to Brahma." Indriya replied, "I request you to permit me to urge him to come back and be a part of the land of Mohoma."

Mohoriti turned towards him with tears in his eyes and hugged him.

"My blessings are with you, Vijay bhava!" He replied.

Chapter-9
Return of Duru

It was twilight and the sun was shining bright, while the birds had started chirping. Cold wind was blowing, when Indriya reached Matsya riding on his horse. His reflection was visible on the water droplets lying on the way.

As he entered Matsya, he could see the progeny of Matsya busy in their morning routine jobs. People had started settling in their shops and were busy in their work. He moved towards the temple at the center, leading his horse.

After he had freshened up, he decided to have some breakfast at the shop next to a temple.

"Do you know anyone with the name, Duru, in Matsya?" he asked a local person.

He thought for a while and said, "I haven't heard about this name; you may check with someone else."

While he was asking about Duru from the local people, one old woman, who was sitting on the stairs of the temple, came closer to him.

"Who are you searching for; Duru?" She asked.

He immediately held her hand as she was unable to stand, "Yes, I am searching for Duru. Do you know him?"

"Come along." she spoke and started walking while being followed by Indriya, leading his horse.

After walking for some distance, she reached a house and asked Indriya to wait. She moved in while walking, slowly.

After a few minutes, Duru came out, walking straight. He had a great build and one could hardly see any effects of age on his body.

Indriya immediately touched his feet and greeted him. Duru blessed him and ask him about his identity.

"I am Indriya, the son of Maaru, your younger brother." he replied joining his hands.

Duru immediately hugged him having listened to his words.

"Don't say 'No', bade Pitashri; I am here to take you to our own land of Mohoma." Indriya insisted.

"Land of Mohoma? How is Pitashri?" Duru questioned.

"He is perfectly fine and, with his permission, I have come to take you back. I request you to not say 'no'. We have built our own tribe by our forefather's name, Mohoma, and it is the time for our family to be together." Indriya explained.

While he was telling, three sons of Duru came out and stood behind him. As Duru saw them, he introduced him to them, "They are your brothers, Durudhan, Asthachik, Karanasura; you have one sister, too, Kriti Shree."

Indriya moved ahead and hugged them while they were still surprised to see him. Suddenly, the same old lady came out crying and hugged Indriya.

Duru consoled her and explained to Indriya, "She is your great grandmother and mother of Pitashri, Mohoriti, Ritikawali. She was in prison since a very long time in Hastinapur and, then, got released considering her old age. She, then, came to meet her old friend, Vanasaki, who was the mother-in-law of my wives' sister. Then, we came to know that she is alive and since then, she has been living with me."

Indriya started crying looking at this family together.

"Grandfather will be happy to see you all. I request you all to come to join the land of Mohoma."

Duru asked his sons to get ready to move to Mohoma. He also asked his son, Asthachik, to call Charayu and Vinashala along with their families to ask them if they, too, would agree to join them in the land of Mohoma.

Charayu and Vinashala were the grandsons of Vanasaki. Vanasaki got married to Majhara, since Mohoma could not return from Trigarta, and gave birth to two sons, Chintan and Mahantam. Further, Chintan and Mahantam had two and three sons, respectively. The eldest son of Chintan was Charayu and the eldest son of Mahantam was Vinashala.

Charayu and Vinashala were also a part of the Matsya army and were related to Duru as his wives' sister was married to Vinashala. Actually, Chintan and Mahantam were also the children of Mohoma and this was a secret she had kept with herself till now.

After a long conversation and discussion, Charayu and Vinashala also agreed to move to the land of Mohoma along with Duru family.

Indriya was extremely happy to have such a big reunion and was overjoyed to take them to his grandfather, Mohoriti.

Next day, they all gathered to start the voyage towards the land of Mohoma.

As they reached Mohoma, Duru and others were astonished to see such a well-planned village.

As they all waited at the center of the village, Indriya went to call Mohoriti.

As he arrived, his eyes were full of tears seeing his mother and his son, Duru.

"Now, the land of Mohoma is complete." he said.

Duru and all their children touched his feet and took blessings.

Vanasaki, who was very old by now, was happy as only she knew that her children also belonged to Mohoma.

It was a night of celebration at Mohoma.

Mohoriti decided to address his people making them aware about everyone and the rules.

"We are the sons of Mohoma and we will live and prosper in the land of Mohoma. I am happy today to have my mother back in the land of Mohoma and would like to welcome my son, Duru, and his family and others who have come to be a part of Mohoma tribe. With you all, our tribe has become stronger and our strength has grown multifolds.

I am proud of Indriya and his thoughts that brought this change in our lives. Going forward, we will emphasize on building our combat capabilities to keep our enemies away and work hard to produce enough food grains for each and everyone in Mohoma.

I am an old man now and I would take care of managing and taking decisions in favor of Mohoma, but I would like to announce the king of Mohoma, under whose directions and guidance, I would like the land of Mohoma to prosper."

The progeny of Mohoma was sure that their king would be Indriya, a man who actually built the land of Mohoma; he was the man who brought everything together. He changed the way Mohoriti was looking at revenge till now.

Mohoriti looked at his progeny and, then, continued, "Systems must be correct and hierarchy must be followed on the path which is correct. We must not be biased to someone who brought us here or for someone who led us somewhere; it must be through a process, which must be correct enough. The process says that my elder son, Duru, who is like a father to Indriya, must rule the land of Mohoma. So, today I declare Duru as the king of our tribe!"

It was complete silence. Everyone looked at Indriya. It was the right time for Indriya to take a decision, which could be in favor of the land of Mohoma.

He smiled and chanted loudly, "Long live King Duru! Long live King Duru!" Looking at him enchanting, the progeny, too, started shouting his name.

Celebration started with dance and music. Everyone was busy welcoming Duru and his family and joining their hands before the new king, when suddenly one fire ball came from the north and exploded at the center of the village.

Immediately, there was a chaos there; everyone started running here and there.

"Warriors, get your swords ready. It's Kimpurushas!" Indriya shouted. Before they could align themselves and get ready for the attack, Kimpurushas were spread all over. It was fire and shout all over; the people were terrified looking at the super humans with head of monkeys and lions.

Indriya and Mohoriti tried to pull their swords and protect

the progeny but it was too late. Within few minutes, Kimpurushas moved away with speed of light, leaving behind fire, and stealing away all the animals. They attacked to warn them to leave the place.

Mohoriti and Indriya moved all around to check what the aftereffects of the attack were. They saw they had destroyed some of their houses and farms and had, also, stolen animals. It looked like they had planned to loot and warn Mohomas.

Mili came running from some distance towards Indriya, shouting to call him. They both rushed towards her along with others to check what had happened and were astonished to see Duru lying down on earth, with blood all around him.

Kimpurushas killed Duru by attacking him with the sword on his throat.

It was a bad time for the land of Mohoma. Their king was killed on the day he acquired his throne. Mohoriti had tears in his eyes and so did the others. The complete progeny went into mourning.

Durudhan, Asthachik and Karanasura were very angry and wanted to take revenge on Kimpurushas immediately. However, Mohoriti advised that to be discussed after they completed the funeral of Duru.

⬧♍♏■♏ 👍♒♋■♑♏

"We must get ready to attack Kimpurushas; they have to pay for our father's blood." Durudhan shouted in anger.

Indriya looked at him and replied while keeping his hand on his shoulder, "Bharata, (younger brother) we must not lose our control. We must think and take actions."

"There is no question of waiting; we are the warriors and we can teach them a lesson." He retorted.

Indriya tried to explain to him again, "We are very few in numbers now and are still in a stage of expanding our tribe; they are well arranged. We might lose again."

Durudhan yelled in anger this time, "You have not lost your father; you are worried more about Mohoma land than our revenge."

Mohoriti, who was listening to this conversation from some distance, interrupted, "I think Indriya is correct; warriors must use their brains, too, to combat. We will build our self and then attack at the right time"

Durudhan was still not in favor and tried to argue but Mohoriti was clear in his words.

He asked Asthachik and Karanasura to call the complete progeny at the center of the land for announcements and discussions.

Soon, everyone was gathered at the decided place.

Mohoriti took the center position and started, "I am sorry for not taking care of you properly; it was all of a sudden before even we could think and plan. But this is a lesson for us. We need to be more organized if we want to sustain and build the land of Mohoma as our place.

It is tough for me and my family to lose Duru, our king, and his space will be forever empty in my life but we have to move forward and look in the direction where we can survive and survive in a better position.

You all came along with me to prosper and it's my duty to take care of you and your family and I can assure you, we will be on top of what we have committed.

As Duru is no more with us, we have to choose our leader, who can lead us in the right direction and make the land of Mohoma prosper.

I would like to hear from all of you, who can be our leader and the king of the land of Mohoma?"

The progeny was silent for some time and looked at each other and, then, shouted in chorus, "Indriya! Indriya! Indriya!"

It was clear what everyone wanted and, so, Indriya was designated as the leader of the land of Mohoma.

Durudhan came forward and hugged Indriya, "You are my elder brother and would like to congratulate you for being our leader and believe that one day you will take revenge for our father and will lead our progeny towards a wonderful life."

Indriya touched Mohoriti's feet and all other elders' present there and took the position of the leader of the land of Mohoma while Mili stood by his side.

Chapter-10
Indriya, the leader

In Hastinapur, Gandhari, who was the daughter of Saubala, the King of Gandhar, which is a province in Afghanistan, was married to Dhiritarashtra. When she came to know that Dhiritarashtra was blind, she, too, decided to deny herself the pleasures of sight. She decided to tie a piece of cloth over her eyes for the rest of her life. Rishi Vyasa gave his blessings at her wedding as 'Be a mother of one hundred sons'. She was a very pious lady and an ardent worshiper of Lord Shiva.

When Kunti gave birth to Yudhishthira, Gandhari became pregnant, too. However, she had an unusually long pregnancy. Frustrated that Kunti's son was the first born, she beat her womb and a hardened gray mass of flesh was delivered. She challenged Vyasa to fulfill his blessing of one hundred sons. Vyasa took the piece of flesh and divided into 100 parts. He, then, put them into 100 pots and tied their mouths and buried them in the earth for a year. Duryodhana was the first to emerge out of the pot. His name literally meant 'hard to conquer'. When he was born, it was a very inauspicious hour. Vidhura and Bhishma advised Dhiritarashtra and Gandhari to abandon the child. He was to bring about the death and destruction of the complete clan. However, Dhiritarashtra and Gandhari's love towards the child was truly blind and they refused to part with Duryodhana. Gandhari, thus, had 100 sons and one daughter, Dushala. Duryodhana and Dushasana were amongst them.

One year had passed under the leadership of Indriya and Mohoma was expanding his prospects. Indriya gazed at the orange sky. The clouds hovering above Yamuna had just parted to reveal the setting sun. One more day under his leadership was arriving to an end, while he stood on the watchtower extending his muscular body over it. The numerous ornaments on his body gleamed in the shimmering reflected light of the waters.

He had perfectly lead his tribe till now. He was more alert than any other day. He looked back at his village and gestured with his eyes.

King Drupad would be visiting the tribe tomorrow to inspect the growth and development done by them. If he finds it good, he might land them more land to extend the development.

He alerted his men tonight, although Panchal army was guarding the borders, to take care of the arrival of their king.

Mohoriti, along with Durudhan and Asthachik, was moving around in the village to inspect the readiness. The women of the tribes were busy making multiple food dishes for the king and were about to work till late night, so that everything looked perfect.

"Indriya! You became a father!" Nadra shouted reaching the watchtower.

Indriya turned towards him and smiled in joy.

He jumped from the watchtower bending his muscular body and hugged Nadra with a smile.

"You keep an eye now." Indriya smiled and handed over the responsibility to him and ran towards his house.

He ran with his full power, to have the first look of the successor of his throne.

"It's a boy." Mohoriti smiled and hugged Indriya.

"He was born in an auspicious hour and will bring luck to our tribe."

Indriya smiled and kissed him on his forehead. The child appeared as bright as the sun looking at him with his eyes wide open

He will be bringing a new sunrise to the land of Mohoma. His small shoulders would grow wide and muscular in future and would take Mohoma to the next level in growth.

He was wrapped in a red silk cloth and wearing a golden anklet. With Chandan mark smeared on his forehead, he was looking like the son of Gods.

"He would be the son of God and would be known in history for his love and sacrifices. He would be the bravest warrior of Mohoma." Indriya looked at him and declared.

💧♍♏■♏ 👍♒♋■♑♏

The progeny of Mohoma was waiting at their huge, strong gate, which opened towards the road made of stones connecting Panchal. With the drums and the traditional songs of Mohoma being played around, everyone was dancing in rhythm carrying flowers in their hands.

Mohoriti and Indriya stood with a garland made of flower in their hand to welcome King Drupad, who would be crossing by the land of Mohoma while going to Hastinapur to meet Bhishma.

Land of Mohoma was decorated to welcome him; it looked like every single stone of Mohoma was thanking king Drupad for giving birth to their land.

Nadra shouted from top of the watchtower, "The dust cloud is visible; King's caravan is on its way."

Music started sounding loud with more energy in place.

As the king's Chariot came to the entry, Mohoriti moved with flowers and tilak in his hand and welcomed the King Drupad, who stood straight with a look of arrogance on his face.

"Good Mohoriti, I am impressed by looking at the development you have made on this barren land". He said.

Mohoriti put his head down and joined his hands towards him.

Drupad decided to walk around the village and check the development made by their tribe. Following him were his troops and some sages, who were travelling along with him.

"How are you managing Kimpurusha? They are very near to you." asked Drupad.

Indriya showed his hands towards the watch tower and explained, "As of now, we are trying to manage the distance with these but we have seen them attacking frequently."

"Last time, they had attacked our women and children, too."

Mohoriti further added, "We are planning to aggressively train our people to combat with them."

Drupad listened to them carefully and said, "Good to listen to your plan. develop a big archery training setup here; take gold from us to setup. Train not only the people of Mohoma but also from other parts of Panchal."

It was a good gift by the king; Mohoma would be the archery training place for complete Panchal. This means youngsters from other tribes will also be coming to learn in Mohoma with Drupad and will help us build our own small unit of army, which could fight against Kimpurusha also.

While Drupad took the seat at the center of the village, everyone present stood around him, praising him to be their king.

Ritikawali, then, came up with Indriya's son in her arms and requested Drupad to give him a name, which could bring him name and fame.

Drupad took him in his arms and asked the sage along with him to predict his future and give him a name.

Sage touched his forehead and blessed him, "He is born in an auspicious hour of moonlight; he will be having a nature as cool as the moonlight but his virtue will be bright as sunlight; he will be a leader and will bring new aspects in Mohoma land. He would be loved by everyone and would spread love in his future. He will be a warrior, who will show his skills in future wars.

He will be a part of making history in future but his fate is such that he will never be known in history. In future, he will take measures which will make Mohoma a prosperous land.

Looking at his effulgent future, we would like to name him Tejaswa."

Drupad handed over him back to Ritikawali saying, "So, now onwards, he will be known as Tejaswa."

Everyone was happy to hear the name and everyone chanted his name along with King Drupad's.

♦♍♏■♏ 👍♒♋■♑♏

In those days, the students went to sages and lived with them until the education was complete. This was called the Gurukul. In the Gurukul, all the students were equal and each had to do their share of work along with their studies. The work would include getting water from the well, chopping firewood, helping in the kitchen, washing dishes, taking the cows out to the pasture, plastering the walls and floor with cow dung, cleaning floors etc.

Somewhere in Hastinapur, Drona reached the outskirts to meet his brother-in-law, Kripa, who was the teacher of Kauravs and Pandavas. He saw some boys playing. While they were playing, their ball fell into a very deep well. The boys gathered around the well, trying to figure out a way to retrieve the ball and were confused on how to do that.

The boys were Kauravs and Pandavas. As they were looking at the ball in the well, Yudhishthira's (who was the eldest among them) ring fell in the well, too. The water was clear and they could see both the ball and the ring in the water. The boys did not see Drona approaching. "You boys belong to the great clan of Kuru; are you not skillful enough in archery to retrieve the ball and the ring?" Yudhishthira turned around and joked, "If you can take out the ball and the ring, we will make sure you get a good meal at our Gurukul." Drona smiled and, then, took a blade of grass and aimed it at the ball. The blade of grass stuck the ball. He, then, threw a succession of blades that stuck to the end of the previous one. Soon, Drona could pull out the ball out of the well. The boys were impressed. "Can you remove the ring from the well too? "They inquired. Drona borrowed Arjun's bow and arrow. He took an aim at the ring and released the arrow. The arrow went through the ring, stuck a stone and rebounded back to Drona who skillfully caught it. Yudhishthira bowed his head in reverence, "O Brahmin, please forgive my boyish impudence. Who are you?" Drona said, "Go ask Bhishma about me. I will wait for you boys right here." The boys ran to Bhishma and told him what had happened. Bhishma welcomed Drona and appointed him to teach Kauravs and the Pandavas.

Chapter-11
Treaty with Kimpurusha

A few years had passed and Mohoma was growing into a perfect Gurukul of Panchal.

It was dark by now with cold breeze blowing. Durudhan was sitting in the room with fire burning in a corner with the woods from the Deodar trees, dried and fallen on earth, collected by his progeny.

In Mohoma, it was a rule, which prohibited the cutting of trees and they needed to be treated as gods. According to the belief, trees were like gods which gave them food and wood for fire. If for some reasons, like construction, some tree had to cut down, a yagna was performed seeking an apology for the mistake.

Durudhan was holding a sword in his hand while staring at the Kimpurusha warrior, who was in his captivity now.

He was more interested in viewing this superhuman, whom he had caught while patrolling in the deodar forest located on the outskirts of Mohoma land.

"What's your name?" Durudhan asked in curiosity, noticing that superhuman regaining consciousness.

He slowly opened his eyes and took a glance at the room where he was locked. He tried to flex his muscles to check if he could loosen the rope tied to him but failed in his attempt.

"For your information, I am from the clan of Kimpurusha; it hardly matters what my name is," the superhuman replied while trying to make himself a little comfortable.

Durudhan came closer to him to have a look at his face, which looked like a monkey's and, then, he turned towards his back and observed his tail.

"Are you a descendant of Lord Hanuman?" Durudhan took back his seat and tried to interrogate.

He smiled and replied, "Every living thing on this earth is a descendant of Lord Hanuman. Why do you think it's only me or Kimpurusha? Our clan was just a medium for him to come to earth for our good and for the overall good of the mankind."

Durudhan moved his sword towards his throat and roared, "And you all are doing wrong against his words!"

Someone knocked at the door, interrupting Durudhan. "Who's there?" he asked from inside the room.

"It's me, Asthachik," a voice answered.

Durudhan stood up and opened the door with a smile. He said, "Brother, I am holding someone from the clan of our father's killer captive."

Asthachik replied anxiously, "Yes, I know, and this message has also reached King Drupad."

"King Drupad! How come he got to know?" Durudhan couldn't hold back the shock.

"King Durmaputra of Kimpurusha, whose territory lies beyond the white mountains, has sent this message to King Drupad. The person whom you have captured is Murmaputra, his brother." Asthachik explained.

He continued, "He has also issues a warning that if Murmaputra is not released, Mohoma will have to pay the price for the same."

Durudhan spoke in rage, "and what about them, who killed our father?"

Murmaputra, who was hearing their conversation, said, "It's impossible for anyone from our clan to kill someone."

"What do you mean?" asked Durudhan stepping towards him.

"We are the descendants of Lord Hanuman. It is a rule in our clan that we could attack to loot but never kill an innocent; we could hit to kill but only if we are in a war and there has been no war with Mohoma yet." Murmaputra explained.

Durudhan brought his face closer to his and retorted, "It's your clan's good luck that you didn't have a war with us yet."

Asthachik interrupted, "Durudhan, you come along with me to Pitamah and Indriya; they are waiting for you in the gurukul camp."

Durudhan looked at Murmaputra in anger and moved a step back asking Asthachik to move so that he could follow.

⬧♍♏■♏ 🖒♒♋■♑♏

Indriya looked tensed and worried sitting on the throne of Mohoma, while Mohoriti stood at the entry of the camp.

"What have you done, Durudhan, captured Murmaputra?" asked Mohoriti as Durudhan entered the camp.

"I captured a man from Kimpurusha, the clan who killed my father. I don't care about his name."

"But this could bring an evil message for our clan, do you realize this?" replied Indriya still sitting on the throne.

"Why are we always afraid of them? We are teaching archery to everyone in Panchal; we have our own unit; why do we have to be scared now? Let's conquer Kimpurusha!" Durudhan suggested.

"Don't talk like kids; we are not alone; we have to think about our progeny, too. We cannot take them to a war situation at a time when we have just started developing." replied Indriya

Durudhan was not interested in listening to anyone at this moment; only revenge was on his mind.

"I am not going to leave him at any cost." Durudhan declared.

"And we must sign a treaty with Kimpurusha; this is my order as the leader of the land of Mohoma."Indriya suggested.

Durudhan looked at Indriya in anger, his eyes turning red and sweat dripping down his eyebrows, and moved out from the camp twitching his *angvastram*.

"We will be going along with Murmaputra to Kimpurusha to have a word with King Durmaputra to reinstate peace between both the clans." Mohoriti told Indriya.

Indriya thought for a while and said, "I suggest Durudhan should also join us so that he could be satisfied; what do you say?"

"I think you are correct." Mohoriti replied in affirmation.

Mohoriti, then, called Asthachik and asked him to bring Murmaputra to them along with Durudhan.

"You may also send our guard to Panchal and inform King Drupad that we are leaving to Kimpurusha for a peace treaty." Mohoriti suggested to Indriya.

💧♍♏■♏ 👍♒♋■♑♏

Next morning, the horses were all set and Murmaputra was about to lead them to his clan, which was situated beyond the white mountains.

They put on their coats made of the skin of deer, as they were expecting it to be cold in white mountain ranges.

"May capturing me lead to a friendly relationship between you and Kimpurusha, Mohoma." Murmaputra climbed the horse and spoke in anger, looking at them.

Indriya avoided replying back to him.

"If I was allowed, you would not have been leaving alive from here." replied Durudhan.

They both knew they were moving for a treaty. Thus, it was just a matter of time when they would talk and get things in place.

After marching continuously for two days, the caravan of treaty immigrants crested the final mountain to reach the outskirts of Kimpurusha, the capital of the White Mountain. Murmaputra had talked excitedly about the glories of his perfect homeland. Indriya had prepared himself to see some incredible sights, which he could not have imagined to have seen in his land of Mohoma. However, nothing could have primed him for the sheer spectacle of what certainly was paradise, Kimpurusha: the land of super humans!

The mighty Yamuna River, a roaring goddess in the mountains, slowed down to the beat of White Mountain as she entered the valley.

She caressed the heavenly land of Kimpurusha, meandering her way into the immense valley.

The vast valley was covered by a lush green canvas of grass. On it painted was the masterpiece of Kimpurusha. Rows upon rows of flowers, all of god's colors, arrayed, their brilliance interrupted only by the soaring deodar trees, which offered a majestic, yet warm welcome into Kimpurusha. The melodious singing of the birds calmed the exhausted ears of Indriya.

Kimpurusha was raised upon a massive platform of a few hectares in size. The platform built of earth towered a few meters in height. On the top of the platform were the city walls, which, too, were a few meters in height. The simplicity and brilliance of the building of an entire city on a platform astounded the Mohomas. It was a strong protection against enemies who would have to fight up a fort wall, which was essentially a solid ground. The platform served another vital purpose: it raised the ground level of the city, an extremely effective strategy against the recurring floods and landslides in this area. Inside the fort walls, the city was divided into various blocks by the roads laid out in a neat grid pattern. It had market areas, temples, gardens, meeting halls and everything else especially constructed for a sophisticated urban living. All the houses appeared as simple structures from the outside.

In contrast to the extravagant natural landscape of White Mountain, the city of Kimpurusha itself was painted only in restrained blues and whites. The entire city was a picture of cleanliness, order and sobriety. Super humans, who were the descendants of Lord Hanuman, called Kimpurusha their home.

The palace of Durmaputra had been built on a separate platform on the southern side of the city. Murmaputra led Indriya and others and asked them to wait till he got the permission for them to enter. He soon returned along with a young commander, who had a face of a lion. The commander gave a practiced smile and folded his hands in a formal Kowtow. "Welcome to Kimpurusha. I am commander, Daksha. You must follow me to meet our king." He said politely.

They entered the palace, which was covered with pure white snow and was guarded by super humans with long hairy bodies. They had adapted to the atmosphere and, accordingly, their body conditions, too, had changed to survive in the cold temperature there. As they reached inside the palace, they saw Durmaputra sitting on the throne, his huge built and long tail was sufficient to explain his powers and capabilities.

"Welcome, people of Mohoma!" he spoke loudly.

Mohoriti and others, too, joined their hands to greet. They were offered seats next to the king for them to sit and discuss. The king continued, "It's not good that you captured my brother."

Indriya replied being a king himself, "So, was it good to regularly invade our land and destroy our livelihood?"

"You all had started interfering in our land area and, so, we had to reciprocate. Your people tried to cut down trees in our land quite regularly, taking away our animals; we couldn't have sat ideal in such a case." Durmaputra put his case.

"OK, so what is the offer of treaty? We are neighbors and will be forever now; so, why not find a solution to this issue?" suggested Indriya .

Durmaputra stood up from his throne and moved towards them. "Let's have a border and make a mandate that no one would be allowed to cut trees and take away the animals. Water from the rivers and their tributaries could be used by both but none of us would be allowed to stop the water."

Mohoriti also stood up and replied, "Agreed. This is what is required to be understood by both of our clans; we agree to this."

However, Durudhan was still angry. He interrupted in between, "What about the killers of my father? I want to behead that person. Only then the treaty could be signed."

Durmaputra looked at him with suspicion, "Who is this now? Who wants to put the treaty on hold in front of the king of the clan?"

"I am the brother of the king and I want revenge" Durudhan responded.

Durmaputra came closer to him and looked into his eyes, "You are standing on my land and daring me! Do you still want to have this treaty? We, the Kimpurusha people, don't kill people. We are the warriors; we kill when we fight and we kill hard. I heard that Duru was declared the first king of your clan and he was killed during our invasion. We immediately investigated with all our people who went to your land that day. We cannot tolerate anything wrong in our policies."

Durudhan stood up in anger and roared, "So what was your finding? Bring that man to me."

"No one from Kimpurusha killed your father; I am sure and, also, can assure you. Go back and investigate in your own clan. You will find the answer there." Durmaputra replied.

Indriya stood up and asked Durudhan to cool down. Durudhan's eyes had turned red due to anger. He was still sure that his father, Duru, was killed by Kimpurusha but he did not have any evidence to prove it. On the other hand, he was standing on their land and taking a cue from their powers, he decided to stay mum at that moment. However, Durudhan's confidence in his clan was shaking somewhere in his mind. He wanted investigations at Mohoma level once they go back.

"We will take your leave now. With a treaty between Mohoma and Kimpurusha, we will follow our words and you must follow yours. We hope you'd understand that we are also warriors and it's better for both of our progenies that we maintain friendly relations with each other."

After the declaration, they hugged each other and decided to go back hoping for the prevalence of peace between the two empires. During their entire journey, Durudhan was silent and was in deep thoughts trying to figure out who could possibly be benefited with the death of his father, Duru.

He looked at the sky, which was dark by now and was filled with the twinkling stars, while constantly thinking over the same thing. He was wondering if Kimpurusha people have not killed Duru, then who that person could possibly be.

Chapter-12
Time for Interrogation

Indriya was sitting on the throne with Mohoriti, Durudhan and other courtiers sitting adjacent to him, trying to investigate the murder of Duru. Indriya looked tensed, lost deep in thoughts. All eyes in the court were on him while Mohoriti tried to figure out the next move.

"I request Indriya and Pitamah to give me the power to punish or take the decision of what needs to be done with the killer, once he is identified." Durudhan requested having stood up from his seat.

"Punishment will be as per our rules and no one will be allowed to do anything on his own." Mohoriti declared and continued, "But, as of now, the more important question is who is the one who betrayed us."

"It would be better to start with the person who saw him first." replied Asthachik, interrupting in between.

"Mili is the first person who saw him dead. She must be questioned first." suggested Durudhan.

Indriya stood up immediately in anger, "She is the first lady of our clan; she cannot be questioned."

"If it is the matter of the clan's security, everyone is equal and any one can be questioned." replied Mohoriti stopping him.

"She is my wife and I am sure she is not involved in this; I must not allow this". Indriya retorted.

"This will stir a revolt, Indriya; I have lost my father and I am not going to leave any culprit." replied Durudhan.

Indriya pulled out his sword and so did Durudhan.

"Stop, both of you; I am still alive to handle such situations among the clan." Mohoriti shouted and continued, "Mili needs to be questioned. If she is not guilty, there's no need to worry".

Hearing Mohoriti, both of them placed their swords back.

"If it's your decision, Pitamah; I would like to talk to Mili first and, then, you can proceed." Indriya requested.

"I am OK, but in that case, you must not ask her if she was involved in this or not. Also, you must not suggest her what she should answer to us. If you can keep your words, we are OK with the meeting," replied Durudhan.

Indriya looked tensed and commented in anger, "I am OK as I am confident about her."

He moved out from the courtroom and started moving towards Mili's room. He was angry, yet confident that she is innocent. He stepped into her room and asked her maids to leave the room immediately.

"I love you a lot, Mili." Indriya came close to her and told her looking into her eyes.

"I know. You came to say this? I am happiest women on this earth." Mili replied.

Indriya moved a step back and turned around to continue, "We met Durmaputra, the king of Kimpurusha, and he confirmed to us that uncle Duru was not killed by them. I don't want any answer from you. I only came to tell you that whatever may be the condition, whether you are right or wrong, I am standing with you and I will stand with you."

Mili's face changed contours; she asked, "What happened; what are you saying?"

"I love you because you always spoke what is in your heart. Remember, I am always with you, on earth or in the heaven. Speak what your heart tells you is right." Indriya tried to explain.

Indriya spoke what he wanted to and moved outside the room without looking into her eyes.

He moved back to the courtroom and asked Mohoriti to proceed with his interrogation while he sat confidently on his throne.

"Asthachik, please go and call Mili, your sister-in-law, to the courtroom" ordered Mohoriti.

Asthachik bowed to him and having taken the permission from Indriya, went to her room. As he reached, he saw that the room's door was shut. He knocked at the door, hearing which Mili permitted him to come in.

"Sister, you need to come with me to courtroom as asked by Pitamah." Asthachik stated.

She stood up and walked towards the courtroom with Asthachik following her.

As she entered, she saw Indriya, Durudhan, Mohoriti and others seated in the court. She bowed before Mohoriti and others and looked into the eyes of Indriya.

"This court has some questions for you. Hope we will get the answers from you, daughter." spoke Mohoriti.

"I am a warrior princess, father, and I will say what I know without any hesitation." said Mili.

Mohoriti looked anxious and concerned for her, but his job was to interrogate her. He started questioning, "As you were the first person who saw Duru killed, did you see anyone running from there?"

"No, father, I did not see anyone running from there." Mili replied.

"You were alone with Duru's body in that room. So, did you reach after he was killed or before that?" Mohoriti furthered.

Indriya interrupted, "Obviously, she reached after he was killed. That's why, she could not see anyone running from there."

Durudhan stopped Indriya, "Both questions have relevance. So, I object and let Pitamah have his questions answered."

"I repeat my question for you, Mili, when you reached that room, you found him dead or alive?"

The sweat on her head was quite visible now; she looked rather tensed. She moved a few steps towards Indriya' s throne and, then, replied while looking into his eyes, "You thought that Pitamah's way to take revenge was wrong. You were the one who made this land of Mohoma. You struggled on the barren land and brought it to this shape; then, why was father Duru proposed to be the king?"

Everyone looked shocked and so did Indriya, while she continued, "Pitamah, I was devastated and broken on hearing your decision to make father Duru as King. Why did you take such a wrong decision? Answer your question, yes, when I reached the room, he was there alive and I found this a very good opportunity to take back the throne for my Indriya. I took the sword lying there and beheaded him." She spoke loud and clear without any fear of death.

Indriya's eyes welled with tears.

"What did you do, daughter!" Mohoriti exclaimed in pain.

Durudhan immediately pulled out his sword and moved towards her, "You have done wrong and I cannot let you go just because you are my sister-in-law." and he attacked.

However, another sword struck his way. Indriya stood up raising his sword in order to stand with her and save her.

Durudhan smiled and moved two steps back, "Look, Pitamah! So, here are the real culprits. The persons, who you trusted, are the real culprits behind your son's murder. Now, I got it! Indriya and Mili are involved together in this plan."

"You are wrong, brother; I was not involved in any plans with her but she is my wife and I will always stand for her" replied Indriya.

Durudhan and Indriya faced off on the court's stone floor. The area was wide enough for two of them to fight, while others would come in action soon.

Indriya's face was scrunched up in anger. He slowly pulled a long sword from his belt, the blade making a hissing whisper as it rubbed against its sheathe. All this while, Indriya was holding Soren firmly in his gaze.

Durudhan bent down and stretched his back. He turned his neck from left to right and cracked a few joints rapidly. Then, he proceeded to do the same with the rest of his body as he loosened up.

"Don't hold back because I am going to break you." Indriya snarled at Durudhan. Mohoriti still followed the rule of one-on-one fight and waited for the result, but he was devastated and was unable to understand who he should support.

Durudhan shrugged his shoulders, smiled, and slowly brought one foot back. He put his weight on it and brought an open palm up.

Indriya turned his head in curiosity.

There was another warrior standing to Durudhan's right, possessing an array of arms. They had everything from sword to archery to various other arms.

Durudhan dipped and weaved right before he was about to reach him and slashed the sword down. He sidestepped to the right just enough and the blade passed from a hair's breadth from his face.

Quickly, before Indriya could respond with a follow up, Durudhan swiftly punched Indriya in the solar plexus, knocking the wind out of the swordsman and stunning him for a moment.

The fight had taken both the men dangerously close to the edge of the court and Durudhan had his back almost to the wall, despite him being counteroffensive.

Indriya was still open for more attacks and Durudhan was yet not done.

The quick blow had opened Indriya up for another attack. He put a simple sidekick into Durudhan's stomach, doubling him over. Durudhan followed that up with a quick rising uppercut.

The crowd watching their fight was about to intervene.

Indriya was pulled off his feet violently and was thrown across the floor. He skid and tumbled along the ground, uncontrolled. He was stopped by the others at the end of the court floor, about five feet from the wall at the back of the throne floor. Indriya looked up and his eyes widened in shock.

Durudhan was about to move with his sword towards Mili. Indriya jumped and caught hold of Mili blocking the sword and shielding from the attacks by Durudhan.

Mohoriti, now, shouted to stop and pulled out his sword. Although, he rose his voice to stop the fight but it more appeared as if he stood in favor of Durudhan. Thus, Indriya decided to move out of room with Mili somehow and run away from there.

He got hold of Mili and shouted at her to run as fast as she could along with him. She jumped towards him while Durudhan tried to smash her with his sword. Indriya ran out of the court holding her hand and dragging her towards the horse standing at the corner of the courtroom.

Durudhan also followed them with other court men. Mohoriti

was also trying to stop them but he seemed to be failing in his attempts.

Indriya reached the horse and, leaving Mili's hand, tried to untie the horse's lead rope.

"Don't worry; we will be out from here soon, Mili." He said in a hurry.

As he untied the rope and turned to check on her, he got shocked to see Mili falling on her knees with her eyes wide open. He immediately caught her from falling on the ground. She was hit by arrows from behind, piercing her body. Blood spurted from each of her wound. He shouted her name in pain while holding her.

She collapsed saying, "I am sorry Indriya, but I love you."

He shouted her name with tears in his eyes. He dropped the sword, which he was holding tight by now, in his hand. He held her body with both his hands and hugged her tight.

He stopped saying anything or even moving his body. It appeared as if all his intentions to live were finished in one shot.

Then, a sword with a sharp blade, flying in air, pierced through Indriya' s neck, beheading him. His head, now fallen on the ground, turned and tumbled many rounds before it finally stopped. His eyes were wide open welling with tears and a pool of blood had now drenched his body. The land of Mohoma had drunk the blood of its own people today.

Durudhan laughed out loud holding his sword dripping Indriya's blood. Today, a brother had killed another on the land of Bharata.

Mohoriti stood stumped; he never had expected what just happened. It was so sudden that he could not even get any time to think over.

While Durudhan stood drenched in blood, Mohoriti anticipated that his next move might be harming Tejaswa. Trying to avert the danger, he rushed towards Mili' s room to check on him. Meanwhile, the supporters of Durudhan had started enchanting his name as the king of Mohoma.

Mohoriti, while still holding his sword, ran towards the room and saw Tejaswa along with Ritikawali.

Ritikawali looked at him and sensed something was not right. Mohoriti pulled Tejaswa towards him and hugged him.

"Son, it's the time for you to leave Mohoma." He said.

"Why Pitamah, are we going somewhere?" Tejaswa, who was just ten years old, asked.

"No, my son, it's not us, it's only you who are leaving. Remember what I am telling you and never forget that." Mohoriti explained.

Tejaswa looked at him stunned, while he continued.

"You are the son of the warriors and you must not fear in any circumstance in life. God is taking your test. Your father and mother are no more but you have to live for them. You must live for Mohoma and fulfill the last wishes of your ancestor, Mohoma."

Tejaswa's eyes were filled with tears, hearing about his family. Even Ritikawali stood shocked and stumped in a corner.

"It's time for you to run. There will be people behind you to kill you, but you must not stop. Run as fast as you can; run to never return; run to fulfill your father's dream."

He nodded his head, with tears in his eyes.

Mohoriti asked him to come along. He took him on his horse and galloped towards the south of Mohoma. His white horse ran very fast. Hiding from the progeny and Durudhan, Mohoriti took him to the border of the land of Mohoma.

In the meantime, Durudhan and his supporters started their search for Tejaswa everywhere in Mohoma.

As they reached the border, Mohoma got down from the horse and asked Tejaswa to take it along and move to the farther point.

Sun was about to set, spreading red color in the sky. It was literally red all over, from the earth to the sky.

"You are a brave boy and I know, one day you will become a brave warrior. Remember, we, the descendants of Mohoma, took birth for some reason and we must fulfill that. I will wait for you in Mohoma. I am sure you will return one day with wide shoulders and a strong body. Never forget that you were the son of brave Indriya, who built the land of Mohoma, and you are the real successor of Mohoma. The progeny of Mohoma and I will wait for his king to return."

Tejaswa stepped down again and hugged him, "Pitamah, I will keep your words and will return one day to land of Mohoma. I assure you that my father and you will always be proud of me."

He climbed the horseback, while holding his sword, and rode towards the south without looking back, as instructed by Mohoriti.

Chapter-13
Eklavya the friend

Durudhan declared himself as the king of Mohoma with the support of his brothers, courtiers and everyone else who considered Indriya a culprit. Mohoriti was not in favor of Durudhan becoming a king, but he didn't have any option here. He, too, believed that Indriya was involved with Mili in the plotting of Duru's murder. Although he was against Durudhan for killing both of them, but Durudhan had a clear justification for this that he took the decision all of a sudden to counter the actions of Indriya to save Mili.

As per him, he, too, didn't want to kill Indriya but it all happened in a sudden fury.

Tejaswa drove towards Vindhya Mountains and hid himself in a forest in a kingdom called Nishadas. The kingdom belonged to a tribe by the same name. Nishadas were known to be the tribes that had the hills and the forests as their abode. They were linked with a king called Vena, who became a slave of wrath and malice, thereby becoming unrighteous. Brahmanas once slew him. Some of the Vena's descendants became Nishadas and some others were called Mlechchhas, who resided on the Vindhya mountains.

Vena was a great king. However, he became evil and corrupt

because of his pride. The creation of the god, earth, became so gloomy and dark that the goddess of earth, Bhumidevi, decided that she would not provide crops and food to humans anymore. She took the avatar of a cow and went into hiding. Meanwhile, a group of rishis decided to save humans and killed Vena out of anger. They, then, rubbed the thigh of his corpse and took out all the evil from his body. Afterwards, they rubbed Vena's arm, and the good, Prithu, emerged. He was Vishnu's incarnate and as soon as he was born, Vishnu's Sharanga bow fell from the heaven into his hands. However, Bhumidevi still refused to give crops to people. It was when Prithu, the son of Vena, threatened to kill her, she gave up, but in return, Prithu was asked to be her eternal guardian. This is why Bhumidevi is also named as Prithvi.

Hiranyadhanus was the commander of King Jarasandha and leader of Nishadas. He was proud of his son, Eklavya. Eklavya was a brave, handsome boy, who was loved by all in the kingdom, but, somehow, he was not happy and this was apparent to his father.

Once, he found his son lost deep in thoughts while other boys enjoyed the pleasures of hunting and playing. He reached close to his son and asked, "Why are you so unhappy, Eklavya? Why don't you join your friends? Why are you not interested in hunting?"

"Father, I want to be an archer," replied Eklavya, "I want to become a disciple of the great Dronacharya who is the great tutor of archery in Hastinapur. His gurukul is a magical place, where ordinary boys are turned into mighty warriors."

Eklavya saw his father; he was silent and worried. He continued, "Father, I know that we belong to the hunting tribe, but I want to be a warrior, father, not a mere hunter. So, please allow me to leave home and become a disciple of Dronacharya."

Hiranyadhanus was troubled, for he knew that his son's ambition was not an easy one. However, he was a loving father and he did not want to refuse his only son's wish. So, he gave his blessings and sent his son to Drona's gurukul.

Eklavya prepared himself and set out on his way. He rode on his black horse, with bow and arrow slung on his back. While he was crossing the forest area of Nishadas, he could smell the aroma of grilled fish coming from the other end.

As he was hungry, he followed the aroma, thinking of getting some food and taking rest. Soon, he discovered a small roof made up of tree branches and dry grass on top of a banyan tree, with fish getting grilled under it, next to its trunk.

He tried to hide behind the bushes to find who the owner of the food was but he could not find anyone except a horse tied at the other end of the tree. He observed it for some more time but he could not resist himself from eating, giving in to his hunger and the aroma that filled the air.

He moved slowly towards the grill and looked around if someone was there. After confirming that no one is around, he pulled the fish from the grill and started eating. The taste was amazing as the fish was marinated with fresh herbs picked from the forest.

He tried to gulp big bites and ate fast before anyone arrived. Once he finished, he turned around to move back but to his surprise, Tejaswa was sitting behind him, watching him silently.

Eklavya as shocked when he saw him and he also fell on his back. He looked at him with fear.

"Don't be afraid; you may have more." offered Tejaswa.

Giving his hand to Eklavya, "Don't be afraid, I am Tejaswa. You can consider me as your friend."

Eklavya was all alone since many days in this dense forest and was happy to see someone of his age he could talk to. He took one more fish and offered him to eat. Looking at his gesture, Eklavya smiled and took another fish and replied, "I am Eklavya, the son of King of Nishadas."

"Oh! My pleasure to meet the prince!" exclaimed Tejaswa.

"I am just a common man like you; don't call me a prince. Call me by my name, Eklavya." said Eklavya.

Eklavya ate the fish offered by him and replied, "I am thankful for your offer. I was very hungry and could not resist myself from eating, but I am sorry, I forgot to ask you. I hope you've got more food to eat."

Tejaswa looked at the fire grill and smiled, "Do not worry, I will catch more."

Looking at the grill, which Tejaswa had kept for himself, Eklavya felt bad and he asked him to take him to the lake so that he could catch fish for him. Tejaswa was happy to hear this and took him to the lake.

While Tejaswa got his fish hook ready, Eklavya pulled out his bow, which he was carrying with him, and walked inside the lake till the water reached his knees. He looked keenly at the movement of fishes in the lake and, in a few minutes, he captured more than ten.

Tejaswa was very happy and amazed to see his skills and clapped loudly.

"So, how did you come into this forest and where are your parents?" asked Eklavya.

Tejaswa was in tears hearing his questions, "I have no one; I came from a far away land."

Eklavya came out of water and kept the fishes on the grass and hugged him, "You offered me food when I was the hungriest in my life; you observed my skills and clapped for me; you are my best friend, would you like to be my friend?"

Tejaswa smiled, too, with tears in his eyes. He hugged him and said, "Thanks for making me your friend."

Sky was growing dark with moon slowly reaching its highest in the sky. The sounds of jackals and lions made the forest appear terrifying. They lit fire under a tree so that they could keep the animals away. They both climbed the roof of the tree house and arranged it to accommodate two people. Eklavya spent that night with him. They both savored a lot of fishes and shared their feelings. Eklavya asked about his family, to which he replied that he was a Shudra and didn't know anything about his family. He kept it a secret that he was a warrior, following the instructions by Mohoriti of keeping himself safe from the outsiders.

The night for them passed counting stars and talking about their families and hobbies.

The next morning, Eklavya prepared himself to move further towards the gurukul of Drona. He thanked Tejaswa and asked for his leave. He told him that he found one of his best friends in life and that he would always remember him. They hugged each other. As he moved, Tejaswa also started following him. Eklavya looked at him and asked him to stay where he was. He explained to Tejaswa that he need not come along with him as he was going to a gurukul to learn. However, Tejaswa, having no other friend and option, kept following him.

After covering a certain distance, Eklavya asked him, “What do you want Tejaswa? Why you are leaving your place?”

Tejaswa looked into his eyes and replied, “I have no family or friends. Please take me along. I will be with you always and will never disturb you. I will also cook delicious fish for you and make you healthy and wise.”

Eklavya was a generous boy. He could not leave Tejaswa alone now. He thought for a while and, then, replied, “OK, you may come along with me, but when I will start my learning in the gurukul, what you will do?”

They started talking while walking together, holding their horses. “I will live outside your gurukul and you can teach me, too, when you have time. When I will cook fish, you may come out to have it, hiding from your teachers.” Tejaswa suggested.

“Ha Ha,” he laughed and they both moved towards the Gurukul in Hastinapur.

The only place where one could get some education was a “gurukul.” A gurukul was residential in nature with the *shishyas* or students and the *guru* or teacher living in proximity, many a times within the same house. A gurukul was a place where the students resided together as equals, irrespective of their social standing. The students learned from the guru and helped him in performing his day-to-day activities, including carrying out the mundane chores such as washing clothes, cooking, etc. The education imparted, thus, was a wholesome one.

When they reached Dronacharya's gurukul, they saw that it consisted of a group of huts, surrounded by trees, flowers and an archery yard. The disciples were practicing to shoot arrows with their bows and the ones in the yard. It was an engaging sight. However, Eklavya' s eyes were searching for Drona. “Where is he? Are you able to see him?” asked Tejaswa.

Without Drona, all his purpose of coming here would be meaningless. Soon, all his worries were subsided. He didn't have to wait for too long. There was this man standing near a tree busy instructing a boy, who was none other than the third son of Pandu, Arjuna. Though Eklavya had never seen Drona before, he put his guess at work. He asked Tejaswa to hide behind the trees and keep waiting there till he returned. He went near Drona and bowed.

The sage was surprised to see a strange boy addressing him. "Who are you, young boy?" he asked.

"Acharya, I am Eklavya, the son of the tribal chief, Hiranyadhanus, from the western part of the forests of Hastinapur." Eklavya replied. "Please accept me as your disciple and teach me the wonderful art of archery."

Drona sighed, "Eklavya!" and continued," if you are a tribal hunter, then you must be a *Shudra*, the lowest social community according to the vedic caste system. I am a *Brahmin*, the highest caste in the kingdom. I cannot teach a *Shudra* boy." Drona was blunt and arrogant in his words.

"And he's also a royal teacher," interrupted Prince Arjuna, who was along with Drona. "Our guru has been appointed by the king to train us, the princes and the highborn. How dare you come inside the gurukul and seek him? Leave! NOW!" he spat out, looking enraged that Eklavya had disturbed his practice.

Eklavya was stunned at Arjun's behavior. He himself was the son of the chief of his clan, but he never insulted anyone below him in such a way. He looked at Drona, with eyes full of tears, for some kind of support, but the sage remained silent, standing with hands folded. The message from Drona was loud and clear. He also wanted him to leave. He refused to teach him and share his knowledge.

The innocent Eklavya was deeply hurt by Drona's refusal to teach him. "It's not fair!" he thought, feeling miserable. "God has given knowledge to all, but man alone differentiates his kind."

He left the place with a broken heart and bitterness towards Tejaswa and sat silently behind the trees.

Tejaswa smiled and asked, "So, you are going to join the gurukul, friend?" and sat in front of him.

"I may be a Shudra but does it make any difference?" he replied in a heavy voice. "I am as strong and zealous as Drona's princes and disciples. If I practice the art every day, I can surely become an archer better than his disciples." He challenged.

Tejaswa understood that Drona has rejected him. He hugged him again and replied, "You are the best and I believe that you will be the best archer one day. Don't be disheartened."

Tejaswa consoled him and asked him to get up and come along with him. Eklavya, having no other option, stood up and followed him wiping his tears. They pulled their horses and moved back inside the forest.

Soon, they reached a lake, where they drank water and sat for some time. Tejaswa tried to console his friend and wiped his tears.

While Eklavya was sad and not interested in talking with anyone, Tejaswa stood to give water to the horses. He untied them and pulled them towards the lake. The bank of the lake was slippery due to wet mud and was also rocky. He tried to control himself but slipped on the wet mud falling on his back. Looking at him, Eklavya could not control his laughter and started laughing. Seeing him laughing, he started this game of standing and falling again in the mud. Each time he slipped, Eklavya laughed louder. He was happy to see his friend laughing and forgetting his insult which he'd just faced.

Suddenly, something struck Eklavya' s mind. He stood up, wiped his clothes and reached near to him. He, then, picked some mud in his hand and started thinking something.

"Tejaswa, do one thing, collect as much mud as possible and bring to that tree." he observed an open space and reached to that place.

Tejaswa could not understand what Eklavya was saying but followed him to keep him happy. He pulled a dry tree branch and twisted it to dig mug. He made a bowl of leaves and used it to pick mud and dump at the place suggested by Eklavya.

While he was collecting mud, Eklavya brought some big stones and placed them one above the other. Then, he started building the statue of someone with the help of mud collected by Tejaswa. Tejaswa kept on watching and supported him. Soon, a statue started taking shape of a sage.

"Who is this, Eklavya?" Tejaswa intrigued.

He moved a few steps back and observed keenly for perfection. "He is my guru, Dronacharya." Eklavya answered.

He made a statue of Dronacharya. He sincerely believed that if he practiced before his guru, he would become an able archer. Thus, though his guru had shunned him, he still held him in high esteem and thought of him as his guru.

"So, what are you planning to do, friend?" asked Tejaswa in curiosity.

He kept looking at the statue and, then, bowed before him, "I will practice archery in front of my guru, Drona, from now onwards."

Tejaswa smiled, "Great! I would help you and practice with you. I hope I can also learn something with you."

They both smiled and hugged smearing mud all over each other.

Day after day, Eklavya took his bow and arrow, worshipped the statue of Drona and started his practice. Tejaswa helped him by complementing him and helping him in his practice. He also tried to learn things which Eklavya was trying to learn on his own. In some time, faith, courage and perseverance transformed Eklavya, the mere tribal hunter, into a new Eklavya, the extraordinary archer. Eklavya became an archer of exceptional prowess, superior even to Drona's best pupil, Arjuna.

Ten years had passed practicing archery and this time had made him perfect. Besides, a perfect bond of friendship had setup between the Eklavya and Tejaswa by now.

One day, while Eklavya was practicing, he heard a dog barking and this was distracting him from his practice. At first, he tried to ignore the dog but continuous disturbance during his practice angered him. He asked Tejaswa to check where the dog was. He stopped his practice and went along with Tejaswa to the place where the dog was barking.

Tejaswa picked up a stone and tried to shoo it away but was unsuccessful in making it stop barking. Before the dog could shut up or get out of the way, Eklavya fired seven arrows in rapid succession to fill the dog's mouth without injuring it. The dog ran away with the arrows stuck in his mouth and, as a result, it roamed in the forests with its mouth opened.

However, they were not alone there practicing. They were unaware of the fact that just some distance away, the Pandava princes were also present in that area of the forest. As fate would have it, that day, they had come with their guru, Drona, who was instructing them about some finer points of archery by making them learn in the real-life condition of the open forest.

As they were busy practicing, they suddenly chanced upon the same dog and wondered who could have pulled off such a feat of archery. Drona was amazed, too. "Such an excellent aim can only come from a mighty archer." he exclaimed. He told the Pandavas that if somebody was such a good archer, then he surely needed to be met with. The practice was stopped in the middle and they all began searching the forest for the one possessing such amazing skills. They finally found dark and skinny man, Eklavya, and his friend, Tejaswa.

Dronacharya went close to them and asked, "Who is the one who showcased such a skill?"

Eklavya bowed his head before him and moved in the front.

"Your aim is truly remarkable!" Drona praised Eklavya, and asked "from whom did you learn archery?"

Eklavya was thrilled to hear Drona's praises. He wondered how surprised he would be if he'd tell him that he in fact was his guru!

"From you, my Master! You are my guru." Eklavya replied humbly.

"Your guru? How can I be your guru? I have never seen you before!" Drona exclaimed in surprise. However, suddenly he remembered something. He remembered about an eager boy who had visited his gurukul several years ago. "Now, I remember," he said, "are you not the same hunter boy whom I'd refused admission in my gurukul some years back?"

"Yes, Dronacharya," replied the boy, "after I left your gurukul, I came to this forest and made a statue of you and worshipped it every day. I practiced before your sculpture. You refused to teach me, but your statue did not. Thanks to it, may be, I have become a good archer."

Dronacharya was surprised by his skills and dedication, "You have become one of the best archers among all my students."

Hearing this, Arjuna became angry. "But you promised me that you'd make me the best archer in the world!" he accused Drona, "Now how can that be possible? Now, a common hunter has become better than me!"

Tejaswa and other princes remembered Guru Drona frequently praising Arjuna saying he had immense talent and that he will be the greatest archer in the kingdom. They waited with bated breath and wondered what their teacher will do now.

Unable to answer Arjun's question, Drona remained silent. The sage, too, was upset that his promise to Prince Arjuna was not going to be fulfilled.

After thinking for some time, Drona asked, "Can you show me my statue, where you practiced?"

"Sure, guru." Eklavya replied and took them to the place.

Dronacharya observed the statue and, then, asked Eklavya, "Where is my guru dakshina? You have to give me a gift for your training." the sage demanded. He had finally found a way to make Eklavya suffer for his disobedience.

Eklavya was overjoyed. A guru dakshina was the voluntary fee or gift offered by a disciple to his guru at the end of his training. A guru dakshina is the final offering from a student to the guru before leaving the ashram. The teacher may ask for something or nothing at all.

"Dronacharya, I'll be the happiest person on earth to serve you. Ask me anything and I will offer it to you as my guru dakshina." he replied.

"I might ask for something you wouldn't like to give me. What if you refuse the dakshina I want from you?" Drona asked in a cunning tone.

Eklavya could not understand. It was considered a grave insult and a great sin if a guru's dakshina was refused. "No! How can I, guru? I am not that ungrateful. I'll never refuse anything that you'd ask for." Dronacharya took a promise from the unsuspecting boy.

Eklavya looked at Tejaswa and expressed his happiness through his eyes.

Drona did not wait anymore. "Eklavya, I seek to have your right-hand thumb as my guru dakshina." he declared.

Silence befell on everyone. Everyone was shocked, including Arjuna. Tejaswa was calling him in his mind asking him to stop.

Tejaswa looked at Drona in horror and disbelief. How could such a knowledgeable sage make such a cruel demand, that too from a mere boy?

For a moment, Eklavya stood silent and looked at Tejaswa. Without his thumb, he would never be able to shoot arrows again. However, the guru must be satisfied. "OK, Gurudev, as you wish." he said. Then, without even slightest of hesitation, Eklavya drew out his knife and cut his thumb!

Tejaswa wanted to stop him, but he could not.

Everyone present there gasped at Eklavya' s act of bravery, but the tribal boy showed no signs of pain and held out his severed thumb to Dronacharya.

"Here is my guru dakshina, Drona," Eklavya said, "I am happy that you have made me your disciple, even if I'm a mere Shudra hunter."

Guru Drona was humbled. He blessed the young archer for his courage. "Eklavya, even without your thumb, you'll be known as a great archer. I bless you that you will be remembered forever for your loyalty to your guru." Drona declared and left the forest.

"What did you do, friend?" Tejaswa asked Eklavya holding his hand and covering it with a piece of cloth.

Eklavya smiled with a deep pain showing through his eyes, "If I had not done this, I might not have been able to survive in this world."

Tejaswa was astonished to hear this; he looked at him in shock while he continued, "Yes, my friend, Guru Drona had promised Arjun that he will make him the best archer in the world and he knows that Arjun does not stand anywhere in front of me. If I wouldn't have given my thumb, he would have got me killed some or the other way. Missing my thumb was just a method to save my life."

"Still, you will never be able to practice archery now." Tejaswa sighed.

Eklavya smiled and said, "If I can become the best by practicing on my own, can't I become the best again by practicing using just my two fingers?"

Tejaswa understood what Eklavya was trying to explain. He smiled and bandaged his thumb after cleaning the blood which was flowing.

"I feel now is the time when we should meet your father, Hiranyadhanus, and take his feedback." suggested Tejaswa.

Eklavya agreed to him and decided to meet his father. The next day, they moved to the palace of Eklavya's father, who was waiting to meet his son.

Hiranyadhanus was overjoyed to see his son back from the forest and hugged him. He smiled at Tejaswa, who touched his feet and took his blessings.

"I am overjoyed to see you, my son!" he exclaimed with a

smile but, then, he observed a deep silence on Eklavya's face.

"What happened, my son?" he asked with curiosity but Eklavya didn't reply.

"What happened to him, Tejaswa?" He furthered his question.

Tejaswa came forward and said, "King, Guru Drona met him and took away his thumb as his guru dakshina."

"What! How could he do this?" his face was red with anger, "I'll not let him go; he needs to pay for this." Eklavya's father was furious and wanted to kill Drona for this.

"Father, please cool down!" Eklavya interrupted, "He wished and I followed what I had been taught by my elders. I am not sad by this but rather I'm worried that I'll have to practice archery all over again using my other fingers."

Hiranyadhanus hugged him back with tears in his eyes, "You are the best archer, my son, and no one can stop you by taking your thumb."

"It's time for you to join the army of our King Jarasandha. He would be happy to have you in his army." Hiranyadhanus suggested.

Eklavya touched his feet and replied, "It would be my pleasure to be a part of his army. Tejaswa, my friend, would also join along with me."

Hiranyadhanus blessed them both and guided for their next move.

Tejaswa also moved forward and touched his feet to seek his blessings.

Chapter-14
Revenge of Drona

Mohoriti felt helpless by now. Sometimes, it used to occur to him that he would be never be able to take his father's revenge. He was broken after Indriya' s death. He missed Tejaswa and was waiting for him to return one day.

Nights had become longer for him now. He was unable to sleep, remembering Tejaswa and Indriya. Ritikawali had grown old by now and, one day, her soul departed to rest in peace.

Durudhan had been ruling the land of Mohoma for twenty five years now and he had contributed to develop his land into a powerful clan. They had fought multiple wars with Kimpurusha in all these years and the treaties, which were signed at the time of Indriya, were all left unnoticed.

The land of Mohoma was no more a happy place. The progeny was living under the fear of the king and was working hard to pay taxes and fulfill the luxurious needs of Durudhan and his sons.

Human trade was happening in full swing during his tenure; everyone was treated as a slave to work hard during the reign of Durudhan.

Mohoriti entered the court where Durudhan was seated on the throne.

"King Drupad has called for help." Mohoriti said.

"Please could you explain in detail?" asked Durudhan.

Mohoriti took his seat and continued, "Many years back, Drupad had expelled Dronacharya from his court when he had come to ask for financial help. Now, he has finished training the princes of Hastinapur and, in return, has asked Kauravs to attack Panchal and capture King Drupad. In the morning, I had received a message from the king to move our army unit towards Panchal and be ready for the war."

"Do we have any other option, Pitamah?" Durudhan questioned.

"Why do we need other options? We are the vassal of Panchal and it's our duty to be on his side at the time of war. On the other hand, we have a good chance to take our revenge from Hastinapur. A long time back, they had killed my nineteen brothers. Now, we have a chance to kill all hundred of them." Mohoriti replied.

Durudhan thought for a while and, then, ordered his army unit to move towards Panchal.

The same day, the army unit was set ready along with Durudhan, Asthachik, Mohoriti and others. They moved towards Panchal in their full strength. Their unit consisted of elephants, horses and soldiers, who were well trained in the unit of Mohoma. They reached Panchal after travelling for two days and saw a huge army waiting for them at the main entrance of the Panchal border.

In Hastinapur, Kauravs had already arrived and were about to attack, while the unit of Mohoma had still not joined the main army of Panchal.

Mohoriti examined from a distance and pulled his horse towards Durudhan, "I think we should wait here only."

Durudhan looked at him and replied, "But we must be with the main army of Panchal and attack along with them."

"Wars are not only won by powers but also by intelligence. When the Kaurav army will reach the middle of the warzone, we will attack from the side. This will land them to surprise and, finally, we will take them off the ground." explained Mohoriti.

Durudhan understood the plan and decided to wait where they were.

With the blow of a conch shell, both armies started moving

towards each other. Panchal army was huge and it appeared as if the Kauravs would not be able to stand anywhere in front of them. Duryodhana, who led the unit, was in front with a cudgel in his hand. He was standing tall with a huge and muscular body, long hair and pride on his face.

Both the armies coincided and, then, a strong wind blew loose sand in the atmosphere giving a signal to the unit of Mohoma to move for the attack. Mohoriti gave orders to his unit to now attack from the side with full strength and hit to kill.

Soon, horses, led by Durudhan and his brother, started galloping and moving in full speed towards the Kauravs. Drupad noticed them and appreciated this move of Mohoriti.

Kaurav army was looking very small in number in front of the huge army of Panchal and it looked like they won't be able to stand for much time. When the sun reached the horizon, both the armies rushed towards each other on the sounds of drums, kettledrums, conches, trumpets and war cries. The flags on the chariots waved with the wind as the beautiful chariots, drawn by the fleet horses, galloped toward the enemy lines. The sun was reflecting off the combatant's beautiful golden armor and as they rushed towards each other, dust rose in the atmosphere.

Panchal army, going as per the strategy of Mohoma, was taking control over Kauravs, when there was a sudden entry of Arjuna, the Pandava, from behind.

Arjuna was the third Pandava and was the best in archery. Dronacharya knew that capturing Drupad would not be easy for Kauravs alone and, so, he had asked Arjuna to go and do this for him.

He entered like a cyclone of arrows raining from the sky towards the soldiers of Panchal. He began aiming at the army men and, soon, began splitting them into two halves.

It was a situation of chaos in Panchal army unit and, suddenly, it appeared that the huge army of Panchal and Mohoma was negligible in front of his expertise.

He fired bows all over the warzone and, soon, reached near King Drupad. Mohoriti rushed his chariot towards him to safeguard his king but the arrows fired by Arjuna struck the wheels of Mohoriti' s chariot making him fly off the chariot and fall to the ground. A second arrow pierced Mohoriti's stomach and passed through to the other side.

Mohoriti was in deep pain, but being an immortal, he resisted dying of it. Arjuna, now, pulled multiple arrows and fired towards Drupad, making him helpless and ready to surrender.

Arjuna captured Drupad and took him to his own palace.

A messenger was sent to Drona to confirm the victory and the arrest of King Drupad. The wounded soldiers were moved to a camp but Mohoriti stood up with the arrow still stuck in his stomach and walked towards the court where Drupad was help in captivity.

His body was covered with blood flowing from his wound, when he saw Drupad sitting on his knees in front of Arjuna.

Then, Acharya Drona entered on his chariot and moved straight inside the court where many courtiers, along with Drupad, were held captive.

Arjuna bowed before Acharya.

"It's the same court and the same throne, Drupad, but I am the king now!" shouted Drona, while he moved and sat on the throne.

Drupad looked at him in anger, but kept quiet.

"Today, I have everything; this Brahmin is having everything and you are sitting in front of me like a beggar." Drona roared.

Drona, then, looked around and saw Mohoriti standing with blood flowing from his body. Drona moved towards him and kept his left hand on his shoulder and pulled the arrow from his body with his right hand. Mohoriti shouted in pain.

"He is the same person who took me out of this court when you asked him to. Today, I am the king; what should I do? Should I ask him to behead you?" Drona said.

Drona moved towards Drupad and sat in front on him and continued, "Remember, pride is a thing which can possibly bring one down to earth from sky and you are the living proof. You had said that friendship happens between equal castes; now, what should I say?"

Drona then smiled, "I still want to be your friend, Drupad, because I am not like you and I don't want someone to come to me someday to take revenge on me as I did with you. From today, we both will be equals. I own the complete Panchal today and I give you the half of it considering you as my childhood friend. This makes both of us as equals now."

Everyone in the court was expecting Drona to kill Drupad, but he returned half of his kingdom and asked Arjun to leave Drupad. He, then, went to him and made him stand on his feet and hugged him.

"Drupad, we are friends now and we are equal now." Drona mentioned again.

Drupad was silent as he had no words to say. Drona took him to the throne and made him sit there. He, then, smiled at him and asked Arjuna to move.

While Drona prepared to move out, Drupad replied sitting on his throne, "Drona, today I am silent because I have been unable to conquer you. Today, I am silent because you have the power of youth, Arjuna, with you but you have committed a mistake of giving me my kingdom back. Remember, I am still a warrior and I will definitely take revenge for this one day. So, either kill me or be ready for my answers."

Drona stopped and, without turning towards him, replied, "I will wait for that day, Drupad. Till then, enjoy your throne."

Drona walked away along with Arjuna and others, while Drupad kept sitting on his throne, angry and devastated.

Drupad asked everyone to leave the court, as he wanted to be alone for some time and think about how he will take revenge for this insult.

Mohoriti, covering his wound with a piece of cloth, also moved out of the court and saw bloodshed and bodies of soldiers, dying mainly of the arrows shot by Arjuna, lying outside the palace. He kept walking between the bodies with his feet getting dipped in the pools of blood formed everywhere.

He kept on walking turning each body and looking at the heads lying on earth, covered with blood. As he walked, he saw the chariot of Asthachik lying in the middle. He, now, moved a little faster to check on him. He got shocked to see Asthachik lying on the chariot with arrows piercing his chest and his body covered with blood. He moved to him and held his head to wake him up but he could not. Asthachik had died in this war.

Mohoriti now worried, started looking for others. He shouted the names of Durudhan and Karanasura but could not hear them. He started running over the bodies turning and checking each, while his hand slipped in blood and tears rolled down from his eyes.

Then, one of his soldiers came to him and with his hand joined and head bowed, said, "Pitamah, I have something to show you; please come with me."

Mohoriti, without asking anything, started following him clearing his path between the bodies and, also, holding his wound. After walking for a few distance, he saw Durudhan, Karanasura and their children's dead bodies lined on a side.

He looked at them in deep pain while his eyes welled with tears. He shouted in pain as all his children had died in this revenge of Drona. His clan was left with no successor and no future. He was living to take revenge on Bhishma and today, someone else's revenge had taken him deeper into this mud of revenge.

He held their bodies in his arms and hugged them. He was left with no one now; he came to Panchal with all his powers and thought he would be leaving now with empty hands.

Chapter-15
Death of Eklavya

Rukmini was a beautiful princess and the daughter of Bhishmaka, the king of Vidarbha. Bhishmaka was the vassal of King Jarasandha of Magadha. She had fallen in love with and had been longing for Krishna. She had been hearing about his virtue, character, charm and greatness. Rukmini's eldest brother, Rukmi, was a friend of the evil King Kansa, who was killed by Krishna and, therefore, he was set against the marriage.

Rukmini's parents wanted her to marry Krishna but Rukmi, her brother, strongly opposed to it. Rukmi was an ambitious prince and he did not want to earn the wrath of Emperor Jarasandha, who was ruthless. Instead, he proposed that she be married to his friend, Shishupala, the crown prince of Chedi. Shishupala was also a vassal and close associate of Jarasandha and, hence, an ally of Rukmi.

Bhishmaka had given in but Rukmini, who had overheard the conversation, was horrified. She immediately approached a Brahmana, Sunanda, whom she trusted, and asked him to deliver a letter to Krishna. She asked Krishna to come to Vidarbha and kidnap her in order to avoid a battle where her relatives might get killed. She suggested that he should do this when she's on her way to the temple or back. Rukmini asked him to claim her to marry her. Krishna, having received the message in Dwarka, immediately set out for Vidarbha with Balarama, his elder brother.

Meanwhile, Shishupala was overjoyed by the news from Rukmi that he could simply go to Kundina and claim Rukmini. Jarasandha, who was not so trusting, sent all his vassals and allies along because he sensed that Krishna would certainly come to snatch Rukmini away.

Bhishmaka and Rukmini received the news that Krishna was coming through their respective spies. Bhishmaka, who secretly approved of Krishna and wished he would take Rukmini away, had a furnished mansion set up for him.

He welcomed them joyfully and made them comfortable. Meanwhile, in the palace, Rukmini got ready for her upcoming marriage. She went to the Indrani temple on the pre-decided day to pray but was severely disappointed to not see Krishna there. As she stepped out, she saw Krishna and he soon swept her into his chariot with him. They both started to ride off when Shishupala noticed them. All of Jarasandha's forces quickly started chasing them. While Balarama occupied most of them and held them back, Rukmi had almost caught up with Krishna and Rukmini. He overtook Krishna near Bhadrod.

Krishna and Rukmi fought a duel, which inevitably resulted in Krishna's victory. When Krishna was about to kill him, Rukmini fell at the feet of Krishna and begged him to spare the life of his brother. Krishna, being generous, agreed to her but as a punishment, shaved Rukmi's head and let him go free. There was no greater shame for a warrior than a visible sign of defeat.

Jarasandha, on the other hand, was angry with the defeat as he had already attacked Yadavs nineteen times and was defeated. His two daughters were married to Kansa and were now widows as Krishna had killed Kansa.

He was burning with the fire of revenge with Krishna. So, he planned to conduct a yagna to please God Shiva. For this yagna, he had imprisoned ninety five kings and was in need of five more. Once he got them, he was planning to perform the yagna, sacrificing all one hundred kings. Jarasandha thought that this yagna would make him a powerful emperor in the entire Arya Vartha and after seeking blessings from Lord Shiva, he would be able to take over Krishna.

Krishna, on the other hand, formulated a plan for eliminating Jarasandha. The Pandava king, Yudhishthira, was planning to make a Rajasuya yagna in order to become the emperor. Krishna convinced his cousin, Yudhishthira, that Jarasandha was the only obstacle preventing him from becoming an emperor. Krishna planned a clever scheme to eliminate Jarasandha by making Yudhishthira's brother, Bhima, wrestle with Jarasandha in a duel.

Jarasandha was also very good at giving donations to charity. After performing his Shiva pooja, he used to give whatever the Brahmins asked for. On one such occasion, Krishna, Yudhishthira's brothers, Arjuna and Bhima met Jarasandha in the guise of Brahmins. Krishna asked Jarasandha to choose any one of them for a wrestling match. Jarasandha chose Bhima, the strongman, to wrestle with. Both of them fought for fourteen days. Bhima lost hope to win the battle and sought Krishna's help. Krishna, who knew about the secret of Jarasandha' s weakness, took a twig, split it into two and threw the left part to the right side and the right part to the left side. Bhima understood the clue and split Jarasandha's body into two and threw them in opposite directions, slaying the king. After his death, the Pandavas released the ninety-five kings imprisoned by Jarasandha and crowned his son, Sahadeva, as the king of Magadha.

Eklavya sought to avenge the murder of Jarasandha by campaigning to destroy Kuntibhoj and every Yadava in Dwarka. He decided to attack the Yadavas and take revenge of Jarasandha, who was killed by Pandavas.

He resorted to a cunning strategy. He provoked Kala Yavana, the king of Mlechchas, to attack the Yadavs. In the war that followed, Yadavs, efficiently led by Balarama and Krishna, routed Yavanas, killing Kalayavana. As Yadavs were returning after this great victory, suddenly Eklavya's forces attacked them. Exhausted Yadavas, being unable to withstand this sudden treacherous attack, came into pressure.

However, standing in front of Krishna and Balarama was not so easy. Krishna, thus, planned and asked his army to move towards Dwarka as he knew Eklavya would follow them.

As they reached the entrance of Dwarka, Sahadeva's army was waiting with full power to behead them.

While the armies were in war, Krishna took over Eklavya all

alone and broke his skull. Eklavya lay on the earth with Tejaswa on his side, when Krishna took an avatar of Lord Vishnu.

Eklavya and Tejaswa understood who he was and bowed before him.

Krishna in his avatar said, "Eklavya, your journey in this body was predefined by the lord. Whatever you did in your life was planned and written in such a way that you will leave a perception and learning for the coming generations on this earth.

The way you worshiped your guru would be an example for the generations to come and will be an inspiration for every student to respect and pray for their teachers, as a guru is someone who would not only teach the lessons of subjects but also the lessons of life. This will also make generations understand the importance of life and skills.

The way you practiced archery and mastered it would be an example to the coming generation that if one visualizes something in his heart, no one can stop him from achieving it.

The way you gave away your thumb to your guru as dakshina would be an example to the coming generation and would teach them to respect and understand the importance of knowledge in their lives.

Your friendship with Tejaswa will be an example to generations that friendship does not look at the walls of caste and money, but is a bond of love and trust between two people.

You were born because your life was a message to the coming generations. You did what you were supposed to do and you are dying not because you did something wrong but because this is also planned to bring an end to the evil on this earth on the next stage.

You will die now and will go to heaven and soon will be reborn as the son of Drupad."

Eklavya understood what he explained and joined his hands in pain and closed his eyes forever.

Tejaswa looked at him and hugged his body and, then, looked at Krishna. He joined his hands and asked, "Lord, everyone on this earth is there for some reason. I am still not able to understand why I am roaming here on earth without any reason. I request you to kill me and give worth to my life"

Krishna smiled and replied, "Tejaswa, you are on this earth for a reason but you need to search for that reason yourself. Every human on this earth has taken birth because of a reason. You have a lot of work to do in the coming days. Your family on the land of Mohoma has a different job to do and that's why you were moved out, as the purpose of your life is different.

The coming days on this earth would be tough and you must play a very crucial role in making people understand what is correct and what is wrong.

At times, you must decide your own fate and choose the path which you feel is correct for the mankind. If you were not required here, I would have killed you today itself but you have a lot of pending work on this earth.

Do your duty and find answers to the questions that I have left open for you. Do your karma and don't expect a result for everything you do. Only then will you find the right path for your karma."

Tejaswa tried to understand what was explained to him. He bowed before the lord and asked, "One more question, my lord, what is the next command for me?"

"I am no one to command. You are the commander of your soul yourself. You need to guide yourself and ask your body to perform as per your orders. You need to find yourself and your purpose of life."

Tejaswa bowed again and joined his hands before him.

"Thank you, my lord." He said.

Chapter-16
Movement to Varnavrata

"King Dhiritarashtra is blind and should now relinquish the throne to Yudhishthira. Bhishma cannot be the king since he has renounced it himself. Our king, Pandu, was the real king and King Dhiritarashtra has been taking care of the empire till the sons of Pandu reach the age to take over. Duryodhana is no good and, also, he is not the eldest amongst all the cousins. Yudhishthira is the oldest one. He is the most capable and the most ardent follower of dharma. If he becomes our king, he will lead us on the path of dharma. On the other hand, I am not sure what will happen to us in case Duryodhana becomes our king." said one of the progeny to others while sitting outside his house in the morning.

The progeny of Hastinapur, by now, was discussing on who should be the next king after Dhiritarashtra. Dhiritarashtra had one more problem other than his blindness. Although he was a very learned and strong man and followed dharma most of the times, yet when it came to his most loveable son, Duryodhana, he always took bad decisions owing to his blind love for him. He liked his brother's sons, the Pandavas, but his weakness of will and doting love for his own children made him a participant in Duryodhana' s evil plans.

The Pandavas were the darling of the public, too. They openly talked about Yudhishthira as their future king.

The political ups and downs had started in Hastinapur and the progeny was in a complete support of Pandavas. This was a posing as a problem for Duryodhana.

Duryodhana complained bitterly to his father, "the progeny speaks such nonsense, father. Do not pay any attention to their views; you are the king and it must be your decision. How can they even think of Yudhishthira as their king? They say the Pandavas are mighty; what about the might of Pitamah Bhishma and Guru Drona, who would always serve the throne of Hastinapur? If Yudhishthira is made the crown prince, it will be a bad luck for Hastinapur's fate. You will be put aside for your blindness, but what about me and our progeny? It is better to end our lives than live here with Yudhishthira as the king."

Dhiritarashtra listened to him quietly and, then, replied, "Duryodhana, do not fill yourself with such hatred. Yudhishthira is your brother and will follow Dharma for as long as he lives. He will never ill treat you or your brothers. I cannot crown you as the crown prince, although you know that is my heart's desire. Yudhishthira has inherited all the good qualities of my brother. Most of my commanders in the army like him; most of my ministers are on their side and so is the progeny. Do not underestimate the power of the progeny to overthrow a king."

Duryodhana was aware about the comments which the progeny made. His rage knew no bounds. Shakuni, his mother's brother, added oil to the fire in him by instigating him. "Your father is blind, so Pandu was made the king. He died without fulfilling his duties as a king. Your father has shown how capable he is in spite of his blindness and has ruled so far and maintained the clout of Hastinapur. Pandu goes off to the forest and Kunti comes back with these five children, how do we know they are the rightful heirs of Pandu? You are not blind, my son. There is no reason why Yudhishthira should be even considered to claim the rights of succession. However, your father is soft-hearted and has accepted the Pandavas. He is raising baby snakes which will one day bite him. Dear son, I have a plan that will kill the Pandavas and their mother, Kunti, and no one will even suspect you. All you need to do is to make your father agree to send the Pandavas and their mother, Kunti, to Varnavrata."

When Duryodhana heard Shakuni's plan for the first time, he was filled with doubts. Shakuni sensed Duryodhana's lack of commitment and confusion. "Dear *Bhanje*, a king must be mighty. No one will believe in your strength if it is not showcased, not even your progeny. The affairs of a kingdom must be kept secret and the earliest indication to the progeny about a wise plan should be at the time of its execution. Evils must be eradicated at the earliest, since even a small thorn, if not removed at the right time, causes a big harm. Strong enemies must be destroyed and even a weak foe should not be neglected, since it only is a small spark that causes a wild fire. Guard yourself against the Pandavas, my future Hastinapur king!"

Duryodhana convinced King Dhiritarashtra to send Pandavas to Varnavrata where annual festivities were being held in the honor of Lord Shiva. Dhiritarashtra affectionately told the Pandavas to go there as the people of Varnavrata will also be very happy to receive the sons of Pandu. The unsuspecting Pandavas were easily persuaded and were happy with the decision. They began their preparations for the journey and took leave from Bhishma, Dhiritarashtra and other elders. Duryodhana was elated and sent his trusted minister, Purochana, to Varnavrata giving him certain secret instructions.

Purochana, being an excellent architect, began building a beautiful palace for the Pandavas at Varnavrata. However, the palace was built with the most combustible materials, like jute, lac, oil and fat. Beds, chairs and other furniture were strategically placed in such places that they could easily be engulfed in fire. The palace was, indeed, being built very skillfully and beautifully. The progeny of Varnavrata praised Prince Duryodhana and King Dhiritarashtra for making such good arrangements for the Pandavas. Duryodhana's plan was to set the palace on fire once everyone was settled in. However, he was unaware that this plan had already been leaked to Vidhura.

Vidhura asked his best and trustworthy soldier, Rajulya, to reach Varnavrata and arrange an architect who is specialized in digging a tunnel. Rajulya took his orders and reached Varnavrata, but he needed to arrange this very secretly so that this information is not leaked to Kauravs.

As he reached there, he presented himself as the owner of a

big land. He said that he is searching for an architect who could build perfect temple of Lord Ram, with tunnels from the temple extending towards various river banks for worshipping.

Most of the progeny suggested him to visit outskirts of Varnavrata, where, recently, an architect had arrived and was building amazing sculptures of gods and goddesses along with multiple temples. His expertise was highly admired by the progeny of Varnavrata.

Rajulya decided to meet him and make him agree for the sake of Bharat varsh. He got into his chariot and reached the desired place as suggested by the people of Varnavrata.

As he reached, he was astonished to see the huge statues of Lord Shiva embossed on the rock hills describing the ancient stories. He could observe multiple small and big temples curved on the rocks and the trees.

He moved out from his chariot and started observing this work of perfection and, also, analyzing the competence of the person to do so. As he moved further deep in the area, he was amazed to see the work of art. Soon, he saw a tall, young and dark handsome man, wearing dhoti and covering his head with a cloth, suspended from the top of the rocks with a string made up of tree branches.

He looked like a hard-working man, who was doing his work with perfection in a hot, sunny day. The sweat dripping from his muscular body was not distracting him from his work.

Rajulya understood that he was the man he has been searching for. He called him loudly, "could you please come down; I would like to talk to you?"

He turned and replied, "Tejaswa, my name is Tejaswa. Wait, I am coming down."

Tejaswa, who moved to Varnavrata after meeting Lord Krishna, had started making statues of rocks himself. He had practiced making statues previously, along with Eklavya, when they had one of Drona. When he came to Varnavrata, he decided to build statues of gods, depicting their stories. He thought may be, someday, he will understand the purpose of his life.

"Yes, sir, please tell me. How may I help you?" Tejaswa came down and started wiping the sweat from his body with the cloth which was tied on his head.

"Good to see your work. I have some work for you, which could earn you a lot of gold." Rajulya said.

"Sir, do you think I am working in this sun, making statues on rocks, for gold? I work for something in which I could search myself, something which could give a reason of my being on this earth." replied Tejaswa

Rajulya smiled, "then, I think I am at the right place."

He sat down on a big stone in the shed of a tree and continued, "Whatever I am telling you must remain between you and I and no one else should come to know about this. Can I trust you?"

Tejaswa smiled at him and replied, "You can trust me; this will not move beyond my heart."

Rajulya moved his eyes to confirm that no one else was present "Duryodhana has prepared a palace in Varnavrata for Pandavas, who will be visiting soon. However, that palace is made up of the most combustible materials like jute, lac, oil and fat. Beds, chairs and other furniture have also been strategically placed so that they could be easily engulfed in fire.

Vidhura, a courtier of Hastinapur, came to know about this and he has asked me to look for someone who could build a tunnel from the palace towards the bank of River Ganga.

This information is very confidential and must not be leaked, as this might also lead to death of the Pandavas. After seeing the perfection in your work, I am confident that you can do this job successfully."

Tejaswa thought in his mind, "It's a great chance for me to take the revenge from my family. If I am able to save Pandavas from Varnavrata and take them to Pitamah Mohoriti, he will be able to take his revenge. I must agree for the same."

"I am ready for it; when should I start my job?" asked Tejaswa with cruel intentions behind.

Rajulya appreciated his decision and opened a map, which was prepared on a piece of cloth, of the palace with all the calculations of the surrounding mapped in the unit, foot.

"This is a map of the palace with the details of surrounding areas; have a look." He said.

Tejaswa looked at the map in detail and, then, suggested, "I will start digging a tunnel from the palace room, as presently it's in construction and no one will notice me since many laborers are working there already. Also, digging such a big tunnel will take time and it would be good to complete the tunnel work at farther end later, so that no one comes to know about this."

He further analyzed the map and informed, "Look at this position; once the tunnel is dug till the forest area, we can do our job without any fear as no one would be there to hear the sound of digging."

"I agree, Tejaswa. I will suggest you to start your work from today only so that it's completed in time." said Rajulya.

"Also, I have one suggestion." interrupted Tejaswa.

"Please tell me." Rajulya asked with curiosity.

"When Pandavas would escape from the tunnel, I suggest you to let me be present at the other end with a boat, so that I could take them to a safe place. You could also assign this job to someone else, but I suggest you should keep this plan between only two of us."

Tejaswa wanted to take Pandavas to the land of Mohoma from there and that's why he put this suggestion forward.

"It's a good idea; I will inform the same to Vidhura; you can start your work." Rajulya confirmed.

Tejaswa folded the map and kept it inside his dhoti.

Vidhura was informed by Rajulya that a person has been identified for the work and he will begin working tonight.

Vidhura warned the Pandavas as they took his leave to go to Varnavrata. "One can escape danger if one forestalls the plans of his astute enemy. There are things sharper than a steel blade and a wise man knows how to guard himself against them. A rat buried in his hole and a porcupine living in his burrow escapes the forest fire. A wise man knows his bearings by looking at the stars and the growth of the moon to the full."

Tejaswa started his work on the same night and continued to dig a tunnel for the next six months. As he reached the last point opening at the bank of River Ganga, he removed the mud from the hole and pushed himself outside. He was happy to see the sun after six long months. Soon, he made the exit hole bigger and wider, so that huge Bhima could manage his exit comfortably. He, then, pulled out the long grass and weeds growing on the side of the bank and covered the exit mouth of the tunnel.

He, then, took his path towards the River Ganga and sat down to wash himself as his body was covered with mud all over. He took the water and started washing his face when he saw a beautiful lady coming out of water.

He realized that she is some goddess and he immediately bowed before her with his hands joined in respect.

"Bless you my son, get up!" she was none other than Goddess Ganga.

"I came to thank you for saving the future of Hastinapur. Your work will be appreciated in history but no one will ever know your name due to the curse on your family. Ask me what blessing you want from me." The goddess said.

Tejaswa bowed before her again and said, "I am thankful I could do something in my life; I request you to bless me so that I can make people aware about right and wrong."

Ganga smiled and blessed him, "I am blessing you with the knowledge of dance and drama; this will help you in fulfilling the purpose you want in the future. You will be excellent in this and no one on this earth will stand in front of you in this knowledge."

Tejaswa thanked her and she went back to water.

Later, Pandavas reached Varnavrata and were astonished by the beautiful palace Duryodhana had built for them. Yudhishthira proceeded to examine the walls and realized they were made up of combustible materials. He told his other brothers and mother to behave in a way that it doesn't arise any suspicion about them being aware of Duryodhan's plan.

From the first day, Bhima and Purochana were conspiring to take over each other. Purochana was waiting to set the palace of wax on fire after the Pandavas slept. However, since Bhima used to be awake all night, Purochana could not get a chance to do so.

Seeing that Bhima never slept even a single night and stayed awake all the time, Purochana asked his wife, a Nishadas huntswoman, and her five sons to come to the palace to help him complete his mission. Her objective was to poison the food given to the Pandavas. Still, Bhima sensed danger and ate the entire food without her knowledge. Since Bhima had already consumed the Kalakoota poison as a child, the poison mixed in the food did not have any effect on him. Later in the night, Purochana, unaware of the fact that the Pandavas were simply sleeping, assumed them to be dead. To celebrate this, Purochana began to drink Suru and, within a few hours, she was drunk. Utilizing this opportunity, the Pandavas set the palace on fire and escaped through the tunnel. Ironically, in the ensuing fire, Purochana, his wife and her five sons themselves were charred to death.

The fire quickly spread across the palace and the villagers of Varnavrata soon came running to put it out. They poured buckets of water but could not stop the fire. They, then, sent a message to the king of Hastinapur saying, "The palace, where the Pandavas lived, has been burnt down. No one has been able to escape alive."

In the meanwhile, the Pandavas passed through the tunnel and reached the other end where Tejaswa was waiting for them on his boat by the bank of River Ganga.

He welcomed all of them.

"My lords, you may change your royal clothes to Brahmins clothes, which I have kept for you behind the trees. This will not let anyone recognize you." He suggested to Pandavas.

Yudhishthira understood his concern and asked his brother to do the same and change their attires.

On the other hand in Hastinapur, upon hearing the message, Dhiritarashtra's heart was warm with joy and chilled with sorrow, while Duryodhana was overjoyed. The royal family at Hastinapur cast off the Pandava's royal clothes in sorrow and performed the rites for the dead. Vidhura was not affected by the sorrow as much as the others and this was attributed to his philosophical bent of mind. However, Bhishma was sunk in sorrow.

Pandavas, along with Kunti, boarded his boat.

"Where are you taking us, young man?" asked Yudhishthira.

"My lord, your life is in danger and I am taking you to the north of Panchal, which is with Drona now. We will go to the land of Mohoma." He answered.

Tejaswa had started sailing the boat amidst the full tides in River Ganga, when Arjuna asked him, "If I am not wrong, I have met you, young man, but I cannot recall where. Are you from Hastinapur?"

Tejaswa, still continuing to sail, replied wisely, "My lord, you had met me when Acharya Drona had asked my dear friend, Eklavya, to sacrifice his thumb."

"Oh! So you are from Nishadas, the hunters?" Arjuna asked again.

"No, my lord, whatever I am today, I am because of Nishadas, but I am not from Nishadas. I came here when I was a small kid, running from my land, the land of Mohoma. I am the son of King Indriya, who ruled and built Mohoma." Tejaswa replied.

Hearing this, Bhima immediately stood up from his seat, went to him and held the rudder along with him to sail along. Looking at him, Tejaswa joined his hands and said, "Lord, please let me do my job; don't make me small by doing so."

"You are also a prince and warrior as us and this makes us equal as per the law." Bhima replied.

"My lord, I may be a prince but I have spent the whole of my life as a Shudra and all that I have understood is that be it Kshatriya or Shudra, we all are humans, and today I am your servant hired by your courtier to take you to a safe place. So, please let me do my job." Tejaswa replied.

Yudhishthira heard his words and replied, "Bhima, he is correct, as he is doing his duty. Let him do his job. If everyone on this earth does his job as a responsibility, there would be no war and bloodshed."

Tejaswa thanked him and continued his duty. The next day, they reached the bank of Panchal forest area and decided to walk further towards the land of Mohoma.

Chapter-17
Pandava in Mohoma

Tejaswa parked the boat in a corner of the bank and took hold of the rudder so that Kunti could step out comfortably.

"We need to walk from here towards Mohoma." he informed everyone.

"But before we start our journey, it would be better if we cook and eat something. I hope you all would also be hungry." Kunti suggested.

"Let me collect some wood for cooking. Meanwhile, you all may take some rest under that tree." Tejaswa suggested.

Arjun desired to join him in collecting wood. So, both of them moved to the other side of the forest. Meanwhile, Kunti started making the arrangements to cook some food.

"We are thankful to you, my friend!" Arjun told him while picking up dry woods.

"I am thankful that you called me friend" Tejaswa exclaimed.

"I am very sorry for your friend, Eklavya." Arjun said with remorse.

"No, please don't be sorry for him. Even he was not sorry for what happened." replied Tejaswa.

Arjuna went silent for some time and, then, replied, "I can't bring him back, but I can give you same warmth of friendship just like him."

Arjuna, then, moved to him and hugged him, "Thank you, Tejaswa."

"Thanks, prince, I am obliged with your friendship." Tejaswa replied.

They, then, picked up woods and reached Kunti. She started cooking rice and some vegetables which had Tejaswa carried with him.

When they were all seated to start their dinner, they saw a group of sages coming towards them. Looking at them coming, they all immediately stood up and bow before them.

"Pranaam, guruvar! Please join us in sharing our food whatever we have and bless us." requested Yudhishthira.

Looking at the gesture, the sages thanked them and had dinner with them. After dinner, Kunti asked them where they are up to and one of the sages replied, "King Drupada of Panchal had been defeated by the Pandava prince, Arjuna, on behalf of Drona, who subsequently took half of his kingdom. To gain revenge on Drona, he performed a yagna called Putrakameshti yagna to obtain a means of besting him. From the sacrificial fire, Draupadi emerged as a beautiful dark-skinned young woman after her sibling, Dhrishtadyumna.

Drupada intended to wed his daughter to Arjuna. However, upon hearing about the Pandavas' supposed death at Varnavrata yesterday, he set up a swayamvara for Draupadi to choose her husband from the competitive contest. We are heading for the same."

After telling this, they blessed them considering them as Brahmins and moved on their way to Panchal.

Once they went off, Tejaswa asked a question to Arjuna, "Why don't you go to Panchal and participate in the swayamvara? Who could be more capable than you?"

"I think he is correct; we must go there." replied Kunti.

Hearing their mother's wish, the Pandavas decided to move towards Panchal.

The next day, when they reached the swayamvara, they saw that a pole was erected at the center of the court above which there was a revolving wheel. A wooden fish was placed in the center of the wheel. At the bottom of the pole, there was a pan full of water. The one who would shoot an arrow in the eye of the revolving fish above while looking at its reflection in the water below would marry Draupadi. This was the condition for the swayamvara of the most beautiful lady. Princes from all over had assembled for the swayamvara. Duryodhana, Karna and Shri Krishna were also present. As the swayamvara began, many brave princes tried to win over Draupadi, but failed to perform the difficult task of shooting in the fish's eye. When Karna came forward to show his skills, Draupadi stopped him and said, "I will not marry a charioteer's son." Feeling insulted, Karna left the court.

When all the princes were unsuccessful in performing the feat, King Drupada became worried about the marriage of his daughter. Suddenly, Arjuna dressed as a Brahmin rose to try the feat. Nobody could recognize him except Krishna. All the princes objected to the participation of a Brahmin in a competition that was meant for warriors. However, looking at the build and the confidence of the Brahmin, no one dared to say anything. Arjuna easily shot in the fish's eye. Draupadi was very happy and she put the wedding garland around Arjun's neck.

Between all the celebrations, Krishna recognized Tejaswa among the mob and moved to him. As he came near him, Tejaswa joined his hands and bowed before him.

"I told you, you have many important jobs to do." Krishna said.

"What is the next order for me, my lord?" replied Tejaswa.

"Just be with them and serve the purpose of your life." replied Krishna and moved away.

All the princes felt humiliated and were also jealous of Arjuna. They attacked him. Bhima came to his rescue. The mighty Pandavas easily defeated all the princes and took Draupadi with them. Tejaswa took them to Kunti, whom he had asked to stay in an empty hut on their way.

When they reached the hut, the Pandavas called out to their mother, Kunti, "Look, Mother, who we have brought along with us." Kunti, who was busy cooking food, replied from inside the hut, "Share it among yourselves." thinking that they had brought food.

When she saw the bride and got to know that she's Arjun's wife, Kunti was very unhappy and said, "As a custom, the Pandavas would have to obey every word that I say. Draupadi will have to become the wife of all the five brothers." Just then, Krishna, who had followed them to their hut, entered. He told Kunti, "In her previous life, Draupadi had worshipped Shiva to get a husband with five qualities. However, Shiva had given her a boon that in her next life, she would marry five men each having one quality." On hearing this, Kunti felt satisfied and declared Draupadi as the wife of all the five Pandavas.

She, then, asked Krishna what was the next order for them, on which Krishna asked them to go along with Tejaswa to the land of Mohoma.

Tejaswa joined his hands and respectfully welcomed them to the land of Mohoma, but before entering, he requested of something from the Pandavas.

"I ran away from Mohoma because my uncles killed my father, Indriya, and they wanted to kill me, too. May be, when they would see me return, they would attack again. Will you be there to save me in such a circumstance?" Tejaswa put his case.

Arjuna came forward to him, "I have called you a friend and I am with you in any circumstance of your life. So, let's move to Mohoma and feel secure."

Tejaswa, who was out of Mohoma for many years, was not aware that Durudhan and his brother were killed by Arjuna in a war with Drupad.

Tejaswa, then, took the position of a charioteer and boarded Pandavas along with Kunti and Draupadi in his chariot and moved towards the land of Mohoma.

The land of Mohoma, which was once the most beautiful and prosperous clan, was now desolate in its curse. Tejaswa's eyes welled up with tears as he reached the main entrance gate of his motherland and was nostalgic to see the watch tower on which he used to play with Indriya.

He remembered his mother, Mili, whom he had left in his childhood, while moving his chariot on the barren land of Mohoma. The progeny looked dull and unsatisfied and this worried him. He believed his uncles had not taken care of the progeny, whom they had brought along with them to flourish.

He, now, moved his chariot fast to reach the palace where once his father use to hold the throne.

He parked the chariot at the center of the empire, the space built for major gatherings, while Pandavas stepped out from the chariot.

Looking at the new faces in the clan, progeny started gathering to the center of the village to know who they were. He kept quiet and remained cautious about the attack from his uncle. As he saw a chariot coming fast towards them creating a cloud of dust, his hand went towards his sword to overcome any unseen danger.

It was Mohoriti dressed in all white, standing still with a bow in his hand as the chariot arrived near them. Tejaswa linked his hand with a smile on his face.

Mohoriti stepped down from his chariot. Though grown old, he still had the same power in his shoulders and spark in his eyes.

Tejaswa moved straight to him and touched his feet.

"Ayushman bhava!" replied Mohoriti and continued, "Who are you, young man, and what your purpose behind visiting Mohoma is?

Tejaswa answered with teary eyes, "You had asked me to return one day with power in my shoulders and a broad chest. So, today I am standing in front of you, Pitamah, your Tejaswa."

Mohoriti dropped his bow hearing his words and extended his arms to hug him, "Thanks to mighty lord for sending you back, my son. Mohoma needed you. My old, aged bones cannot hold the burden of this clan anymore."

"I had to return one day to my land." replied Tejaswa and, then, he turned towards the Pandavas and continued, "Pitamah, they are Brahmins who have come along with me and they will take rest in our land today."

Mohoriti joined his hands and greeted them, not knowing that they were Pandavas, and asked one of his courtiers to take them to the guest room and take care of them.

Pandavas followed him, while Tejaswa joined Mohoriti to his court.

Mohoriti was overjoyed and took him to his court. While they were moving, Tejaswa was worried about Durudhan and his brothers and in curiosity, he asked, "Where are my uncles? Are they still after my life?"

Mohoriti stopped as he reached near the throne. He asked him to go and sit on the throne. Tejaswa, who was confused, kept looking at him.

"You are the real king of Mohoma! I kept this throne vacant for you after all your uncles died in a war with Drona." Mohoriti explained.

Tejaswa was shocked, "What? All of them died in a war!"

Mohoriti took him to the throne and made him sit on the throne. Taking a long breath and he, then, told him about the war in which Arjuna took over Drupad, resulting in the death of all his uncles.

Tejaswa listened to it carefully and, then, replied "I know you are waiting for your revenge from Hastinapur and, so, I have returned to you. Hope your revenge is fulfilled once you kill the Pandavas."

"What do you mean, Tejaswa?" asked Mohoriti.

"Yes, Pitamah, the Brahmins who have come along with me are none other than the Pandavas, whom I escaped from Varnavrata and brought to Mohoma for you. Now, you can take your revenge and hurt Bhishma deep in his heart."

However, before Mohoriti could take any decision, a porter outside his court announced the arrival of Dhrishtadyumna, Drupad and Krishna. Mohoriti was surprised to hear the announcement and took his way towards the main door to welcome them.

After greeting them all, he welcomed them to his court.

"Please call the Brahmins who have arrived at your palace." asked Dhrishtadyumna

Hearing his words, Mohoriti asked his servants to call them to the court. Once they arrived, Dhrishtadyumna joined his hands and said, "The great Pandavas, I came to know that it's you who have married my dear sister, Draupadi. I followed you to know how you are taking care of my sister."

"Arjuna, you put me in prison but that was the fate of God and I forgive you for that. I know my daughter can never get better husband than you." replied Drupad

Drupad played a very political game to bring Pandavas on his side to take his revenge on Drona, who had won half of his kingdom with the help of only Arjuna, but now Drupad was having all the Pandavas on his side.

"I declare today that I'd arrange a big fat wedding of my daughter along with the Pandavas and would invite kings from all the clans and kingdoms to give you blessings." announced Drupad.

Now, Mohoriti needed to take back his decision of attacking the Pandavas as Draupadi had married them and she was the daughter of Drupad, who had allotted to them the land of Mohoma. He couldn't betray his king.

Krishna, who was aware about everything, smiled and decided to meet Mohoriti and Tejaswa that night.

Chapter-18
Krishna and his plan

Mohoriti and Tejaswa were sitting in the court room discussing the way he'd spent all these years far from Mohoma, when Krishna turned up in the room.

Looking at him entering, they greeted him. Krishna smiled and asked them to take their seats.

"You have not slept yet, Dwarka Naresh?" asked Mohoriti.

"Foreseeing the upcoming ups and downs in our land, how could I sleep?" replied Krishna.

"But, now, everything looks perfect. Pandavas are saved from Varnavrata and could be king soon." Mohoriti stated.

"The road to perfect living is never easy, Mohoriti. Who knows this better than you?" replied Krishna and continued, "Do you think Duryodhana will grant them what they want so easily and he will not create any troubles in the way? Also, if everything ends so well, how will you be out of your family's curse?"

Mohoriti asked in a surprised tone, "How come you know about our curse, my lord?"

"You just called me 'lord' and, now, you are asking how I came to know about your curse." Krishna replied.

"So, what is the next order for us? Please suggest the road

ahead." Mohoriti requested.

Krishna stood up from his seat and said, "Human beings are born with some special qualities, like jealousy, envy and many more. At times, these are exaggerated to meet the needs of earth. If earth will be filled with devils, gods must come here to kill them. So, the time will progress to clean the earth. Soon, the time will stop ticking and a situation will come when the family members would kill their family to keep themselves alive. People will be drinking each other's blood to get rid of their thirst; there will be hue and cry all over. In a little while, there will be orphaned children and many widows in every state, but that will be for a change. You know, an eagle, when old, searches for the top most peak of a mountain and, then, scratches his wings with his beak till not a single feather is left. He, then, breaks his nails and finally breaks his beaks hitting it hard on the rock and sits there for months without food and water to get a new birth with new feathers, nails and beak. Similarly, there will be pain and blood to get the new birth of the mankind."

Mohoriti joined his hands, "So, what are the orders for us, lord?"

"I am no one to order you. It's your soul who would order you. Take the right decision at the right time. Move along with time. Today, Pandavas are at your doorstep. Be with them; they would need you in future and you will need them in future." explained Krishna.

He, then, turned towards Tejaswa and held his shoulder, "You have a lot to do in your life; I told you once. Bringing Pandavas safe from Varnavrata was not the only job for you."

"So, what is next order for me, lord?" asked Tejaswa.

Krishna said in a serious tone, "As I see, Pandavas would be requiring a huge army support in future. You need to start working on it from now."

"No one has had a bigger army than the Yadavs on this earth and when your army is with them, what else they require?" asked Mohoriti.

"You didn't hear me carefully. I said the time will turn. Who knows I will be with them or not; who knows if my army will be with me or who knows will Tejaswa be with you. Time can change anything; so, we need to be prepared for every turn of time. Now, Tejaswa, you must lead the way to extend your clan. You must look out for the expansion of the Mohoma's area. You need to fight wars; you need to get married. Play all the diplomatic and strength games but, also, extend your army and one day your army will be a back up for the Pandavas."

Tejaswa pulled his sword and went on his keens holding the sword with both his hands, "I promise you, lord, that the coming days of my life will be spent moving only towards one goal. Bless me to achieve my targets."

Krishna blessed him to conquer the world.

"Why not start from now? You can never conquer Kimpurusha alone but you have Arjuna with you now. Use him and get it with you." Krishna smiled and left saying that he is feeling sleepy now and that they both talked too much.

The next morning, Tejaswa requested Arjuna to help him invade Kimpurusha, as it was the kingdom because of which he'd lost his father, Indriya. Arjuna, having considered the efforts made by Tejaswa to save them from Varnavrata, agreed to help Tejaswa.

Drupad also decided to support Mohoma with his army of Kshatriyas to conquer Kimpurusha. Arjuna led the huge army of Kshatriyas and the unit of Mohoma towards the white mountains of Kimpurusha.

Draupadi, along with Kunti, came forward with a tray made up of mud, with vermillion and flowers placed on it. She put tilak on the forehead of Mohoriti and, then, of Arjuna. She, then, reached Tejaswa and started putting tilak when Krishna smiled and commented "Draupadi, you received Pandavas as your life partners and Tejaswa as a brother."

Draupadi smiled and nodded, "Brother, hope you win every battle of your life."

Tejaswa bowed and thanked her.

Krishna, then, asked Arjuna, through a gesture of his eye, to come aside. Arjuna understood and moved aside, where Krishna was standing. He smiled at him and, then, explained, "You know, Arjuna, why I asked you to go on a battle just the next day of your marriage?"

Arjuna kept quiet and stood with his hands joined before Krishna.

"The future is tough, my brother, and the one who prepares

initially, succeeds later. In the coming times, there would be a war and now is the time for you to get your preparation started, right when your enemy thinks you are nowhere in front of him. You are a great archer but no war could be won just with the powers in one's shoulders. Wars are won by strategies and moves and the game is always on the side of the one who moves first.

The land of Mohoma is not only a clan but also a land for your war preparations. Politically, use this clan to grow your strength, which will serve you in future when required."

Arjuna bent down on his keens and asked for his blessings and moved towards his army. He, then, looked at them and ordered to start moving towards the White Mountains.

It will take almost two days to reach the white mountains and would be a tough terrain for them to fight in snow and cold breeze, whereas Kimpurusha were experts in fighting in the extreme conditions of cold.

The movement of such a big army could not be kept hidden and, soon, Durmaputra, the king of Kimpurusha, came to know about the movement of Mohoma's army towards them.

"I knew we are breeding snakes with us." Durmaputra told his commander in anger.

"They are not alone, but are accompanied by the Panchal army of the Kshatriyas. I have also heard that they are being led by the Pandava, Arjuna."

"I have heard about Arjuna quite a lot but he did a big mistake by planning to conquer us. Let's plan out better." replied Durmaputra.

He, then, moved towards the sand and clay model of Kimpurusha and showed a valley between the two white mountain ranges.

"They will be entering from the valley area as the other entry is completely covered with snow and they are not expert in snow walking. Ask our troops to hide above the valley on the peak points and provoke an avalanche once their entire army passes by the valley. It will be a panic situation for them and after that, once they try to gather themselves, attack from our best archer troop. Every arrow from the top will slit their bodies into parts."

Commander understood the plan and took his permission to move his troops towards the peak of the valley. This plan was great and could easily stop the entrance of a huge army. Durmaputra knew the strength of his clan and how to use it when required. They immediately took the action and placed their archer troops at the peak point, waiting for Mohoma army to reach.

The next day, when Mohoma army reached to some distance from the White Mountain valley, Mohoriti came near to Arjuna and said, "I have a suggestion, if you allow."

"Please do suggest." replied Arjuna.

"By now, the Kimpurusha army would have come to know that we are coming towards them and if I would be their commander, I would definitely try to stop us from entering the valley by some sort of a planned attack. Also, I would have taken the benefit of height to conquer." Mohoriti explained.

"Then, what do you suggest on our movement plan?" asked Arjuna.

"Let's send a small troop from the entry of the valley, while the bigger portion of our army would climb the mountain range and try to make a surprise attack." replied Mohoriti.

"But will it not be tough for our soldiers, who have not fought in such adverse conditions?" Arjuna asked.

"We will place our camps here with only the troop which will go through the valley. Kimpurusha army, who would be monitoring us, would feel that we are camping here while the remaining troop will get some time to climb the ranges. We must try to reach the top before our ground troop enters the valley, so that we can withstand the attack and save the lives of our soldiers, too." explained Mohoriti.

Arjuna understood the plan and asked him to camp at the present position as per the plan, while they, along with the bigger troop, would move on the other side to start climbing the mountain range.

It looked like their plan was working as Kimpurusha commander was worried thinking why they were camping at the entry of the valley.

In the next two days, the rest of the troop, along with Mohoriti, Tejaswa and Arjuna, climbed the mountain, but to their surprise, Durmaputra was ready to welcome them there with his troop of super humans, who immediately rolled heavy rocks and burning balls towards them, making them unstable. They had not planned for this. At the same time, the troop at the ground level had started marching towards the valley going by the plan. As they reached the center of the valley, Kimpurusha army evoked avalanche with a blow of snow towards them. Most of them got burnt alive in the avalanche, after which Kimpurusha army rained arrows on them, leading to pool of blood flowing in the snow making the White Mountains turn to red.

Arjuna heard the sounds of soldiers crying and shouting. It looked like his army was hit hard by Kimpurusha's. It was a huge loss of Kshatriya soldiers but this challenged Arjuna's proficiency. He, then, along with Tejaswa and Mohoriti, opened the war on Kimpurusha with great slaughter of Kimpurusha soldiers.

War continued for three long days with loss and slaughter of Kshatriya's and Kimpurusha's soldiers but finally Arjuna managed to hit hard his arrow on the chest of Durmaputra leading to his death.

Finally, after three days' collision involving a great slaughter of Kshatriyas, Arjuna brought the region under his complete sway.

He declared Tejaswa as the new king of Kimpurusha, which would now be a part of the land of Mohoma.

When Dhiritarashtra heard that the five Pandavas were alive, he invited them back to the Hastinapur kingdom. However, in their absence and having considered them as dead, Duryodhana was succeeded in being made as the crown prince. On the return of the Pandavas, the issue of returning Yudhishthira's crown to him was raised. Dhiritarashtra led the subsequent discussions into ambiguity and agreed to a partition of the kingdom "to do justice to both the crown princes" on the suggestion of Bhishma and Vidhura. He retained the developed Hastinapur for himself and Duryodhana and gave the barren, arid and hostile lands of Khandavaprastha to the Pandavas.

Pandavas cleared this forest to construct their capital city called Indraprastha. This forest was earlier inhabited by Naga tribes led by a king named Takshaka. Arjuna and Krishna, along with the support of Mohoma clan, cleared this forest by setting up a fire. The inhabitants of this forest were displaced. This was the root cause of the enmity of the Naga Takshila towards the Kuru kings, who ruled from Indraprastha and Hastinapur.

Lord Indra was the protecting deity of Khandava forest, which is why the region was known as Indraprastha. When the forest was being burnt, Indra attacked Arjuna with his bolt (Vajra), injuring him.

However, with help of Krishna, the Pandavas successfully developed their land and built a great and a lavish city, which was considered as comparable with the heavens, and, thus, this city came to be known as Indraprastha.

Chapter-19
Helpless Tejaswa

Mohoriti, being an experienced man, understood what Krishna explained to him and, so, he decided, along with Tejaswa, to expand the land of Mohoma to multiple clans, either by war or by diplomacy. His idea was to first try out the diplomatic way to build a friendly relation with the other clan and if that was not possible, go for war. However, he ensured time was utilized for the expansion of Mohoma.

Mohoriti decided to move to Chedi tribe and tried to convince the clan of Madhyadesa to become their allies. Their king, Sisupala, had allied with Jarasandha, but after the latter's death, his son, Dhrishtaketu, had become the king of Chedi.

King Sisupala was born with three eyes and four arms. His parents were inclined to cast him out, but were warned by a heavenly voice against doing so, as his time had not come yet. It was also foretold that his superfluous members would disappear when a certain person would take him into his lap and that he would eventually die by the hands of that same person. Coming to visit his cousin, Krishna placed the child on his lap and his extra eye and arms disappeared. This also indicated that Sisupala's death was destined to happen by the hands of Krishna.

Later, Sisupala's mother made Krishna, her nephew, take a vow that he would pardon his cousin, Sisupala, for a hundred offenses. When Yudhishthira underwent the Rajulya Yagna, he sent Bhima to obtain the fealty of Sisupala, now the king after his father's death. Sisupala accepted Yudhishthira's supremacy with no protest, and was invited to the final ceremony in Indraprastha.

At that event, the Pandavas decided that Krishna would be their honored guest. At that time, Sisupala insulted Krishna for being a cowherd and worthless to be honored as a king. At the same event, he committed his hundredth sin and was pardoned by Krishna. When Sisupala insulted him again, considered as his 101st sin, Krishna released his Sudarshana Chakra on him and killed him on the spot.

Dhrishtaketu was ruling Chedi when Mohoriti, along with Tejaswa, arrived with an offer to ally.

Mohoriti offered a treaty in which Mohoma would supply apples and dry fruits to Chedi kingdom from the recently acquired Kimpurusha kingdom to become their friendly allies. Chedi kingdom, which was almost in the middle of Bharat, was deprived of dry fruits and apples and, thus, it agreed to their proposal for a business ally.

Moving further with the strategy, the land of Mohoma allied with many other tribes like Asmaka, Kanana, Karusha and Kashi.

While in Hastinapur, reeling under the loss of half of the land of Hastinapur, Duryodhana' s jealousy and rage was further fueled by the Pandavas' success and prosperity. Eventually, Shakuni sired yet another ploy and got Duryodhana to invite the Pandavas over to his court for a game of dice (gambling). Shakuni was a master at gambling and owned a pair of dice which magically did his bidding.

Many kings of the ally kingdoms and tribes were also invited to enjoy the game. Mohoriti, along with Tejaswa, also joined as a viewer. It was the first time that Mohoriti was visiting Hastinapur after he had left chasing Bhishma.

On the entrance of the place where the game of the dice was being conducted, the name of each invitee was being announced so that everyone is aware who all have marked their presence to witness the friendly match between Kauravs and Pandavas.

As Mohoriti's name was announced, it immediately clicked

Bhishma, but hearing the introduction of Mohoriti as belonging to the land of Mohoma and being an ally of Indraprastha, he understood the political move of Mohoriti behind coming to Hastinapur without fear.

Mohoriti entered and moved straight to Bhishma with his head up, looking straight into his eyes.

He reached him and joined his hands, "Accept my kowtow, great Devavrata."

"It is amazing to see you Mohoriti after so many years. I am more surprised to see you walk in without any fear of me." replied Bhishma.

"I was never afraid of you, Devavrata, but was waiting for right time. I still remember how you killed my father and nineteen brothers." Mohoriti retorted.

Bhishma stood from his seat and looked into his eyes, "If you were not an ally of Pandavas, I would have killed you here completing the figure to twenty."

"Time changes, Devavrata, and I still assure you that I will be a reason of your death." replied Mohoriti in confidence.

"Take your seat and be our guest, as we don't attack our guests." replied Bhishma in anger.

Mohoriti turned and took his seat placed in the arena for viewing the game of dice.

Bhishma stood up from his seat and moved to Arjuna, who was standing along with his brothers and Krishna. Looking at Bhishma coming to them, they did a kowtow before him, on which he blessed them.

"I would like to tell you, Arjuna, beware of Mohoriti. He is that weed, which eats the tree that supports him in growing." Bhishma spilled over what he had in his mind and moved back to his seat.

Krishna smiled and turned towards Arjuna, "This game will help you understand what must be your future of ally or friendship with anyone. So, concentrate on the game and let the time decide, not your elders."

While Krishna was explaining Arjuna, Balram, the elder brother of Krishna, came to him and informed that the evil Salva, the king of Soubha, is about to attack Dwaraka. Understanding the crucial situation, Krishna used this as a pretext and left Pandavas and proceeded to fight with Salva, along with his brother Balram.

The game of dice began and, very soon, Yudhishthira started losing all. He first lost all his wealth to Shakuni. Then, he placed Nakula as a bet and lost him. Then, Sahadeva, Arjuna, Bhima and finally, Yudhishthira placed himself as a bet and lost.

Tejaswa was able to see what was going on in the court but was bound to keep quiet as no one was allowed to speak or interrupt in the game. Till now, he was feeling pity for his friend, Arjuna, but, then, something happened which ashamed him to be their ally.

When Duryodhana provoked Yudhishthira, he placed Draupadi, whom Tejaswa considered as his sister and held in high regards, on the bet.

His eyes welled up with tears; he was surprised to see how low Dharma raj could go to play a game of dice. He imagined that he would have cut his head if this was a condition in front of him but would never place his wife on bet.

Finally, Yudhishthira placed Draupadi as a bet and lost. Duryodhana, then, with a cunning smile on his face, sent his charioteer, Pratikami, to bring Draupadi to the hall. Draupadi told Pratikami that she couldn't come to the hall of the Kauravs. Duryodhana got angry with this rejection and sent his brother, Dushasana, to bring her. Dushasana moved a step ahead in misbehaving and held her by her untied hair and dragged her to the hall.

Draupadi felt devastated. This had put a lot of questions related to Dharma to Bhishma and the other elders. She asked them what right Yudhishthira had to place her as a bet; she was his wife and no husband has the right to place his wife on bet for his pleasure. She asked how the elders of Hastinapur were tolerating that evil game and the disrespect being shown against the women and daughter of Hastinapur and the queen of Indraprastha. Bhishma and others behaved strangely and told Draupadi to ask Yudhishthira for all the answers. Yudhishthira just kept quiet with his head bowed down. Tejaswa, who was monitoring this incident, felt scorned by the Pandavas. At that time, Vidhura stood up, joining his hands and declared that the entire incident, which took place, was extremely Adharmic. He told Draupadi that the great injustice was being meted out to her as a woman and that the entire hall was engulfed by Adharma.

Karna was trying to provoke the Pandavas, who were sitting like pets and letting all these monstrosities to go on. Karna could not do anything directly for Draupadi because he was bound by his friendship to the Kauravs, although he wanted to. Also, if he had tried to intervene, people would raise questions and gossips that Karna has a soft corner for Draupadi. In reality, he did have a soft corner for her and, that is why, he was extra careful to not let his feelings show. He thought that the only way he could stop all this was by inciting the Pandavas. Karna, then, made a very cheap statement at Draupadi. He told her that all her husbands were now a slave of Duryodhana and, therefore, she should now live in the palace of Duryodhana. Duryodhana, then, in order to split the unity of the Pandavas, told Draupadi that if one of the younger Pandavas told everyone that they did not have any respect for Yudhishthira, he would release her. Bhima got extremely enraged at this and stood up in anger. He got up and told everyone that Yudhishthira was extremely respected by all of them. Bhima declared that in Kshatriyas, strength determined superiority and seniority and, by that measure, he was the guru of everyone there. Therefore, his word should be taken.

The entire hall panicked at the anger of Bhima. Bhishma, Drona and Vidhura all tried to pacify Bhima and asked him to sit down. Duryodhana, going further in insulting, showed his thighs to Draupadi and patted on them. Bhima, at that point, made a vow that he would kill Duryodhana by breaking his thigh. However, Duryodhana still continued with making poisonous statements. He told the Pandavas to keep Lord Krishna as a bet in the game, since they had nothing else left. At this, Bhima's anger got out of control. He made a terrible vow to crush the head of Duryodhana with his foot and smash him.

Karna, once again, asked Draupadi to enter the palace of Duryodhana. Enraged, Bhima and Arjuna rushed towards Karna, but were stopped by Yudhishthira. Duryodhana, then, asked Dushasana to take away the royal clothes of the Pandavas and give them forest garbs to put on. Duryodhana, then, ordered Dushasana to disrobe Draupadi.

Dushasana began to pull the saree of the empress. Bhima, then, made another terrible vow that he will rip apart the chest of Dushasana and drink his blood.

Draupadi, then, went into a trance praying to Lord Krishna, who granted her one saree after another, protecting her. Dushasana kept disrobing Draupadi but as soon as he was done with that, immediately, a new saree appeared. Finally, Dushasana collapsed. Duryodhana, then, asked Draupadi to be taken to his palace. Draupadi made a vow that Bhima would kill Duryodhana, Arjuna will kill Karna and Sahadeva will kill Shakuni.

Dushasana started to pull Draupadi to the palace. Bhima looked at Arjuna and told him that he had had enough and he could no longer remain quiet when his wife was being dragged away. Bhima got up to destroy all the Kauravs.

Suddenly, the people in the hall started hearing ugly crying of foxes from a distance. Dhiritarashtra heard this sound as well and asked Vidhura about it. Vidhura replied that is an extremely evil omen and that the entire Kauravs clan will get destroyed if Draupadi is not released and pleased with the boons.

Dhiritarashtra, who was extremely scared by now, ordered to immediately release Draupadi. When pressed to accept boons, Draupadi asked only for the release of the Pandavas.

Finally, the Pandavas were released and had to go to the forests for twelve years and, then, to a hiding for further one year. If they were discovered during the hiding period, their twelve year plus one year punishment would reoccur.

The Pandavas left the hall, where the game was being played.

As they were leaving the hall, Yudhishthira kept his face down. This was to ensure that his gaze full of anger doesn't fall on Duryodhana and burns him alive. The compassionate Yudhishthira realized this and kept his face down.

Bhima left the hall with both his shoulders hunched up to indicate that using just the power in his hands, he was going to destroy them all. Draupadi left the hall leaving her hair untied. This was to indicate that all the Kaurav women would meet the same fate of having to leave their hair untied, i.e., widowhood.

Arjuna left the hall and kept sprinkling the entire route with sand. This was to indicate that he, just like the countless grains of sand, would release countless arrows at the Kauravs.

Nakula and Sahadeva left the hall with their heads down in

shame.

The official priest of the Pandavas, Dhaumyacharya, left the hall chanting the mantras meant to be chanted during funerals. This was to indicate the fate that all Kauravs would meet.

Thousands and thousands of progeny of Hastinapur followed the Pandavas on their way to the forest along with Mohoriti and Tejaswa.

After reaching at some distance on the outskirts of Hastinapur, Arjuna called Tejaswa and Mohoriti, "You have seen what Duryodhana did in the dice game and, soon, the time will come when we will take revenge for this."

Mohoriti joined his hands with his head bowed, "I understand your pain and no punishment can get their sins washed off. What is the order for us?"

Arjuna continued, "We will be in exile for the next thirteen years. During this time, you have a big task to do. Get ready with an alliance of maximum clans you can. The first thing that we'd do once we are back would be a war with Kauravs."

Mohoriti assured him while Tejaswa kept quiet; it seemed like he was lost deep in his thoughts.

They finally moved into a forest beginning their wait for the war and completing their vow.

Chapter-20
Tejaswa moved from Mohoma

The court room of Mohoma was set with Tejaswa on the throne and Mohoriti, along with the other courtiers and sages, present to discuss on the next political move of the land of Mohoma keeping in view the political changes in Hastinapur.

It was sure by now that the war would happen after thirteen years and it was to be decided in this court room who must Mohoma support. After what happened in the game of dice, the progeny was already divided in supporting Kauravs and Pandavas.

Though many of them had sympathy towards Pandavas, even Kaurav's supporters were not less in number and as a clan, it was important to hear the voice of the progeny before making any important political move.

Mohoriti stood up from his seat and started addressing, "My lord, respected Acharya's and my dear progeny of Mohoma, we all know what happened in Hastinapur and it's for sure that after thirteen years from now, there would be a war between Pandavas and Kauravs. However, I suspect this war would not be limited to two brothers but many kingdoms and tribes will also be a part of it. What we are going to discuss now would have also become a point of discussion in many clans by now and everyone would be getting prepared for a war which would happen after thirteen years. You all would be thinking why I am discussing about a war which will take place thirteen years from now, but I have a point to make here.

We are an ally of Pandavas and, since last few years, we have been making a lot of diplomatic moves to create allies with different clans. Why I am discussing this is because Arjuna asked me to continue with these diplomatic moves so that we could be ready for a war situation.

On the other hand, our ideologies are always against Bhishma and looking at the present situation, it is sure that if a war happens, Bhishma will be supporting Kauravs as they hold Hastinapur and Bhishma, as per his vow, will continue to serve Hastinapur. Bhishma, as a matter of fact, also owns the throne there.

And we, as Mohoma people, must be supporting Pandavas, who will fight against Kauravs and Hastinapur."

Tejaswa interrupted in between, "Pitamah, I disagree with your point." Mohoriti was shocked to hear him. He continued, "Why should we support them? Yes, I was the person who brought them here but, now, I am ashamed about it. It would have been better if they would have been burnt in Varnavrata."

"What are you saying, Tejaswa?" asked Mohoriti.

"I am correct, Pitamah. They sat in the game of dice like ducks, while Draupadi, my sister, was insulted in front of them."

"But they had won against Duryodhana in the past; how could they resist, then?" asked Mohoriti.

"I will put my question differently. Why did they go to play the game of dice, when they knew that Duryodhana is always against them and Shakuni is an expert in dice game?" questioned Tejaswa.

"They were asked by Dhiritarashtra, the king of Hastinapur and their uncle." told Mohoriti.

"Wow! They can insult their wife in court but cannot say no to their uncle, who is always against them. I do not buy this point. Yudhishthira is a man of Dharma; what happened to his dharma when he placed his brothers and wife in the game as bets." replied Tejaswa in anger now.

The conversation was growing warm by degrees between them, when one of the courtiers stood up and replied to Tejaswa,

"So, do you want to say that Duryodhana did correct with them?"

"I am not saying he did right or wrong but whose mistake was it? Let me ask you a few more questions. Did Duryodhana do wrong by inviting Pandavas for the game of dice?"

Courtier replied, "No."

"Yes, for this question, the answer would be 'no' because Pandavas had full rights to say no for the game but they, too, were interested in playing the game of dice. They are warriors and they could have asked Duryodhana to have a game of warriors instead but they accepted the offer to play this game." replied Tejaswa and further asked his second question.

"Yudhishthira was losing the game and he had already lost his wealth and kingdom; then, why did he place his brothers as bets one by one? Did Duryodhana place them on bet or did he forced him to do so?"

On this question, the courtier replied, "The game's rule was 'till you have anything left, you cannot stop the game' and, so, he placed his brothers."

"Why did he agree to such a rule? Rules are set in the start of the game. Yudhishthira, being such a learned man, must have understood this but he kept mute; do you still say it was mistake of Duryodhana?" answered Tejaswa.

Courtier replied, "No."

"Now let me ask you another question. Why did he place Draupadi in the bet when he knew he was losing the game? Even if he would have won Draupadi, still she would have been the wife of a slave of Duryodhana; do you believe this could have been avoided?" Tejaswa furthered.

"I agree to your point." Replied the courtier.

"I have another question for you. Seeing their wife getting insulted, they kept quiet. Did Duryodhana stop them from taking any action? They are warriors and would have easily taken over every other warrior present in the game room. Why did they not take any action?" asked Tejaswa

Courtier had no answer and Tejaswa understood and continued, "I had seen your wife last evening at the river side; she was taking bath. I would like to tell you that she is one of the most beautiful women I have seen in my life naked." Tejaswa commented.

Hearing this, the courtier shouted at Tejaswa and pulled out his sword.

"Pitamah, King Tejaswa is crossing his limits; please ask him to take his words back." The courtier warned.

Tejaswa smiled and replied politely, "I am sorry, Sir. I hurt you, but look, you, being my courtier and standing in my court, pulled out your sword having heard from me that I saw your wife naked. How come the Pandavas kept silent when their wife was actually being stripped naked in front of thousands of people? This is my question to you."

The courtier placed his sword back and was silent again.

"And here's my last question to you. Why did they agree to play one last chance, when they knew that they have lost everything and finally took thirteen years of exile? They must have learned at least something from what happened." Tejaswa asked his last question.

However, this time, the answer came from Mohoriti, who was listening to the argument since long, "Because they respect their elders. They know they must respect the words of their elders and follow them. They played again because they wanted to obey their uncle."

"So, how was Duryodhana wrong in this?" asked Tejaswa to Mohoriti.

"Duryodhana was wrong because he planned the game of dice; he is wrong because he insulted everyone; he is wrong because he insulted Draupadi." replied Mohoriti.

"But who started this, Pitamah?" asked Tejaswa and continued, "Drithrastrya, being elder to Pandu, must have been the king initially in place of Pandu and if he is the king, then, obviously his son must be his successor. Then, what is the problem with the Pandavas?"

"Yudhishthira is elder to Duryodhana and he must be the successor." replied Mohoriti.

"Pitamah, this problem was resolved when Pandavas were given Indraprastha. They must have not accepted the game of dice and it's their mistake. If they wouldn't have accepted that, today we would have been discussing the progress of our clan and not about the war. It's because of them that the complete Bharat is now getting worried about the war and its effects."

"Whatever, now what has happened cannot be changed, that time has gone. We cannot stop the war, which will definitely take place. The matter of our discussion should be whom we should be supporting, Pandavas or Kauravs." replied Mohoriti.

Tejaswa looked towards the courtiers and replied, "If you ask for my opinion, we must support Kauravs, who did what was correct as per their strategy. Yes, they did some things wrong, like insulting a woman, but placing your own wife on bet is a much bigger mistake and, so, we must support Kauravs."

He looked towards the courtiers, who were looking forward to the decision of Mohoriti whom they trusted more by then, for their reply.

Mohoriti, now, stepped down from the platform where he was seated and came to the center of the court, "I have been living since three generations to take revenge on Bhishma. Our tribe was built to conquer Bhishma someday and, somehow, we have moved forward in our strategy till now so that I could go back to Hastinapur and face Bhishma. Everyone, who is born in Mohoma, knows that the land of Mohoma is for revenge on Bhishma. Mohoma, my father, died because of Bhishma. How can we support Kauravs who will be definitely backed up by him? According to me, the land of Mohoma can never support Kauravs."

Listening to his words, other courtiers started murmuring among themselves and, then, they all recalled his words together in the court, "The land of Mohoma cannot support Kauravs; we will be supporting Pandavas." They all stood up in support of Mohoriti.

Tejaswa looked at them and, then, pulled out his sword. While holding it with both his hands, he kneeled down before Mohoriti and said, "Pitamah, I love you, but I cannot compromise with my thoughts and this is what I have learned while I grew up all alone in a forest, where I took all the decisions trusting what I felt was right. Today, my heart says I am correct to not support Pandavas and I will follow my heart, once again. I request you to please grant me the permission to leave the throne and go my way to a place where I can support Kauravs." saying this, he bowed again.

"You will fight against Mohoma?" asked Mohoriti in low tone.

Tejaswa stoop up and looked into his eyes, "I will fight against

Pandavas and not against Mohoma. I would like to request you if, during the war, you find me standing with arms against you, please do not hesitate to hit me hard."

"Bless you my son! May you find me standing in front of you in war and your hands remain stiff while beheading me." replied Mohoriti and hugged him.

While some of the courtiers wanted to be in support of Tejaswa, but looking at the majority, they remained neutral and supported the other side.

Even Mohoriti was upset with the decision of Tejaswa, but for him the thing more important was the land of Mohoma and ideology behind its formation. He declared that Mohoma would be working hard in the next thirteen years to be an ally with maximum number of tribes and get ready to fight from Pandava's side. He also declared to his progeny that for the next thirteen years, extra food grains and other food materials will be collected as tax to save it for progeny; the food might be required in huge quantity if the war continues for long.

Extra focus will be given on development of arms and ammunition and, so, production of iron and other metals will be focused upon. As per him, Mohoma needs to become one of the biggest arms producing tribe in the next thirteen years.

Tejaswa was disheartened to have decided to move away once again from the land of Mohoma, giving the throne to Mohoriti. He decided to move to Hastinapur and observe the conditions and search for his own path.

Chapter-21
Effect on Progeny

Vidhura walked to Dhiritarashtra to discuss the matter of concern, along with Bhishma. Both joined their hands before him as they reached.

"Is everything fine, Vidhura? I am worried seeing you both together coming to visit me." Dhiritarashtra said.

Vidhura looked at Bhishma and replied, "everything is not perfect, Maharaj, the progeny is worried that the incident that happened will definitely lead to war in the coming years. They are worried for their family members and loved ones. Many Janpads have already started gathering food and valuable materials for future."

Dhiritarashtra smiled and stood up while holding his hand, "Don't worry, Vidhura; I am sure this war will not happen. Duryodhana will find them out in the last year of their exile and they will go back for the next twelve years."

"Do you want them to go for further exile, Maharaj?" interrupted Bhishma.

Dhiritarashtra was puzzled by Bhishma's question. He replied, "No, No, definitely not. They are like my sons and I want them to be back as soon as possible."

"Then, if they are back, why do you think there will be no

war?" asked Bhishma.

Dhiritarashtra showed himself as helpless once again and took his seat. He said anxiously, "Then, what to do, Pitamah, I am unable to understand."

"This is the problem, Dhiritarashtra. You are dwindling between the rules and your love for Duryodhana and this has created a complex situation. However, remember there will be a war and I believe no one would be able to stop it." replied Bhishma

Dhiritarashtra, then, ordered, "Vidhura, you take my order. Let us be ready for the war; my order must be announced to the progeny."

"Please let me know your order; I'll get it announced." replied Vidhura

Dhiritarashtra thought for a while and, then, dictated, "As Hastinapur may enter into a war with Pandavas in future, the following guidelines must be ensured. Every male child, who would be born from now, must join the army; he would be fourteen when the war would start. Every male child who is ten years old now must join army immediately. Manufacturing of arms and ammunition must be insisted and the progeny involved in it must be allowed a month's food stock from our palace.

Every year half of the wealth of Hastinapur must be invested on war preparation. The progeny must work extra hours daily to produce food to overcome its storage. One third of the food produced every year must be stored for the future.

Construction of river canals must be initiated for the movement of army units. We need to be prepared for what might be coming to us."

Vidhura heard his announcement and replied, "But, Maharaj, this will create a panic situation among the progeny. If one third of food is moved to storage, the progeny might be left hungry. I am not authorized to say, but it's wrong. I request you to please relook into the announcement."

"I am the king, Vidhura, and I understand what is right and wrong for Hastinapur; everyone must understand that they are what they are because of Hastinapur. It's our duty to be ready for any danger it might face."

Looking at his harsh and arrogant words, Bhishma stopped from what he was about to suggest to him. He bowed his head and moved along with Vidhura.

Under the fear of a war, the progeny began getting worried for their family and loved ones as they knew no matter who wins, the effect would be faced by both the sides. The biggest concern for them was the lives of their loved ones, which held no value in front of the message from the king.

With the sound of drum beats, everyone in the market of Hastinapur got conscious and came closer to the messenger to hear the announcement. One of the courtiers from the court of Dhiritarashtra announced the order of the king and this immediately created a hue and cry among the progeny.

Tejaswa, who heard the announcement, also got worried.

"I became father today only; now, this means I have to get my son trained for army." replied one of the progeny.

Tejaswa, who heard him, replied, "So, you don't think we, too, have to share equal responsibility to safeguard our kingdom?"

"This is not safeguard. The king himself landed us in this problem. He should have stopped that game of dice. It's a matter of two brothers; we poor people will be killed because of them." He replied.

Tejaswa heard his words and got confused looking at the condition of the progeny, who were living in fear because of the actions of the royal people.

Many clans stopped trade with a few other clans, which produced those food items which could not be stored. This resulted in surplus production of the perishable items in those clans. Also, since it was a time when barter system was prevalent, they were not able to get things, which previously they exchanged against their produce.

As years passed, some of the clans faced severe food issues and they decided to ally with Hastinapur, so that their progeny is not deprived of food. They started moving their army units towards Hastinapur to join the Kauravs army.

A similar strategy was executed by Mohoriti in Mohoma; he supported multiple clans to get their alliance.

Tribes like Andhra, Abhisara, Karnapravarna, Kitava and many more joined hands with Kauravs whereas Kuninda, Chola and many more joined Pandavas as a result of the efforts of Mohoma.

It was a time of uncertainty when both the parties were moving in every direction to make alliance politically or diplomatically.

Tejaswa was deeply impacted with the changes and sufferings of the progeny. He himself supported Kauravs, although he had a soft corner for the Pandavas. His major concern after hearing the discussions of the progeny was that people were confused on what to believe or who to support. Although he knew that the opinions of the progeny hardly mattered but at least if their doubts were cleared, they would support Hastinapur with a smile.

He was sitting under a tree at the center of a temple when suddenly some of the people, who were supporting different strengths, started fighting. They were very loud; one party was justifying Kauravs as right and perfect whereas the other was shouting for Pandavas. This was not the first incident in last few years. Such fights had happened multiple times and many people had lost their lives in them.

Children had started playing games dividing themselves into two different armies, Kauravs and Pandavas, and fighting using fake arms.

Tejaswa could not sleep that night thinking what he must do to make the progeny aware and positive towards Kauravs.

He remembered the words of Krishna, "You have a lot to do in the coming years." and these words kept him awake the whole night, thinking what he must do. While he was thinking and watching the stars, he could hear some villagers singing the psalm of Lord Brahama nearby.

He stood up and walked to those people, who were sitting under a tree in front of the temple and singing psalm from Ramayana. He, too, sat in front of them, enjoying the cold breeze blowing there. After sometime, he smiled; he had gotten an answer for what he was waiting for. He understood it's lord who has showed him the path.

He decided to do street plays and sing psalms describing the story of Kauravs and Pandavas for the progeny. He thought that he would spread the positivity about Hastinapur and Kauravs. He was not sure if it will work but at least he wanted to try out.

The next morning, he reached the river bank early in the morning, took bath and got ready for doing something new for the progeny. He colored his face with white lime stone powder and drew stripes of yellow and red color, extracted from the flowers, on his cheeks using his fingers. He carried a dice made up of stone with him and moved towards the market area of Hastinapur.

He reached the center of the market and, with shy eyes, looked around. He saw people busy while shopping; some of them were even observing his colorful getup. He smiled at them and climbed the elevated bandstand.

"Come on, my friends, come on my people; here I am singing loud and clear." He enchanted in a loud voice, making himself audible to most of the people present. His look attracted them and many of them turned to see what he was about to depict.

He stood in the center with progeny gathered around him, consisting of males, females and children.

"I am Kalu Kumar, whom people also called Tejaswa." He started narrating the story in the tone of a song and gave himself a new name, Kalu Kumar.

Progeny laughed on the way he started, but he looked confident in depicting what he wanted to.

"This story is very long,

But I will sing in short,

Two brothers lived once, the elder one blind and the younger one strong,

Everyone felt the blind elder is of no use, so, they made younger one the king,

The younger one died early, so the blind became the king,

Tell me my audience, what was the mistake done by the blind king?"

The progeny replied with smiles on their faces, "No, he did what he should have done."

Tejaswa continued singing the song, along with a dance performing the actions to keep them engaged.

"Now, both brothers had sons,

The younger brother's son wanted the throne,

While the blind king was still alive,

The blind king's son interrupted,

Did he do any mistake if he interrupted?

Tell me my audience; was it a mistake done by the blind

king's son?"

The progeny replied with smiles on their faces, "No, he did what he should have done."

Tejaswa explained the complete story of Pandavas and Kauravs in the form of dance and song. His story favored the Kauravs and left a positive impact on the progeny.

His dance drama was loved by the progeny and he was highly appreciated for his efforts and excellent storytelling skills. He felt satisfied, as he had found a new way to put his thoughts to the progeny of Hastinapur.

Now, this dance and drama became his daily routine of life. He started presenting his thoughts in different songs, making the progeny get inclined towards Kauravs. Soon, his songs became so popular that villagers started singing his songs in temples and gathering.

He left a positive impact in the atmosphere of tension among the progeny. Now, even the progeny started believing that whatever their king is doing is right. He also developed a sympathy factor for Dhiritarashtra among the progeny. Soon, the progeny started following what orders the king had floated. He developed a feeling of patriotism among them.

Soon, he extended his borders and started performing for the nearby tribes in Hastinapur and became famous as Kalu Kumar.

One night, when he finished his performance, he went to a river bank to wash up his body color. He sat down and started pouring water on his body when he heard the sound of ornaments and sniffed the smell of flowers. He turned to check if someone is there but he could not see anyone.

While he started his job back, he saw a beautiful lady wearing ornaments and flowers in her hairs coming and sitting at some distance from him.

He saw her but tried to ignore her and continued washing himself.

"You sing beautiful songs." she spoke softly.

Tejaswa heard her but tried to ignore. Having received no reply to her compliment, she said again, "I like your stories."

Tejaswa stood up and started moving without replying to her or looking at her. Looking at his arrogance, she stood up and replied loudly this time, "Why are you so arrogant, Kalu Kumar?"

Tejaswa stopped with his back towards her and replied with a pause "I am not arrogant; you are very beautiful and I am afraid if I'd look at you or speak to you, I might fall in love with you."

He paused and waited for a reply, but this time she came in front of him and said, "So, look at me and fall in love."

She invited him with a proposal.

"Who are you lady, so beautiful like a nymph?" he questioned her looking into her eyes.

She showed some arrogance now and turned her back to him. He could, now, see her beautiful shoulders decorated with white flowers.

"Won't you answer me, nymph?" Tejaswa asked.

She turned towards him once again and replied with a smile, "I am not a nymph; I am Madhurika, the daughter of the commander of one of the army units of Hastinapur."

"You are the most beautiful girl I have ever seen, Madhurika, and your name is a rhythm to my songs. May I hug you and believe that I am not dreaming?" he replied.

She closed her eyes and expressed her acceptance for a hug. He walked two steps closer to her and touched her shoulders with his fingers. He felt the warmth of her body.

"You are like a soft flower." he told her softly and, then, took her in his arms hugging her. She, too, hugged him expressing her love towards him.

She, then, pulled herself out of his embrace and ran away telling him, "I have to go home; my mother would be waiting. I will wait for you tomorrow right here."

Tejaswa, filled with her fragrance, smiled on hearing her words and replied to her loudly, "I will wait for you tomorrow."

Chapter-22
Encounter in Kekaya

Kekayas was an ancient clan attested to have been living in the north-west, between the rivers, Gandhar and the Beas. They were the descendants of the Kshatriyas. It was ruled by Vrihatkshatra, along with his four brothers, and was one of the important clans with a strong army. Both, Kekayas and Mohoma, wanted to be allies for the benefit of a huge army and warriors' expertise in sword fights.

Tejaswa, who by now was a renowned storyteller, was often called by different kingdoms or clans to know the exact story of Pandavas and Kauravs. Kings started taking decision of alliance on the basis of his depiction of the story.

His skills were so perfect by now, that Kauravs were already running high in number of allies and this was not hidden from Duryodhana, too.

Vrihatkshatra, the king of Kekaya, invited Tejaswa for his performance before he could take a decision of alliance, as Mohoriti was about to visit him with a proposal.

The court was set and Vrihatkshatra and his four brothers were seated along with their guest, Mohoriti, when Tejaswa entered the court with his body painted and covered in multiple colors to recite the story.

He bowed his head in front of all, with a special look of extra respect towards his great grandfather, Mohoriti. He, too, blessed him open heartedly. Vrihatkshatra was still unaware about Tejaswa being related with Mohoriti.

The king asked Tejaswa to start the performance. He bowed and replied in respect.

It was a big day for him today. He needed to give his best, not only because he wanted Kekaya to support Kauravs, but also he thought that his performance might compel Mohoriti to change his decision of supporting Pandavas.

Using fantastic expressions, eyes movements and dance moves, Tejaswa started his performance with a song telling the story and explaining what was right and what was wrong as per his point of view.

The prince of Kekaya was impressed by his performance and felt like entering an imaginary world of Hastinapur.

Once the performance was over, Vrihatkshatra asked his courtier to fill bags of Kalu Kumar with gold and silver but hearing this, Tejaswa, who was also known as Kalu Kumar, joined his hands and asked, "Maharaj, I request you to listen to what I want."

Vrihatkshatra, who was impressed by his performance, told him that he could ask for what he wanted.

"I am not greedy for gold and silver, my lord. I dance and perform so that everyone could know the truth; they could take the decisions not out of any sympathy or word of mouth but after knowing the complete story. I hope you liked my story depiction. I only request you to support Kauravs; they are the ones, I believe, who did what was correct." replied Tejaswa.

Mohoriti, who had watched the complete performance, interrupted, "Excuse me, Maharaj, forgive me for interrupting in between your conversation but please do not just commit something on the basis of a performance by a dancer, who is expressing his views. Think politically, also taking in view the future of the progeny."

"However, whatever he had presented had a point and it looks like Kauravs were correct on their side." replied one of the brothers of the king and continued, "I, too agree, with Kalu Kumar's story; why couldn't Pandavas live in Hastinapur as other ninety nine brothers of Duryodhana were living. If they were so polite and perfect, why did they have a problem in accepting Duryodhana as their king? They could have let him be the king and they could have lived as princes along with the other ninety nine."

Vrihatkshatra also put forward his point of view, "But, I feel Pandavas are correct; their father was the first king and Yudhishthira is the eldest. So, he must be the king; even Kauravs could live peacefully as prince. Why do they want the throne?"

"The matter is not about the throne but about the process. It's always seen that the eldest son of the present king becomes the successor. Look at our case. You were declared as the king after the death of our father and we respectfully accepted it. Similarly, Duryodhana, being the eldest son of the present king, must be the king." replied one of the brothers of Vrihatkshatra.

Vrihatkshatra further explained, "There is a difference in our case. We are real brothers, born from the womb of the same mother; but, in Hastinapur, it's different."

"I do not agree with this; the system that were made by our ancestors are perfect and we must follow the same. I support Kauravs and would like to hear from my other brothers, too, on what they think in this matter." replied one of the brothers.

Except king Vrihatkshatra, the other four princes voted in support of Kauravs. King Vrihatkshatra was not in agreement.

"I respect you, my brothers, for your point of view and would never want to burden you with my thoughts. I suggest you four, along with your territories, could support Kauravs, while I, along with my territory, would support Pandavas. What do you say, my brothers?"

After some discussion, it was decided that Vrihatkshatra will support Pandavas while his brothers will be the allies of Kauravs.

Mohoriti thanked Vrihatkshatra and decided to move to a different tribe for discussion. While he was boarding his chariot, Tejaswa reached him, touched his feet and asked for his blessings.

"How are you, Pitamah?" Tejaswa asked.

Mohoriti hugged him and said, "I would have been fine, if my Tejaswa was with me".

"I miss you too, Pitamah, but I cannot compromise with my thoughts." Tejaswa explained.

"I understand you, my child; I heard about your approach

to put forward your thoughts and I appreciate your efforts. We are humans and can only do our work. Let us leave the conclusion in the hands of god." replied Mohoriti.

Mohoriti stepped in his chariot, looked into the eyes of Tejaswa and said, "Remember, we are only the chariots of this war. History will not remember who pulled the chariot but will remember who stood on the chariot with a bow in his hands. However, if the chariot is not perfect, no wars can be won. In future, we would be called as the chariots of this Mahabharata."

Mohoriti, then, turned around and, soon, his chariot moved to the next destination, leaving Tejaswa behind with his thoughts.

Twelve years had already passed and, soon, the last year was about to start, when Pandavas were supposed to live in exile, hiding and if they were found, their punishment would reoccur.

Chapter-23
Mohoriti meets Lord Shiva

Kamyaka Forest was situated on the western boundary of the Kuru Kingdom, on the banks of the Sarasvati River. It lay to the west of the Kurukshetra plain. It contained within it a lake called the Kamyaka Lake. The Pandavas, on their way to exile in the woods twelve years ago, left Pramanakoti on the banks of the River Ganges and went towards Kurukshetra, travelling in the western direction, crossing the rivers, Yamuna and Drishadvati. They finally reached the banks of the Sarasvati River. There they saw the forest of Kamyaka, the favorite haunt of ascetics, situated on a level and wild plain on the banks of the River Sarasvati abounding in birds and deer.

Mohoriti moved from Kekayas towards the Kamyaka forest to meet Pandavas and update them about the progress, after which they would be going to hide.

Pandavas, who were living in a small hut abounded by flowers and forest, saw chariot of Mohoriti coming towards them.

Mohoriti joined his hands while he stepped down from his chariot.

"Pranaam, Mohoriti, hope you would be having some good updates" asked Bhima.

"We have progressed well in our ally; yesterday, we had Kekayas agreeing to ally with us. I thought of meeting you before you go into hiding. Do you have any plans where you will be going further?" asked Mohoriti.

"Actually, we were waiting for your information on alliances to decide where we will be going to hide. Based on your suggestion and support, we will decide our next step." replied Yudhishthira.

Mohoriti, immediately, pulled out a document, which had a map of Bharat. He laid it down on earth and started marking their allies on it. He marked them with three different colors, red, blue and green.

"These are the clan, which are in alliance with us. Red are those, whose positions are still unclear like Atavisavara, Adhiraja. Blue are the ones supporting both of us and green are the ones who are supporting only us and among them, if you'd ask me, I will suggest Kasi, Virata, Chedi as our strong supporters."

Yudhishthira looked at the map in deep thoughts and said, "The Virata king is old and hospitable and he will be best suited for our purpose," Yudhishthira, then, said, "Mohoriti, apart from us, it's only you who knew where we will be hiding for next one year and there are chances Kauravs would try to get information out from you by any means. I would suggest, for next the one year, you must go to the Himalayas"

"As you order, my lord!" replied Mohoriti and left for Himalayas as ordered.

The Pandavas, then, discussed what disguise each one would take during this period in Virata.

Yudhishthira said, "I shall go to Virata as a Brahmin, by the name of Kanka. I shall be a courtier and would play dice with the king to generally please him. If questioned, I shall say that I was formerly with the Pandava king, Yudhishthira."

The other four brothers chose their own disguises.

Bhima said he would become a cook in the Virata household, calling himself Vallaba. "Besides pleasing his majesty's palate," Bhima said, "I shall also entertain him in sports as a wrestler; this way, I would also practice for the same."

For Arjuna, the curse, which he had received from the Apsara Urvashi, that he would lose his manhood for a year, came in handy.

He thought of serving the Virata royal ladies in the disguise of a eunuch. Eunuchs were often engaged in various capacities in the women's apartments. Assuming the name of Brihannala, he thought of teaching dance and music to the women of the royal household specialized in tabla, thanks to the knowledge he had received in arts from the Gandharva Chitrasena.

Nakula would join Virata as an expert on horses. He decided to take care of the royal stable, breed quality horses and train the equines. His name would be Granthika.

Sahadeva would use his knowledge of cattle breeding. Under the name of Tantripal, he would seek employment with Virata and take charge of their cattle.

Draupadi had her plan ready. She would become a Sairindhri or a beauty specialist, attached to the queen, Sudeshna. If asked about her previous employment, she would mention that she was in the service of the Pandava queen, Draupadi

Just before parting, the sage Dhaumya advised the brothers on how they should carry themselves while in disguise. "Draupadi's position would be vulnerable." he explained the Pandavas. "There may be bad elements in the court of king that would be attracted to her and may try to take an advantage of her beauty. You should keep a close watch over her without giving away your identities. You should serve the king in a way you expect your servants to serve you. Do not either rebel against the king or try to excel him in any department; always remember you are his servants. Be ready to please the king always, but in ways that are truthful. Use the clothes that are provided to you and be content with whatever rewards you receive and live in same conditions as servants live. As soon as you reach Virata, hide your weapons in a safe but handy place. God be with you."

Everything moved according to their plan. Having reached Virata, they hid their weapons on a huge Sami tree, which had twisted branches, in the outskirts of the city. They hung a corpse on the tree, so that the smell of the rotting body would keep people away.

Yudhishthira prayed to the goddess Kaali along with his brothers before entering Virata. Pleased with the prayer, the goddess appeared before the Pandavas. She blessed them and said, "You will have my protection. During the year to follow, no one would be able to discover your identity."

One by one the Pandavas infiltrated into Virata's court and took up the positions they had planned. Virata king was impressed by Kanka, and made him his companion and advisor. Bhima approached the king who was pleased with his appearance and culinary talk. He was made supervisor of the royal kitchen and as a wrestler.

Draupadi entered the city and was wandering near the palace. The queen took notice of her and had her brought to her presence. Learning that she was a skillful Sairindhri, Sudeshna engaged her as her personal hairdresser and care lady.

Nakula and Sahadeva followed and got installed as supervisors in the equine and bovine departments of the kingdom, respectively, as per the plan.

Arjuna appeared at the gate of the city in the guise of a eunuch. His masculine frame, despite definite feminine traits, intrigued the monarch to whom he was taken. Arjuna explained that he was of the neutral sex and was well versed in dance and music. He could be the princess Uttara's guru in music and dance. After ascertaining the truth about his gender, the monarch sent him to the maidens' apartments.

On the other hand, as suggested, Mohoriti moved to Himalayas and decided to practice austerity to please Lord Shiva; also, he knew no one will take a challenge to wake up a sage in austerity. He took a position with both hands up and joined, standing on his one feet, enchanting OM from his soul.

He continued practicing austerity in extreme conditions of cold and wind without water and food for the next eight months in the same position enchanting OM.

Lord Shiva, who was passing by along with his wife Parvathi, heard the sound of his soul and came to him.

"Open your eyes, devotee." Lord Shiva asked.

Hearing his voice, Mohoriti opened his eyes, which were closed since last eight months. It took him strength to open his eyes which were frozen in the snow. He took a relaxed position, joined his hands and sat on his knees.

"I am blessed to have your Philosophy." replied Mohoriti.

Lord Shiva and Goddess Parvathi smiled, "I am happy to see your austerity; ask me what you want."

Mohoriti joined his hands, "Lord, please stop the war that knocks at our door."

Lord Shiva understood what he wanted. He replied, "Ok, if you can get build koti (crore) of my statues in next four months, your wish will be fulfilled. I will reappear on the last day of the fourth month, if the figures would have been met."

Saying this, Lord Shiva disappeared.

Mohoriti was very happy to know that if he would meet figures, he could get this war canceled. On the other hand, he was worried how he will build these statues in such a short span of time.

Mohoriti knew making a koti statues would not be an easy task and Tejaswa was an expert in statue making. If he would help him, he would definitely complete the figures. He reached to meet Tejaswa and explained to him that he understood that their ideologies did not match but at least he could help him in making statues of Lord Shiva for a cause of dharma. He avoided informing him the real reason behind building the statues.

Tejaswa, who respected his Pitamah a lot, agreed to him and decided to build statues in Unakoti hills, which were hills of soft rocks. He explained Mohoriti that if they build statues in that place, they wouldn't have to waste time in searching and collecting rocks, which were available in plenty there, for making the statues.

Chapter-24
Curse of Golden Deer

Tejaswa and Mohoriti reached the rock hills of Unakoti to the north east of Bharat and started making statues. While Tejaswa worked on carving statues of Shiva on big mountain rocks, Mohoriti tried to make stone statues of a smaller size.

Every day, they worked continuously to complete the task and counted them when they rested at night. Slowly, that barren rock hill started looking like a temple of Lord Shiva, with every size of the statues of Lord Shiva along with Parvathi, Ganesh and his son, Kartika.

It was the last night of the fourth month, when Mohoriti counted the statues.

"It's only one less than a koti statues, Tejaswa. Hope we have managed it." He said.

Tejaswa, who was still carving the last statue, replied with his eyes still on his work, "Pitamah, you can go to sleep now, I am working on this last statue and would complete it shortly."

Mohoriti smiled and relaxed moving to their hut to take a nap, while Tejaswa continued his work.

He was busy carving the expressions of Lord Shiva, when he heard cracking on one statute which was placed at some distance. He kept his instruments and rushed there to check what has happened. To his astonishment, one of the Koti statues was broken from the center. While he was checking the loss, he heard another sound of breaking of the rocks. He left the existing stone and started checking the next. To his surprise, one more statue was broken. He examined it closely with firelight in his hand and observed footmarks on the statue of some animal. He understood that there was some animal which was hopping around the area and unknowingly breaking the statues.

While he was still examining the loss, he saw a bright golden light from the back of a huge statue of Lord Shiva and heard the sound of animals running on the rocks. He could not let all his efforts go to waste; so, picked up his bow and arrows and moved to check what was there.

With his bow and arrow all set, he moved with his pressed feet to avoid any sound. He started following the yellow light, which was moving very fast from one position to another. He followed the light to avoid further loss, as time was running. He, soon, realized that the light had stopped and he could see the shadow of a deer from behind the rocks. He took an aim and pulled the string of his bow to shoot. The arrow took pace and, soon, he saw in shadow the deer tumbling down to earth.

He ran towards it and saw a golden deer lying down there with his eyes still blinking. He stepped closer to her and saw her still alive. He pulled another arrow to his bow and shot at her to kill her completely.

This one pierced her body, leading to a pool of blood. Then, suddenly, the yellow light converted into a beautiful lady standing in the complete dark atmosphere in front of Tejaswa.

"Who are you, Devi?" he asked in astonishment.

"I am a celestial nymph, Devapima, from the court of Lord Indra."

Tejaswa bowed his head again hearing her words as she continued, "About two hundred years back, I did a mistake and laughed at lord Indra and he cursed me to be born as a mortal. I requested him to send me on earth as a beautiful deer and he agreed and told me that one day a king will come and kill me and only then you will be back to heaven and your curse will come to end. However, your forefather, Mohoma, didn't let it happen and I took rebirth as a golden deer again and waited till you, his fourth generation, came and kill me."

She continued while Tejaswa kept listening, "I am thankful to you for releasing me from this mortal life. I will be going back to heaven in peace now. You can ask me for one wish as thanksgiving."

Tejaswa still standing having his hands joined, looked into her eyes and replied, "I request you to take your curse back from my family." He pleaded.

Looking at his request, the nymph, Devapima, replied, "I cannot take the curse back, but you will be able do it yourself. I can show you the path; now, it will be your karma to get rid of this curse. Later on, you'd have to decide about your life or death. Your life would continue your family's curse while your death will bring it to end. Your life will give you those chances and you need to decide what is correct for you."

She blessed him and turned back to the sky, leaving the atmosphere dark again. While Tejaswa thanked her, he saw the first morning sun ray hitting the tallest statue of Lord Shiva. It was early in the morning and his koti statues were still not complete. As he turned back, he saw Mohoriti standing behind him.

"I missed completing the last statue, Pitamah." he informed still sitting on his knees.

Mohoriti looked him in anger, with his eyes red and wind blowing in his long hairs.

"You didn't miss my son, you intentionally missed the same. It is visible to me that you not only left one incomplete but also broke many of the ready ones."

"No, Pitamah, that is not true." Tejaswa replied but he stopped giving any explanations to him because he didn't want Mohoriti to get worried for him.

Mohoriti turned his face from him and replied, "You are a true Kaurav now; it's deep in your blood now. You can never play a fare game, son. I, somehow, forgot that you are from Hastinapur and would be expecting a war not peace."

Tejaswa, still sitting on his knees with tears in his eyes, said, "Forgive me, Pitamah, please!" he pleaded but Mohoriti didn't turn his face towards him and moved back to his way to Mohoma.

Tejaswa decided to go back to Hastinapur and do his duty, which he felt was correct.

Chapter-25
Tejaswa joins Hastinapur Army

After returning from exile, Arjuna's son, Abhimanyu, was planned to get married to Uttara, the daughter of Matsya king.

After Abhimanyu's marriage ceremony, there was a royal festival and everyone was pleased that the son of Arjuna was united with the daughter of King Virata from Matsya Kingdom. This was altogether a political move to bring Matsya on side of the Pandavas and build pressure on Hastinapur.

The next day, all the kings, who had assembled for the Pandava's cause, came to Virata's imperial court to discuss the future strategy. The court room had present King Virata, King Drupada, Satyaki, King Yudhisthira, Bhima, Arjuna, Nakula, Sahadeva and Mohoriti. Also present were Lord Krishna, the supreme personality of godhead, and his very powerful brother, Balarama. From the Yadu house came, Pradyumna and Samba. Arjun's son, Abhimanyu, was present, along with the sons of Draupadi appearing like their fathers in power. Drupada's sons and Virata's sons were also seated in the court. They all talked on varied subjects for some time, and after conversing with each other, they sat in a thoughtful mood to plan their next move for Pandavas.

Lord Krishna sat in the middle of the assembled kings, like the full moon shines among many stars in the sky. With his lotus like eyes and bluish complexion, he was attracting the minds of everyone present in the court. After due contemplation, Krishna spoke, "It is known to all that the Pandavas were unfairly defeated in gambling by Suvala's son, Shakuni, and, thus, exiled out of their kingdom. They were, then, exiled to the forest for a period of thirteen years, which they faithfully carried out. Dhiritarashtra's sons still maintained their illicit desires for complete sovereignty of the world; although, the sons of Pandu also had a right to share the half of the kingdom as Pandu, their father, was the first king to hold the throne of Hastinapur. What Duryodhana exactly thought was not completely known; so, what opinion could be possibly formed? Therefore, a competent person, who could go to Hastinapur and induce the Kauravs to give half the kingdom to the Pandavas, was to be selected".

After listening to the words of his younger brother, Baladeva, the carrier of the club and plow, spoke to the assembled kings, "You have heard Krishna's advice, which is pregnant with virtue and is beneficial to both Yudhishthira and Duryodhana. Dhiritarashtra's sons should give half their kingdom joyfully so this quarrel could be settled. It is known that when Yudhishthira was in possession of the throne, he unnecessarily engaged in gambling, even when he was not able to play the game well. He foolishly gambled away his kingdom, and no blame can be put on Shakuni; he only played his game, in which he was perfect. Therefore, the messenger should approach the sons of Dhiritarashtra with words of humility intended to pacify Duryodhana. Nothing can be gained by war with the Kurus.

After Lord Balarama finished expressing his opinion, Mohoriti rose up and condemned Lord Balarama's words, which favored Duryodhana. Mohoriti spoke, "With his deceitful nature, Duryodhana tricked the sons of Pandu out of their kingdom. Instead of facing them on the battlefield, they chose to cheat them out of their kingdom by throwing the dice. They are cowards of the highest order. Why should Maharaj Yudhishthira, who is entitled to the ancestral throne, humble himself before the uncivilized Duryodhana, who tried to see the Pandavas' beloved wife stripped naked in the imperial court. They should either give back the kingdom or be ready to fight. Who can withstand Arjuna on the battlefield? Who can stand in front of Lord Krishna as he wields his Sudarshana Chakra to destroy the entire array of the Kurus? Who can withstand the tenacious Bhima, with mace in his hand, ready to destroy the ranks of the oncoming enemy? There is no need to approach them like beggars. Either Maharaj Yudhishthira gives back his kingdom this very day, or Dhiritarashtra's sons will lie on the earth slain by me!"

After Mohoriti' s speech, the eminent king, Drupada, gave his opinion, "You have spoken well. Never will Duryodhana agree to give up his kingdom by peaceful means to them. Dhiritarashtra will agree with his son's wishes, and Bhishma and Drona will follow out of stupidity for sure. Karna and Shakuni will certainly join forces with Duryodhana out of folly. The words of Baladeva are, indeed, righteous, but Duryodhana should never be addressed in mild words. Sweet words are never spoken to a snake, but a weapon must be used to kill it. An envoy should be sent to Duryodhana demanding half the kingdom. At the same time, a message should be sent to all the kings of the earth, where Mohoriti has already done alliances and the ones who favor Yudhishthira's cause, asking them to come here to support us."

Lord Krishna, then, gave the final opinion, "King Drupada's words are thoughtful and meant to promote the interests of Pandavas. However, our relationship with both, the Kauravs as well as the Pandavas, is equal. We have been invited here for the marriage ceremony of Abhimanyu. The marriage ceremony is now complete, and we should return to our kingdoms. Since you, King Drupada, are the eldest and most respected amongst us, you should send a message to Duryodhana, requesting for half the kingdom. If Dhiritarashtra's son would make peace, then there should be no hard feelings on either side. However, if Duryodhana refuses to make peace with Pandavas, then after calling others for war, you must also call us. The wicked will have to face the onslaught of the Gandiva bow as well as my wrath".

Saying this, Lord Krishna made preparations to leave Virata. After the departure of Lord Krishna, the supreme lord of heaven and earth, King Yudhishthira, along with King Virata, began making the preparations for the war. King Drupada sent for one of his most trusted priests and gave him a message to be spoken in the midst of the Kaurav leaders. The priest, then, departed to Hastinapur with a peace message.

Meanwhile, the Pandavas continued with their preparations for the future war, knowing well the mentality of their cruel cousin. Arjuna, then, left for Dwarka in hopes of obtaining favor of both Krishna and Baladeva. When Duryodhana learnt about the Pandava's intentions through his spies, he also set out for Dwarka. Both Arjuna and Duryodhana arrived in the city of the Yadus on the same day. When they arrived, Lord Krishna was sleeping; they both entered his room together. Duryodhana sat at the head of the bed whereas Arjuna sat at Lord Krishna's lotus feet. When Lord Krishna awoke, he saw Arjuna first, seated at the end of the bed. He greeted both Arjuna and Duryodhana and asked about their welfare. Duryodhana, then, solicited Krishna, "I am requesting for your support for a future war. You bear a similar relationship with both the families. Since I have come to you first, please follow the path of virtuous men. You are listed on the top of all who are righteous, and, therefore, I ask you to assist me at this time."

"It is, indeed, true," Krishna replied, "that you have come to me first. However, I have cast my glance upon Partha (Arjuna) first. Since you both have come here, I shall lend my assistance to both of you. Those who are junior in years should have the first choice. I have a body of soldiers known as the Narayana, which has one million men, that is one choice. The other choice is me. However, I will not fight in the battle. Arjuna, you may choose between me and my men. Since you are the youngest, you may pick first." and he smiled.

When given the first choice by Krishna, Arjuna chose his most intimate friend, Krishna. Joyfully, with the only option left, Duryodhana chose Krishna's division of troops, shunning the personal power of the supreme personality. After this meeting, Duryodhana went to Balarama, the possessor of infinite power. Duryodhana explained how Krishna was chosen by Arjuna, although he himself would not fight. Duryodhana, then, requested Lord Balarama to fight for his cause. Hearing his appeal, Balarama replied to Duryodhana, "When we were present at Abhimanyu's marriage ceremony, I spoke in your favor. I showed affection for both the parties, although Krishna did not agree. Krishna has now chosen Arjun's side, and under no circumstances I can fight against him as he is my younger brother. Therefore, I will fight neither for Kauravs, nor for Pandavas.

Somewhere in Hastinapur, Tejaswa was waiting that night to meet Madhurika. It was a pleasant atmosphere with slightly cold wind blowing carrying the fragrance of flowers spread all over. It was dark and the sound of insects was breaching the silence around.

Tejaswa was in deep thought of Madhurika, when he heard the sound of a galloping horse. He smiled to know she is there but, to his surprise, she was not alone today, but his father, commander Siyarakot, was along. He stood up from the bridge on which he was leaning till now and turned towards them.

"Young man, she informed me about you and your desire. Who doesn't know you; even King Duryodhana once enquired about you, appreciating the great moral support you are giving to the progeny of Hastinapur in this tough time." Siyarakot spoke after coming near to him.

Siyarakot was a tall man with wide shoulders, long hair and dark beard. His crown, made up of gold, was shining in the moonlight. Madhurika stood hiding herself behind his father's bulky body. She looked beautiful even when worried and scared and Tejaswa fell in love once again looking at her.

"Thanks for giving me this honor!" he replied joining his hands.

Siyarakot, then, smiled, "But do you know that I am the commander of the Kuru army. How can I allow my daughter to marry someone, who just dances and acts in front of the progeny."

Tejaswa looked down, while his hair waved in the cold wind, and, then, turned his back to him, making a swift movement and pulled out his sword. Before Siyarakot could guess and take an action, Tejaswa placed his sword on his neck, "I dance to help the progeny relax, but you don't know that I use swords to relax myself."

Seeing his body posture leaning back and hands holding the sword on his neck with a single movement, Siyarakot smiled while Madhurika got afraid.

"I am impressed, young man, but just this demonstration cannot allow you to win my daughter." He said.

Tejaswa moved back his sword and holding it in both his hands, he kneeled down with his head bowed and asked politely offering his sword back, "Then, how can I make her mine?"

Siyarakot held Tejaswa's shoulders and asked him to stand up.

Looking inti his eyes, he replied, "Join the army of Kauravs and if they win against Pandavas, Madhurika will be yours forever."

Tejaswa looked into his eyes with confidence and asked, "When can I join your army, do let me know?"

Chapter-26
Conflict in soldiers

Tejaswa joined the army unit of Kauravs and was asked to move to Kurukshetra, as all the efforts put into reinstating peace were failing. Krishna himself tried to be a peacemaker and reached Hastinapur but peace talks failed when Duryodhana tried to imprison Krishna. Now, war was definite to happen. All the important arrangements had been started to be made.

Soldiers started visiting their families for one last time because they didn't know what would be the end of this war. Hue and cry was audible from almost every next house of every kingdom.

Yudhishthira had commanded the army to move to the holy Kurukshetra field and arrange themselves in proper formations. Pandavas had seven akshauhini (battel formation) divisions of troops assembled for the victory. The names of the leaders of these seven divisions were Drupada, Virata, Dhrishtadyumna, Sikhandin, Satyaki, Chekitana and Bhima. All of them were seasoned veterans in wars and were skilled in the use of weapons.

Mohoriti was the commander of the akshauhini division of the Drupada army and leader leading his unit.

All the kingdom Generals made preparations to move their

army units to the holy Kurukshetra, where great sages had performed austerities and sacrifices, both in the recent times as well as in the ancient ages. They were being followed by millions of men, who were uttering war cries. The Pandavas, along with the other distinguished Generals and commanders, made their way to Kurukshetra. The ladies, led by Draupadi, remained in Upaplavya, the capital of Virata. The Pandavas army appeared like a vast ocean and as it headed for Kurukshetra, it appeared to cover one point of the horizon to the other when viewed at from a hilltop. Upon reaching Kurukshetra, Yudhishthira asked the troops to encamp on that part of the field, which was leveled, cool and abounding in grass. Lord Krishna and Arjuna blew their conch shells producing a rumble that sounded like a thunder. Hearing this, the Pandava army was filled with joy and motivation; the message of arrival was sent to Kauravs army, which had camped on the other end.

On the side of Kauravs, Bhishma was placed as the commander-in-chief. When Bhishma was officially placed as the commander-in-chief, the complete Kaurava army was overjoyed, because they knew the power of immortal Bhishma. The sound of the conch shell made the musicians play their instruments and blow their conch shells louder. Suddenly, rain began to fall, making the ground muddy. Fierce whirlwinds rose and earthquakes shook the ground, making all the warriors sad and upset. Extraterrestrial voices could be heard and meteors started falling from the heavens. Jackals and crows howled fiercely and loudly, indicating the arrival of a great calamity.

Kauravs also organized their eleven akshauhini divisions on the plane of Kurukshetra. There were hundreds of thousands of huge tents that were stuffed with food and drinks of various kinds, Suru being the most prominent of them. There were also beddings made up of grass and clothes for the tired and wounded. There were thousands of Vaidya (physicians) to take care of those who fell ill during the battle. In the armies of both the sides, there were hundreds and thousands of chariots loaded with different kinds of weapons. There were also tents erected to repair the chariots that were damaged in the battle. The chariots of both the armies were loaded with quivers of arrows, javelins, long handled spears, barbed darts, heavy maces, clubs made of wood and metal, long ropes, pots filled with poisonous snakes, clubs having iron spikes, swords, short and long bows, battle axes, forked lances and extra armors. Each chariot was made of the sturdiest material and, also, was intricately carved. The pearls and other valuable gems were also embedded in them in an artistic way. There were characters embossed on the chariots with gold and silver. Four horses of the best breed were yoked to each chariot. Each chariot was supplied with one hundred bows.

There were, thus, thousands and thousands of chariots surrounded by innumerable elephants. On the back of each of the elephant, there rode eight warriors. Two of those warriors were armed with hooks, two were excellent bowmen, two were first rated swordsmen, one was armed with a lance and trident and one was the mahout to drive the elephant. There were countless elephants like these and each was carrying incalculable weapons on his back. There were also hundreds and thousands of horses which were trained well. The horsemen were skilled in the use of the bow and arrow, javelin and sword while riding. The foot soldiers were numbered in millions.

According to their divisions, they wore armors of different kinds and carried weapons of diverse capacities. In each convoy, there were ten elephants and each elephant was assigned with ten horses and around each horse, there were ten infantrymen to guard them. In the reserve army that was kept for any emergency, there were fifty elephants to guard each chariot and onto each elephant there was a hundred horsemen and around each horseman, there were allotted seven foot soldiers. In this way, the Kauravs army had designed their strategy to position for the fight.

Tejaswa shared his tent along with three more soldiers named Arjveer, Durkal and Narayan. Durkal and Narayan were from Narayana sena from Krishna's Dwarka. They actually supported Pandavas but were forced to fight from Kauravs' side, as Krishna had gifted his army to Duryodhana.

It was a dark and cold night and the sound of beating iron to prepare bows could still be heard. The sounds of discussions on hot topics among the soldiers were audible from almost all the camps.

"Lord Krishna took a decision to move us with Kuru. He should have kept us with him." Durkal started the conversation in their camp.

"You are from Narayan sena and would always stay the same.

However, remember that Krishna has played a very intelligent game." replied Arjveer.

Other soldiers in the room came near to him and asked in curiosity, "What game?"

"See, he is not fighting the war. This means he will be safe in the war and, obviously, he knows when Bhishma is the chief of Kurus, his army is in completely safe hands. So, the crux is that he saved his complete clan very intelligently." Arjveer explained coolly to others.

"I don't agree with you," interrupted Tejaswa and continued while he stood up and took a seat near to him, "Krishna is the lord and yes he tried to save his people by handing them to Kurus but he hasn't saved himself. He couldn't leave Pandavas, his cousins, bare handed and, so, he gave himself to them without caring for his life."

"But I still feel we are not safe. I, somewhere from my heart, support Pandavas." replied Narayan.

"You are a warrior. Don't be afraid. Fight for your army and fight for yourself." replied Tejaswa.

"Dear, when you know that your biggest motivation is supporting the other side in a war, how can you find the motivation to fight? We fight for our lord or King Krishna, but as he is favoring Pandavas, our heart is somehow aligned with him."

While this whole conversation was going on, Karna, along with Siyarakot, was on an inspection of the camps and he overheard the discussion, which led him to think about the motivation for soldiers. Karna immediately moved towards the camp of Duryodhana along with Siyarakot having crossed the multiple camps of soldiers, chariots parking area and the unit of arms and ammunition center. The camp for kings and Generals were separate from those of the soldiers and were vast in size and structure.

Duryodhana's camp was huge and had a capacity of two hundred people. It had multiple rooms for discussions, war planning, sleeping and advocacy (court room). On outside, it was beautifully decorated with carvings of ancestors of Kuru and their stories. On the inside, it was built in white with firelights placed at every corner and a model of Kurukshetra built with mud and sand placed in the middle. Duryodhana was wearing black dhoti and angvastram with a lot of ornaments, which made him look like a perfectly strong king.

He was holding a dummy soldier in his hand and placing it on the model to plan some new formation to attack Pandavas.

"Friend Duryodhana, we have a situation here." Karna told Duryodhana as he entered his camp along with Siyarakot, the commander of one of the units.

"What happened, Karna, why are you so worried?" Duryodhana replied while taking off his angvastram from his neck. Duryodhana was taller than Karna; he stood in front of him with his strong and broad shoulders to discuss more.

"Friend, I was on routine inspection of our soldiers and their camps. Strangely, I overheard multiple conversations among our soldiers, mostly from the camps of Narayan sena, which we got from Krishna, and some other tribes' camps, which are supporting both Pandavas and us. Those discussions made me understand that even if we have a very big army, most of the army men are either confused or are supporting Pandavas. Soldiers fighting without soul are soldiers without arms."

Duryodhana listened to him carefully and gave a thought to motivate his army.

"Siyarakot, you had once informed me about Kalu Kumar, the man who danced and acted and was working to motivate our progeny; you had also mentioned that he seemed successful in doing so. Can we can call him to Kurukshetra?" He asked him.

"My lord, Kalu Kumar has joined my army unit before we came here, he is already available." Duryodhana answered.

"Oh! Great, send a message to him, that I want to meet him immediately." Duryodhana replied.

Siyarakot immediately sent his messenger to the Tejaswa camp and asked him to reach camp of Duryodhana. Hearing his message, Tejaswa dressed up and went running towards his camp.

He was excited to meet Duryodhana, whom he was publicizing since many years, and had a dream to meet him face to face. As he entered his camp, he joined his hands and bowed before Duryodhana, who was waiting for him to sit on his throne.

"Welcome, Kalu Kumar, I have heard lot about you and was impressed to hear about your dance and drama performance to depict my story and it's interesting to know that you are a warrior, too." Duryodhana welcomed him with a smile and motivating words.

"It's my pleasure, Maharaj, for your words; do let me know your order." Tejaswa said.

Duryodhana now stood up from his throne and came near to him, to further motivate him, "I heard my soldiers are still confused whom to support and it is obvious, Pandavas have created a myth among people that they are so nice and perfect and it's me who is troubling them. You tell me Kalu Kumar, am I wrong? What mistake did I do? I am the son of the present king and, as per the rules, I should be the next king." Duryodhana continued while Tejaswa heard him "Still I gave them Indraprastha from my kingdom, Hastinapur, which Yudhishthira lost in the game of dice. Why am I being blamed for it, if he was not competent to play the dice, why did he bet for everything he had? He is elder to me; he could have stood and left the game but actually he was enjoying the game."

Duryodhana had tears in his eyes with his head down, "It hurts me to see my own brothers standing in front of us for a war and why? Just because I am not giving them five villages? So cheap! The progeny needs to understand that I gave them Indraprastha and what they did, they lost in a game of dice. Now, if I again give them five villages, they may again go and lose it in game of dice to another kingdom. How can I just let my land go in a game of dice? No, I can't do this to my Hastinapur."

Tejaswa heard him, "You are great my lord; please suggest me your order."

Duryodhana turned towards him, with putting his hand on his shoulder, "You need to present a dance and drama for soldiers tomorrow and show them the real picture, which they have not seen yet. I am just a warrior and could not express my feelings of how much I am hurt with this war but how the Pandavas have dragged me into this."

Tejaswa took his orders and replied, "My lord, I take your order and would assure you that tomorrow would be my best and final performance before the start of the war. After this, everyone in your army would love to be with Kurus."

He bowed again and requested for his leave. Duryodhana smiled and blessed him for his success.

"Karna, tomorrow would be an actual war of ideologies between mind and soul and I hope Kalu Kumar would win the same." said Duryodhana.

The next day, just before the day one of war, the stage was set for a motivational event. A big elevated stage was built so that the event is visible to all the soldiers. Once the order was received from each unit chief, the soldiers started arranging themselves near the stage. Stage was lighted with firelight all around, with huge statues of Bhishma, Dhiritarashtra and Duryodhana placed at each corner.

Tejaswa entered the stage with his body painted in white, with his face designed for two characters. He was tall with muscular body; his body cuts were made visible by the colors on his body; his long hairs were tied up with red colored rope, making him different from all others present to witness the show.

He started his performance with a song enchanting the story of King Shantanu, followed by Kurus and explained perfectly the story of Duryodhana in a motivational way. His performance started leaving a deep impact on the mind and soul of all the soldiers, making them understand the reason of war and presence of each one of them for that. It was a deep silence once he finished his performance and after a few seconds, a sound came from somewhere between the mob of soldiers, "Long live Duryodhana! Long live Hastinapur! Long live Bhishma!" and soon millions of soldiers started repeating these words, with energy and full confidence. Duryodhana was amazed to see this response and he looked at Karna with a smile. Bhishma was the one who still somewhere in his heart supported Pandavas.

Duryodhana, then, decided to come on stage and address his soldiers, "Thanks, my people, for your support and belief in me and Hastinapur. We are here in this situation because of the people camping on the other side of Kurukshetra and I assure you they will pay for their sin from tomorrow.

I love them, they are my brothers but I cannot compromise on the fact that they wanted to divide Hastinapur. They tried to intimidate me that if will not give them five villages, they will take us for a war. Can you trust me as your king, if I kneel down in front of them and give them five villages just because I am afraid of war? I don't think anyone of you deserves this insult for your king.

They came first, asking for the throne and we agreed to give them even though the process says it's wrong, but they went off hiding to Mohoma and Drupad, claiming I tried to burn them in Varnavrata. I did my best and developed a palace for them, with new architectural technology suggested to me; how would I know if that would not work. They created a story behind the incident that I did the same to get sympathy of Drupad as they were afraid that Drupad has Dhrishtadyumna now and he could take revenge of their attack on Drupad. I still welcomed them to Hastinapur with open arms and gave them Indraprastha, a part from my kingdom, but they were not satisfied with that.

Yes, I called them for a game of dice but not because I wanted their small kingdom and just imagine, why would I take their kingdom when l already have a bigger and prosperous kingdom than theirs. I never asked him to bet for his brothers and wife but he did because he wanted to play more.

Yes, I agree I insulted Draupadi but why should I not have done this? She insulted me when I visited Indraprastha; she teased me and my father by saying a blind's son is blind.

I still say, one can clap only using both the hands and if I did wrong, they provoked me to do things wrong and today if we are in position of war, it is because of them.

When I have Bhishma, Drona, Karan and many brave and excellent warriors with me, along with the soldiers who are not less than any of these warriors, why I should be afraid of them. We will fight till our last breath, we will fight till last drop of strength in our muscle, will fight even till one of us is left and will help them to reach heaven. Are you with me in this pious work? Are you with me to clean this earth? Are you with me for creating a peaceful Hastinapur?" he roared loud and clear and, in return, the soldier's motivational level boosted up, and this was quite visible from the response in sound of them, which was audible till the camps of Pandavas.

Krishna turned out from his camp hearing the sound of soldiers of Kurus and said smiling, "The heart of progeny is like clay. It could be molded to any shape as desired by the leaders; they just want smile, food and family and they can do anything for them."

Chapter-27
War begins

Next morning, both the armies stood ready for combat on earth of Kurukshetra, and they faced each other like two gigantic oceans. The whole Bharata had concentrated his warriors on this sacred Kurukshetra field, so huge was the army of both the parties. Only women and children were left in their homes for praying. The Kurus and the Pandavas made certain rules of warfare before the battle. Persons who were equal should fight against each other and if having fought fairly, the combatants withdraw, there should be no fear of another attack. A chariot fighter should fight with a chariot fighter, and one riding on an elephant should fight with another riding on an elephant. One riding on a horse should fight with an enemy riding on a horse, and infantry soldiers should fight with infantry soldiers. No warrior should strike another who is not prepared or panic stricken. One who was engaged with another, or one seeking shelter, or one retreating, one whose weapon was rendered unfit, or one who had no armor would never to be attacked. Those who carried drums and those who blew conches, should never be assaulted.

Mohoriti was happy with these rules as he was the chief of one the units of Drupad called Mohoma and also drove on his chariot, making himself eligible to fight with Bhishma.

Then, the great Bhishma, the grandfather of the warriors, blew his conch shell whose sound could be heard till other planets, making a sound like the roar of a lion, giving Duryodhana and complete Kuru army a confidence of joy. After that, the conch shells, drums, bugles, trumpets and horns were all suddenly blown, and the combined sound was tumultuous. On the other side of Pandavas, both Lord Krishna and Arjuna, stationed on a great chariot drawn by white horses and flag with Hanuman, sounded their transcendental conch shells. Lord Krishna blew his conch shell, called Pancajanya; Arjuna blew his, the Devadatta; and Bhima, the voracious eater and performer of herculean tasks, blew his terrific conch shell, called Paundra. King Yudhishthira blew his conch shell, the Ananta-Vijay, and Nakula and Sahadeva blew the Sughosa and Manipuspaka. Other kings present in the war blew their respective conch shells. The blowing of these different conch shells became uproarious, vibrating both in the sky and the earth.

Yudhishthira, then, loudly exclaimed, "Anyone amongst the army of Duryodhana who would like to fight from our side, we will accept as an ally!" There was a moment of silence, Mohoriti was expecting if Tejaswa would change his mind but he remained silent and, then, Yuyutsu, one of Dhiritarashtra sons by a Vaishya wife, said, "I will choose your side if you will accept me." Along with Yuyutsu moved Narayan, friend of Tejaswa. Tejaswa help his hand and tried to stop him with requesting him through his eyes but he untied his wrist and moved to Pandavas.

Under Bhishma's command, Dushasana advanced with his troops, bearing the great Bhishma at their head. The Pandavas also advanced with cheerful hearts, desiring battle with their grandfather troop. With Mohoriti leading the Panchal troop, the army of the Pandavas, accompanied by the tumultuous blowing of conch shells, bugles and trumpets as well as the beating of drums, encountered the troops of Dushasana with their full force. The uproar of the soldiers was deafening, and Bhima roared like a tiger heading towards them. The thunderous war cries of Mohoriti's voice rose above the sounds of the instruments and the clashing armies. His voice sounded like thunderbolt in sky. Indeed, the war cries of Mohoriti were so loud that the horses and elephants on both sides passed stool and urine. Mohoriti assumed an awful form and fell upon army unit chief of one of the clan leader. Duryodhana, Durmukha, Dussaha, Dushasana,

Vivingsati and Chitrasena, pulling back their bowstrings, released snake-like arrows desiring to end Bhīma's life. Joining Bhima in the encounter were the five sons of Draupadi, Abhimanyu, Nakula and Sahadeva. The commander in chief of Pandavas, Dhrishtadyumna, also joined happily in that combat. He rushed against Duryodhana penetrating them with his pointed shafts from both the ends. The moment both the armies collided, a dust cloud rose up into the sky covering the battlefield with darkness, which was visible from galaxies.

The sound of the troops running and colliding, the twang of bowstrings, the tread of the infantry, the furious sounds of the horses and elephants, the falling of weapons and Gada, the clash of weapons, the sounds of elephants rushing against one another, and the clatter of the chariots mingled together and produced a loud uproar, causing earth to shiver.

Ganga's son, Bhishma, rushed towards Mohoriti, taking up a bow that resembled the rod of death. And Mohoriti, taking up his bow, rushed to Bhishma with great fury. Finally, he got a chance after many generations. Bhishma, although piercing Mohoriti's body with many arrows, could not make him waver, and the son of Mohoma, Mohoriti, also could not make the son of Shantanu, Bhishma, falter.

The mighty bowman, Tejaswa, battled with the Andhaka ruler, Rajdvala. Soon the King of Andhaka cut off the standard and overthrew the charioteer of Indriya's son. Tejaswa was outraged and pierced Rajdvala with six arrows. With another arrow, Tejaswa cut off the standard from his chariot and killed his charioteer.

Bhima struggled in battle with Duryodhana. Both of those mighty warriors covered each other with hundreds of arrows and Gada. And Dushasana, rushing against the mighty warrior Nakula, pierced him with many sharp arrows, shot one another by another. Laughing at Dushasana's prowess, Nakula cut off his standard and bow and struck him with twenty arrows. Dushasana, however, countered and killed Nakul's horses and cut his standard from his chariot.

Bhishma, exhibiting extraordinary powers, approached the Pandava army and began to rain arrows in thousands upon the great warriors. He, first of all, met with the son of Subhadra, Abhimanyu, who was supported by Arjuna, Virata and Dhrishtadyumna. Horsemen, chariot fighters and elephants fell fast before the onslaught of the immortal Bhishma. Arjuna requested the Lotus eyed Krishna on seeing his soldier retreat, "O Krishna, guide my chariot to great Pitamah". He was protected by Drona, Kripa, Salya and Vikarna.

Hearing wish of Arjuna, lord Krishna moved that beautiful chariot in line for challenging Bhishma. Arjun's chariot was drawn by spotlessly white horses of celestial origin with Hanuman roaring from the banner striking terror into the hearts of the Kauravs army. Seeing Arjuna coming, Bhishma released seventy arrows. Drona assailed him with twenty five and Kripa with fifty more. Salya released nine arrows, and Drona's son released sixty. Arjuna neutralized those arrows and pierced each of the great warriors with many shafts. All the arrows released by Bhishma were repelled by Arjuna, and all the arrows released by Arjuna were torn to pieces by Bhishma. Neither could gain an advantage over the other, and all, including the heavenly lords, wondered at the display of powers. Bhishma could not be defeated by Arjuna, and Arjuna could not be made to quit by the immortal, Bhishma. While these two combatants were fighting with their celestial weapons and countering each other, other warriors from both the sides began to kill one another with sharp edge scimitars, axes, javelins and innumerable arrows.

There was fierce fighting between Drona and the son of Mohoma, Mohoriti. Both were greatly provoked remembering the past incident when Mohoriti shattered him out of Panchal, and both released divine weapons, hoping to slay each other. Somehow Drona managed to kill Mohoriti s horses and the charioteer. Mohoriti descended from his chariot mace in hand on earth, indicating he was ready to fight on foot. But before he took another step forward, Drona shattered the weapon to pieces with his deadly arrows. Mohoriti, then, took up a large scimitar and a beautiful shield marked with a hundred moons and curved with sun. He assaulted Drona, and each step caused the earth to tremble. Drona, however, checked Mohoriti with arrows used for short range conflict. The son of Mohoma deflected those arrows with his shield, using his dexterous arms. Finding Mohoma in the struggle, coming to Mohoriti's aid, Bhima struck Drona with twelve arrows, and quickly took Mohoriti onto his chariot, saving him from certain slaughter.

On the other hand, Tejaswa, still on foot, holding his deadly sword, began to wander the battlefield slaughtering elephants and making a wide path of flesh and blood wherever he went. Holding great scimitar, he cut chariots in two, horses from the middle, and heads, arms and thighs were seen flying in all directions, from his scimitar wherever he went. His scimitar appeared like a discus destroying the whole foot army of Pandavas. Anyone, who was foolish to approach him, shouting battle cries, was sent to the other world. He turned about, and jumped high, rushed forward and rushed backward, constantly keeping his sword in a circle. That grinder of the foes slaughtered elephants by cutting off their legs, trunks and heads and sometimes severing them down from the middle. He moved on the battlefield, sometimes dragging the chariot fighters from their chariots, and sometimes trampling over infantry. Sometimes, he would be so provoked that he would crush foot soldiers into balls of flesh. No one could stand before the son of Indriya as he slaughtered on the field of Kurukshetra.

On end of day one, King Yudhishthira greatly mourned the loss of so many soldiers on the first day of the battle. Seeing Bhishma slaughtering his army, he went to Krishna and spoke his heart out, "Pitamah is consuming my army like forest fire consumes grass. No one can stand before him when he releases his celestial weapons upon our soldiers. Everyone in Kauravs army can be defeated, but the mighty chariot fighter, Bhishma, cannot be stopped. I am unable to watch as my best warriors are getting slain by him. I shall, therefore, give up for my rights, and save these great warriors from the fire of the colossal, Bhishma. Suggest me, what I can do prevent this slaughter? Although Arjuna is our only hope, I see that he is indifferent, for although we are being slaughtered by Bhishma and Drona, he does not take action. Endowed with supernatural powers, Bhima alone is extinguishing the enemy troops. But at this rate it will take a hundred years to defeat the enemy. Krishna, please find the person who can stop Pitamah and the great Drona, so that after war, our kingsmen and progeny can live happily in our kingdom."

Seeing Kunti's first son conquered by despair, Krishna smilingly instructed him, "Do not grieve, chief of Bharata, especially when your warriors are great bowmen and archer. May be you didn't notice but I didn't miss the chance to admire immortal Mohoriti, slaughtering

Kauravs with his powers today."

Krishna took a seat under the tree and Yudhishthira sat next to him; he continued, "Let me tell you the story behind Mohoriti. He is the son of a great warrior and friend of your ancestor, King Shantanu, exiled out from Hastinapur by Bhishma considering him as the successor of Hastinapur in his absence. He is immortal and possesses the same powers as Bhishma, gifted by Lord Parshuram. But somehow curse to his family could not let him do what he was supposed to. I can't say if he can be reason to kill Bhishma but definitely he can stop Bhishma from ending the war on the second day itself. If Pitamah can slay our troops, we have Mohoriti to slay Kaurav's troop. I suggest you to let him take over on troop reduction of Kauravs like Pitamah is doing for us."

Yudhishthira, then, requested chief Dhrishtadyumna, "In a previous age, there was a formation spoken of by Brihaspati, the priest of the demigods. It is known by the name of Krauncharuma and it will help us to rout our enemy. Tomorrow before the sun rises, arrange our troops in this formation, with Mohoriti taking over the troops of Kauravs."

As asked by King Yudhishthira, Dhrishtadyumna arranged the phalanxes in the proper formation before the sun appeared on the horizon. He placed Arjuna, the carrier of the Gandiva bow, in the forefront of the whole army. King Drupada, surrounded by many phalanxes, became the head of that formation. The two kings, Kuntibhoj and Saivya, became the two eyes, and Nakula and Sahadeva were placed on the right and left wing of the formation. On the joints of the wings were placed ten thousand chariots and at the head of the formation were placed a hundred thousand. A hundred million chariots were placed in the body of the formation and in the neck was placed a hundred and seventy thousand chariot fighters, all led by Mohoriti, the son of Mohoma. On the joints of the wing as well as the far edges were placed hundreds of thousands of elephants. The rear of the formation was protected by Virata, the ruler of Kashi, and the King of the Chedi. Thus, the Pandavas army waited silently for the dawn of the second day.

With dawn of the second day, the Kauravs saw the commanding formation created by the Pandavas. In the presence of all his important generals, Duryodhana spoke encouraging words, "Each of the Kaurav warriors present in Kurukshetra here is capable of killing the Pandavas in battle. How more effective will you be if united against this vast army in commanding formation? Let us now make arrangements to counter the vast array of the Pandavas."

Upon hearing the desires of Duryodhana, Bhishma and Drona formed an array to counterattack on Pandavas. Hundreds of millions of soldiers were lined up for combat, and they filled the earth from one horizon to the other. The leaders of the mammoth divisions were Bhishma, Drona, Kripa, Salya, Duryodhana, Sala, Shakuni, the ruler of the Kambhojas, Vinda and Anuvinda, Kritavarman and many others.

Then, Krishna blew his conch shell and was followed by the other great warriors. Conches, drums and kettledrums sounded in thousands, and the tumult was uproarious. In response to the Pandavas battle cry, Bhishma and Drona sounded their transcendental conch shells, creating fear in the hearts of the enemy. The sound of these conches was tumultuous and weakened the hearts of the enemy's soldiers. All the warriors in the Pandava army sent up war cries that caused the very earth to tremble. Both armies, while advancing towards one another with upraised weapons, uttered thunderous shouts that shook the earth.

The two blood thirsty armies met with a forceful impact, causing a huge dust cloud to rise into the sky. Arrows like lightning bolts were scorching through the sky severing the heads, arm, and legs of the approaching enemy. Mohoriti, as guided, exhibited gruesome prowess and approached the Kuru army. He began to rain arrows in thousands upon the troops. The Kuru soldiers wavered upon seeing the fierce Mohoriti releasing arrows like thunderbolts from the sky. Horsemen, chariot fighters and elephants fell fast before the onslaught of the invincible Mohoriti.

From this point on, the battle went on blood-thirsty. Mohoriti became superhuman and created a scene of terror among the enemy's troops. Krishna was correct on his words, thought Yudhishthira. From his chariot, he rained a shower of arrows upon all the warriors in the Kuru army. The King of the Kalinga's, Shrutayus, and his son, attacked Mohoriti, to stop him and pierced him with their shafts. They managed to kill Mohoriti's horses, and became confident of victory;

Sakradeva assaulted Mohoriti, deciding to send him to Yamaraja. Mohoriti countered those weapons with his own excellence, and took up a huge mace, which he released it with tremendous force. That mace scorched through the air, and simultaneously killed the charioteer of Sakradeva. The mace was thrown with such power that no one could distinguish the body of Mohoriti any longer.

Enraged on the battlefield and fighting alone, Mohoriti took up an immense scimitar and shield, and ran into a troop of thousands of men shouting fierce war cries that terrorized the hearts of the enemy. The ruler of the Kalinga's, Shrutayus, was furious, and rubbing his bowstring, released a deadly arrow hoping to kill Mohoriti. While that arrow was scorching through the air like a meteor, the powerful Mohoriti cut it in two with his huge sword flying in air. When that weapon was baffled, Mohoriti sent up a loud roar that deafened the enemy's ears. The ruler of Kalinga was further enraged and released sixteen barbed darts toward the son of Mohoma. Mohoriti smiled and shouted and cut them into fragments with three swings of his might scimitar.

The Kalinga army, seeing Mohoriti alone fighting with tens of thousands of men, thought that he was not a human being but a celestial, immortal warrior. Rushing at elephant of one of the Kuru' s warrior, Mohoriti jumped onto his tusk and then onto his back, and with one swing of his sword, he divided that warrior from the middle. One half fell off one side of the elephant, and the other half fell off the other side. With a thunderous roar, Mohoriti raised his mighty sword, with blood served from Kuru's.

When the entire Kaurav's army was routed, Bhishma said to Duryodhana, "The immortal son of Mohoma, blood thirsty of Kuru since decades, is annihilating our troop as he alone is able to do. Today, he cannot be subdued by any means. He appears to be the lord of death in human form today. Our soldiers are running from the battlefield in his fear. The sun is now setting on the horizon, and I think now is the time to withdraw our troops for the day." Having made his decision, the mighty chariot fighter, Bhishma, ordered the withdrawal of the troops by sounding his conch shell, thus ending the second day of the terrible war. The Pandava army also withdrew with joyous hearts, remembering the feats of Mohoriti.

Chapter-28
The Night before the third day

Mohoriti poured water on his head seeing the huge amount of blood, which covered his body as a result of the slaughter he did for the whole day of thousands of soldiers, getting washed. Water flowed from his face dropping from the long white beard, cleaning his body but not his soul.

Dressed up in a white dhoti, he decided to visit the temple of Lord Shiva on the bank of River Ganga. The temple was common to both the armies and was visited by soldiers and warriors after day was called off from the war. As per the war rules, no one was supposed to attack their enemy in temple area or anywhere after the war is called off for a day. Lord Shiva is equal to everyone and everyone was allowed to visit him without a fear of attack.

As he entered the premises of the temple, the soldiers of Kuru gave him side look, looking at him with enmity but unable to do anything then. He carried holy water of Ganga and flowers for Lord Shiva. He entered temple, performed rituals and worshiped for some hours. The day had gone dark by now, with cold wind blowing from the side of river Ganga. While he moved out, he still carried the image of super humans along with him; his white dhoti waved with the flow of the wind. He walked slowly trying to answer many questions running in his mind, when someone called him from the back. He turned around to check and saw Tejaswa standing with his hands linked. He moved to him and touched his feet. Mohoriti blessed him and asked him to stand up.

"Pitamah, I wanted to share with you something." He said.

"Carry on, my son" asked Mohoriti.

"I killed the golden deer, which cursed your father, Mohoma, and this has led to the end of our curse." informed Tejaswa.

Mohoriti heard it with no expressions on his face and, then, replied, "Curse will be over by itself, when I will kill Bhishma tomorrow."

"Your revenge of ego will be over by tomorrow, not the curse of your family." replied Tejaswa smiling at him

"What do you mean by that?" he asked him.

"Yes, maybe you get success in conquering Bhishma, but will that uplift the curse of our family? The curse says that our life will be affected and directed as per changes in life of Kurus. This means either you kill each and every Kuru, including Pandavas and their sons, or end your family to stop this trend." Tejaswa explained and continued, "What will you do, Pitamah? Do you have courage to kill them all? Actually, you are confused on your target; you are not sure if you want revenge or you want the end of curse."

Mohoriti looked at him with deep thoughts and continued, "I don't understand what your revenge is for. Bhishma killed your brothers because you tried to take his position; then, how come Duryodhana is wrong in defending Pandavas. He is doing the same, what you tried to do long back, i.e., protecting his position. You were neither the son of King Shantanu nor held any position in his court. How could you expect yourself to be his successor? You, the son of Mohoma, lived your life in a wrong perception and motivated your family in the way you wanted; you are responsible for death of my father, Indriya, and mother, Mili. You are responsible for death of Duru and Maaru. You are responsible for death of each and every one in our clan."

Hearing his words, Mohoriti shouted loud, "Stop Tejaswa, else I will forget that we are standing in front of Lord Shiva."

Tejaswa stopped and looked at him with calm eyes, "Pitamah, you are coward and afraid of listening to the truth of life. I pity you because you will be taking revenge for something which you don't deserve."

Tejaswa moved after completing what he wanted to say, leaving Mohoriti standing still, talking with his soul.

Krishna, along with Arjuna, stopped Tejaswa on his way back to his camp, "Tejaswa, I overheard your conversation with Mohoriti. Remember, I told you that you have a lot of work to do. Do you think this was one of them?"

"Pranaam, Lord Krishna, and mighty prince, Arjuna! How come this could be part of that? I provoked him to stop slaughtering; this is against your army." Tejaswa explained.

Krishna, lotus eyes smiled, "Yes, I appreciate your acting skills; you provoked him keeping in view the way he fought today but you forgot that he is a warrior and fighting is his duty. He is not a dancer, who will be affected by your acting and will change his way to fight."

"I don't know, but I want this curse to be over. I know he cannot kill each and every one in Kuru but if he does, then this curse will hunt our coming generation." Tejaswa replied anxiously.

Krishna moved around him with a smile, "So, what do you want, victory of Kauravs or end of this curse?"

"Not sure, but I want both I suppose and I am sure my life can bring an end to the curse." replied Tejaswa in a confused state.

"Everyone on this earth takes birth with a goal, which is defined before his birth. Concentrate on your duties, the goal will be achieved by itself." explained Krishna in a simple way and left questions for him to think over.

Krishna, then, smiled and moved giving his last words, "I am tired after the whole day of moving chariot as directed by parth. I need some rest; you think and find your answers."

On their way back to Pandavas camp, Arjuna asked Krishna, "I could not understand what you explained to Tejaswa. How can he, just a soldier, be so important for us, that you guided him in this detail."

Krishna continued walking with firelight in his hand, smiled and replied, "If only high rank warriors decided the outcome of a war, the soldiers wouldn't be needed. Any soldier can someday take rank of a warrior. Every soldier plays important role in a war. Tejaswa plays an important role in motivating Kaurav's army. If he stops his motivation, we succeed in reducing their troops to half its size."

"But you appreciate that he provoked Mohoriti, who is our best warrior in winning over troops." anxious Arjun asked.

"In wars, you may have to lose your best warrior to win over the strength of enemy, I did the same." smiled Krishna moving on, while Arjuna still stayed confused about his strategy.

When the night passed away and the dawn appeared with the first ray of sun, the great grandsire of the Kuru dynasty, Bhishma, gave orders that the army to be arrayed in the Garuda formation today. The beak of the bird was the Bhishma himself; Drona and Kritavarman were the two eyes. Ashvatthama and Kripa Acharya were the heads and they were supported by the Trigarta, Bhurishravas, Jayadratha, Sala, Salya, Bhagadatta clan kings and the troops were the neck of that great bird. Duryodhana and his brothers, along with Shakuni, constituted the back of the bird, and Vinda and Anuvinda, the Kings of Avantipura, were the tail of the bird. The two wings of that formation were the numerous divisions of troops under different generals.

Considering the array formed by the Kauravs, Arjuna, in consultation with chief Dhrishtadyumna, arrayed their troops in a counter formation that resembled a half moon. On the right side of the moon was the mighty Mohoriti supported by Drupada and Virata. Dhrishtadyumna and Shikhandi took their positions in the middle of that formation surrounded by the Chedis, the Karushas and the Kashis. Next to these great warriors was King Yudhishthira as well as the five sons of Draupadi and the son of Arjuna, Iravan. On the far left side of that moon were Arjuna and Bhima.

Then, the rivalry between the two great forces, Kauravs and Pandavas commenced. Each rushed at the other eager to kill. The two armies clashed, and the deafening sound of steel and weapons could be heard in all directions, from earth to sky. A large number of elephants and chariots on both sides rushed at one another with the intention of slaughter and blood. As on the previous days, the sounds of the drums, kettledrums, conches, rattling chariots, clashing weapons, and the war cries of the foot soldiers combined together to produce a thunderous sound that weakened the hearts of gods too. Mohoriti, the son of Mohoma, began killing soldiers in hundreds and thousands causing a great carnage on the field of battle, as his previous day, showing no effect of provocation done by Tejaswa. Unable to tolerate the power of Mohoriti, the unlimited Kauravs army attacked him. Simultaneously, they released thousands of arrows, javelins, darts, swords, scimitars, maces and battle axes. Seeing that curtain of weapons coming toward him like a hurricane, he checked it with his celestial weapons, gifted by Parshuram. He, then, released countless arrows that created a massacre among the Kauravs troops. Unable to confront Mohoriti, Kauravs immense army broke its formation and began to flee. Bhishma, then, came forward to rally the troops, and also Duryodhana encouraged the soldiers to return to their positions.

However, Mohoriti caused carnage of dead bodies to float in the ocean of holy land of Kurukshetra. Releasing his lethal weapons, he severed the arms, legs and heads of the Kuru troops. So quick did he sever their heads that the trunks remained on the chariots still grasping weapons or armed with bow and arrow. His bow was drawn in a full circle, and he was releasing continuous lines of arrows in all directions. He looked like he was taking revenge than actually fighting for Pandavas. The Kuru army could not tell where Mohoriti was for he appeared to be in all directions. At one moment, he was on the west, and the next moment, he was on the east. Not one of the Kuru tribe kings was able to get close to him; such was the prowess he exhibited. They could not tell where he was, but they could only see that the whole sky was filled with his arrows and burst of blood and dust. Not one arrow released from the bow of Mohoriti missed its target. With a single arrow, he was killing the gigantic elephants that tried to block his way. Four or five soldiers, riding on the same elephant and encased in mail, were pierced at the same time with one arrow.

That army was so completely routed that no two persons were seen close to each other; all had fled from the battlefield. The only thing left was a vast ocean of blood, severed bodies, broken weapons, shattered chariots, dead horses, and dead elephants. The Kuru soldiers were throwing away their weapons and running from the battlefield, saving themselves from the hurricane of Mohoriti.

Seeing the devastation of their army, Duryodhana told Bhishma, "The hour has come, Pitamah, to fulfill your vow to stand by the side of Hastinapur. He is the man, who tried to kill your father, King Shantanu, years before. He is the man, who tried to take your position as his son. He is roaring in front of you again; destroy him, before he succeeds in his plans."

Thus provoked by Duryodhana, Bhishma said to his charioteer, "Take this chariot to where Mohoriti is present. I will force the immortal Mohoriti from his chariot and take his life." His charioteer directed the chariot towards the spot where the son of Mohoma was releasing his arrows, leading to slaughter. Sighting Bhishma coming forward to challenge Mohoriti, Tejaswa moved towards them from behind. Foremost of all the warriors, Mohoriti saw Bhishma coming to oppose him and released thousands of arrows by invoking his celestial weapons. At one point, the chariot of Bhishma could not be seen, so heavy was the power of his weapons. However, Bhishma cut his bow in two with a single arrow. Picking up another bow and stringing it quickly, Mohoriti roared and stretched that bow to its fullest. Bhishma, the father of all warriors, was not affected by his exhibition of powers and he cut that bow into two. Mohoriti applauded Bhishma exclaiming, "O Devavrata, such a mighty feat is indeed worthy of you. I am pleased with your fighting. Continue to attack to the best of your ability."

Bhishma attacked Mohoriti and covered him with a curtain of arrows. Mohoriti countered and pierced Bhishma with seven shafts, filled his banner and pierced the chariot rider with three shafts. Then Shantanu's son placed on his bowstring an arrow capable of killing his enemy. However, Bhishma cut the arrow and the bow which was in Mohoriti's hands. Throwing aside the broken bow and arrow, the son of Mohoma took up a sword and shield, and descending from his chariot, ran at Bhishma. Whirling his sword and shield, he jumped onto Bhishma chariot but Tejaswa, breaking rules of the war, interrupted in between and knocked Mohoriti, saying sorry in low voice. Mohoriti roared in anger and pulled Tejaswa up by his hair and threw him to distance; then, rushing back towards him and raising his sword, he severed Tejaswa's head.

Realizing that he killed his great grandson in agony and fury of revenge, Mohoriti's strength diminished and his celestial weapons would no longer come at his command. Remembering the great curse of golden deer, he cast aside his weapons and sat down with eyes wide open. He fixed his mind on the saying of Tejaswa when he met him last night and turned his thoughts completely away from battle. For some time, he went through each and every face in one go from his family and remembered what he got after a long wait of revenge.

Duryodhana reached on his chariot to the spot and asked Bhishma to kill him and send him to Yamraja. On which Bhishma replied "He is not holding his weapons now, he is not fighting now; this is against the rule of war. I don't kill weaponless soldiers."

Bhishma turned his chariot and moved to attack in different direction, followed by Duryodhana.

Observing Mohoriti, the demigods and rishis confirmed his meditation by saying, "Your departure from this world is close at hand now, son of Mohoma. Withdraw your heart from battle and thoughts of revenge." With these words, a fragrant and auspicious breeze filled with water particles from holy River Ganga began to blow in all the directions. In the heaven, Mohoriti heard the sounds of conch shell, drums and bugles. Showers of blood, then, began to fall from the sky upon him. All this was only seen by Mohoriti who now thought of attaining the kingdom of God.

Chapter-29
Krishna explaining Mohoriti

The war was called for the day, leaving Mohoriti still in a state of meditation, holding the soulless body of Tejaswa, with its head fallen at distance. Blood flow from his neck had almost stopped; though, a few drops could still be seen falling slowly.

It was dark by now and hills of the slaughtered body parts lying all over could well be seen. Jackals and other animals had now entered the holy land of Kurukshetra in search of fresh, slaughtered meat of humans. Smell of burning human bodies could be smelled, with fire fumes at every near distance is visible.

Broken chariots, pooled with blood and body parts of horses, elephants and soldiers were spread all over.

Sound of pain of the soldiers, who were still alive, could be heard in dark. These soldiered were being looked for by the surviving one with firelights in their hands. Vultures enjoyed fresh meat in night, picking up human body parts and taking them to the treetops and hill tops. Soil was wet with blood and was licked by animals to fulfill their thirst for blood.

Time felt less to collect and cremate body parts of slaughtered warriors. Celestial cry was heard in the complete night, a cry on mass death and slaughter. Yamraja was too occupied to collect souls turning back to him. Wind was blowing warm in the month of winters because of heat of burning chariots and human bodies. It was tough to identify body parts if it was of a soldier or archer or king. At last, it was only blood and dismantled flesh from a body.

Krishna walked back in war field, and reached Mohoriti, having crossed the bodies on his way. Mohoriti was still in a state of meditation, thinking about the past, which could not be changed by now.

Krishna touched his shoulder bringing his consciousness back, and saw him still silent.

"You need to cry Mohoriti, tears can bring out your soul's desires" but he still kept quiet, without shedding a single drop of tear or moving, while he held Tejaswa's blooded body in his hands.

Krishna looked at him and then decided to show him what Tejaswa felt in his last time and why he took such a decision. With his divine powers, he blessed him with divine eyes to watch past from the mind of Tejaswa. Soon, white light spread in dark field of Kurukshetra, centering the head of Mohoriti. Time rewinded to Unakoti after Tejaswa met celestial nymph, Devapima.

"Tejaswa left for the forest of Madhuvan to meet Sage Vyasa, to understand the meaning of the words of celestial nymph, Devapima. After travelling for four days bare foot, he reached the forest of Madhuvan, which was dense and covered with long deodar trees. He was tall, with broad shoulders, wide chest and a muscular body. He hung bows on his back with bare sword in his hand and moved cutting weeds and unwanted branches on his way. He stopped in the middle of his way to take a sip of water that he had collected from the tributaries of River Yamuna. He kept stopping in between when he saw the rays of the sun, which managed to breach the dense coverage of leaves, to get himself dried up, as he was wet after swimming in River Yamuna to reach the forest area.

His foot was bleeding but his inner pain was much strong than what he felt in his foot. Time was running short; he already missed a chance to stop war, as he could not complete koti statues in Unakoti. Things would have been different, if he could have managed the same. He looked at the fallen tree branch and sat there, rubbed some leafs to paste and implemented on wounds on his bare foot. Looked up and around again and again, hearing sound or roar of tigers or Hoo-ah-hoo...Hooo...Hoooo...Hoooooooo sound of owls. Bad signals were flowing high as darkness taking over control on complete Bharata. If war is not stopped, soon the complete earth would be in state of hue and cry of dark tears flowing from the eyes of the widows and the orphaned children's. He could not stop to waste his time; he needed to travel to meet Sage Vyasa.

He stood back and moved towards the center of the forest, where there was a Gurukul of Sage Vyasa. He crossed the waterfall, flowing with white stream of cold water and saw the Gurukul covered with lust green trees, with small gate made of woods in between. As he entered the gate, he saw multiple cows fed by sages with green grass. Some of the students in his Gurukul were carrying water and somewhere sitting under a big banyan tree, he was studying Sanskrit mantras. He kept walking, observing them all. He was feeling cold , with blood still flowing from his wounds. He pulled back his sword and started moving to old sage relaxing under one of the trees.

"O, guru, help me, I came from far to meet sage Vyasa, please guide me his way"

Sage opened his eyes and directed him towards east, where there stood a tall, old sage, with wide eyes and long beard. His face was having a spark of knowledge and greatness.

As Tejaswa reached him, without turning, he spoke "I know Tejaswa, why you are here?"

He turned to him smiling, with his wide eyes.

Tejaswa touched his feet and asked, "Please oblige me with answers of questions running in my mind and heart, O guru."

Sage Vyasa smiled and replied with glory, "your answers will be in the questions, which I would ask you. Our soul is capable enough to give every answer within; no sage or learned person can answer, questions of our soul." He continued with his question then, "Do you really support Kauravs?"

Tejaswa thought and replied from his heart, "I supported Kauravs and I am supporting Kauravs because my inner turmoil says they are correct in their ways."

Vyasa asked his second question, "Do you think, Mohoriti's feeling of revenge with Kuru is justifiable?"

"Keeping myself in his position, a person who has seen his father Mohoma and nineteen brothers slaughtered in front of him, it looks correct but if I think from my heart and logics of processes, he is exaggerating his desires."

"You are correct my son, he desired to marry Satyavati; he desired to be the successor of the throne of Hastinapur and having a desire is not a problem. Every human being, who has taken birth, will have desire and he will do his best to achieve his desire. Mohoriti did the same and there is nothing wrong in it. May be if your family would have not been cursed by celestial nymph, Devapima; he would have left his desire or would have not thought of revenge but because of curse, his mind, body and soul forces him to take revenge." Sage Vyasa replied

Tejaswa heard him sincerely and then questioned, "I am having his blood in my veins, I must also be having equal curse as he had, why I am not able to think as he did or my father did?"

Sage Vyasa now smiled, "Every human who takes birth, comes with a future, which was written by all mighty Brahama, and no curse is bigger or can effect what is written by him. And who says you are not affected by that curse. Only a feeling of revenge is missing in your heart, which is your inner strength, expressed stronger than curse."

Tejaswa then questioned him further, "You are the one who knows everything of future; please suggest me what must I do and what is correct"

Sage Vyasa thought for a while and replied "Time is approaching, when sky will turn dark, sun will have lost his glory, clouds will shower blood, human parts will be eaten by animals and human will slaughter human like vegetables and no one could stop that, because that is planned by Gods themselves and that would be start of Kalyug. Whatever you do, you can never stop what is designed by God himself and this is destiny. But you have an option to bring your family out of this curse at least." He further continued

"You need to fight against Mohoriti; he is immortal and possesses same powers as Bhishma, if they both fight against each other war will never come to end, but can lead to the end of this earth and creation. Vasudev Krishna told you once, that you have bigger things to do and today I will tell you what bigger thing you need to do. You are the only person who can stop Mohoriti to leave his weapons. Mili, your mother

knows this as this was curse given to her by one of the Naga Sadhu, when she was young, who was of the age of her great grandfather and she laughed at that Naga Sadhu, looking at him naked, polished in ashes, that her son would be killed by his great grandfather. To avoid such instance, she wanted Mohoriti to follow his husband, your father, Indriya and so she killed Duru to let Indriya be King of Mohoma. She always thought, if you being son of king, Mohoriti will never attempt to kill you, in any conditions. Her mother's love led her to death, unknowingly that it will still happen."

Tejaswa linked his hands, "Do let me know guru, what next is hidden for me."

Vyasa continued "Soon time will come, when two extreme powers will come face to face, huge thunder will happen, clouds will go dark, human blood would flow like river stream, which you need to monitor. Mohoriti and Bhishma will turn their celestial weapons on each other, creating loud noise and thunder. That would be time, when you need to stop Mohoriti. You might have lost your life but that would be end of curse, too. You and Mohoriti are only left in your family, so once you reach heaven there is no scope of curse to follow."

"Someone needs to pay for jobs done by their ancestors and you are the chosen one. You will not only end curse to your family but will help in winning truth over sin and lie. You would be the reason of victory of truth on this earth."

Tejaswa still continued with his hands linked towards the great future depicter, "Thanks for giving me path of my life, I will end my life for truth to win; I ensure you, there will be no tears in my eyes when I take nap of death. Thanks again for your answers." He touched his feet and asked for his leave. As he turned sage Vyasa told him one more thing "Son, in future, I will write story of this war between Pandavas and Kauravs, named Mahabharata, so that coming generations must know what happened in fight of truth and lie but I am sorry I would not mention anything about generations of Mohoma, considering it's quite possible, story of Kuru Kingdom will be faded in front of sacrifice and efforts of your family. But remember, behind every successful kingdom and his king, it's his progeny who leads them to success and you are progeny of Kuru, which will be praised, blessed and prayed in coming generations forever and ever."

Tejaswa then moved to Hastinapur carrying his bow and arrows on his back, thinking of building future for the coming generations by losing his life. He was sad after hearing future but happy to know his part in victory of truth. His eyes were wet with tears, when he reached Hastinapur and waited for Madhurika.

That day, he was sad, with tears in his eyes but confident on his take away. Silence was obstructed with sound of waves of River Ganga, hitting the port. He could see them coming towards him, while next wave followed behind it, just like if first fails, second follows it to support, but in his case, if he fails, there is no fall back. Fisherman on his boat was sailing at the far end, while moon glittered in the sky. He was finding himself in a similar position, trying to take his position, with glittering smile and instructions given by Lord Krishna.

"What are you looking at so deeply, when I am still in front of you" interrupted Madhurika with her beautiful voice. He turned towards her but today his tears where shadowing her smile of love and this was quite visible, behind his long hairs, which where flowing in air. He was silent, with lot of words buried beneath.

She understood, seeing his eyes; she understood the storm within his heart. He wanted to hug her with passion but something was stopping him. He knew he can't live forever with her. He knew his expectation to have family and children with her were no more feasible. He turned back to hide his tears.

"Your wounded toes are telling much more than your eyes. I love you, speak to me." she asked him coming step forward towards him.

"If I look at you, I will fall in love with you more and I don't want that now."

"And why you don't want to love me anymore; did you find someone more beautiful than me?"

"May my eyes burn, if my heart even thinks that someone else is more beautiful than you. You are in depth of my heart and no one can replace your space there in but I am puzzled." replied Tejaswa still looking at the river waves.

He turned towards her, "I love you more than myself and that's why I want to marry you. But I am puzzled thinking what will happen if war happens, I don't want you to be widow."

"I love you and can do whatever you say, no matter if you love

me or not." she replied.

He hugged her but his eyes still said something else. He knew if he goes directly to join Kuru army, he would have been thrown out considering him as a dance and drama expert. He wanted her to bring her father Siyarakot, who was commander in unit of Kuru army, so that he could enter by his source in his unit.

He knew he can't marry her; he knew he can't love her; he knew he will die in some days and was guilty of using her but destiny wanted the same. His heart was bursting when he was telling a lie to her in tears. He wanted to cry loud, he wanted to curse his destiny, when he is so close to one he loves a lot on this earth but could not accept her love in return.

Latter, he joined Kuru army and still continued to motivate army men by his dance and drama, which he actually did to provoke Mohoriti against him.

On last night, he saw Mohoriti moving towards the temple; he followed him. He observed Mohoriti furious actions in Kurukshetra warfield and monitored his own death time. He knew time has come to stop him, time has come to release curse, time has come to give final performance but he also knew how much Mohoriti loved him. He will never kill him if not provoked. He already did provocation since long by cursing Pandavas whom he was supporting but final provocation performance was must. He met Mohoriti outside the temple and cursed him by saying he is responsible for death of his family members, he cursed him for death of Indriya, he cursed him that he is behind revenge, which pierced Mohoriti's heart deeply, resulting in slaughter of Tejaswa today.

When Tejaswa's head was cut into parts, his brain still functioned for some time and spoke these words in his mind, "I am sorry Pitamah, for making you responsible for my death but my father Indriya would be happy today. I am sorry for hurting your feeling hard last night but your father Mohoma would be happy today. No one will remember me, I would be nowhere in history but I am happy to be a part of the victory of truth. My soul will meet Mohoma in heaven and would take his blessings after completing his immature job. Nothing results in the fight of revenge and nothing would be recovered in the fight of revenge, all would be left in ashes.

I am sorry Madhurika for not being able to forget you. I am sorry for loving you. I am sorry for leaving you alone. I am sorry for using you but I hope you would feel proud of me one day. I would still love you from the sky. I would still hug you when wind would blow. I would still kiss you when the flowers would touch you and I am sorry for still loving you and he rested in peace."

White light which was enlighten by Krishna stopped with a loud burst of Mohoriti crying, shouting the name of Tejaswa, which could be heard till sky and deep into earth. While holding the body of Tejaswa still in his hands, he cried loud.

"Forgive me, my son; forgive me, I am your transgressor." he cried while Krishna observed him and gave him time to bring out his pain.

Mohoriti, with his hands full of blood, hugged the body of Tejaswa with a cry. He, then, stood up keeping his body with care on side, tottered to pick up his head which was lying at some distance. He picked up his head with care and sat keeping it in his lap. He rapped his head while singing a song in the voice of cry, which he used to teach him when he was a child and lived in the land of Mohoma.

Soldiers watching him from some distance could not stop their tears, while Mohoriti, an unbeatable warrior, lost everything in this war.

He, then, stood again and kept the head of Tejaswa joining to the body and touched his head saying to go to sleep as it's dark now.

He, then, bent on his knees, with hands linked and approached Lord Krishna and offered the following prayer to him, with tears in his eyes, "Through Your grace, O Krishna, I have received understanding for my son's feelings. O foremost of the Yadus, O lotus-eyed Lord, I repeatedly offer my humble obeisance's to you. You have been glorified as the Supreme Lord of sky. The great sages and Brahmanas know you by many names. O Creator of the world, you are the soul of complete universes, and you are the support of this manifested creation. You are Vishnu, Hari, O Krishna. You are the Lord of Vaikuntam and the foremost of all beings. Previously, you have taken birth as Prishnigarbha, the son of Prishni and Sutapa. Another of your names, O Lord, is Triyuga. You are the Lord of the senses and are, therefore, known as Hrishikesha. You are the great swan, Hamsa Avatar; the boar, Varaha; and the half man, half lion, Nrisimhadeva. You are the sun, the moon and the firmament. You are the chief of the celestials, Indra, and you are the beginning, the middle and the end of all creations and this universe. You are Dhruva, you are Garuda and you are the great sage Kapila. You are the Super soul in the heart of every living and nonliving being. Obeisance unto you, O Lord, who wields the Sarnga bow, the Sudarshana discus and the Kamodaki club. Please help me to death now. I have no interest in living on this earth, taking burden of so many deaths and slaughtered bodies on my shoulders. O Krishna, let your Sudarshana discus take my soul and let me rest in peace."

Krishna came near to him and wiped his tears with his angvastram "Stop crying O brave warrior, Tejaswa did what was planned for him in sky and you are doing what is written for you. My dear Mohoriti, how have these impurities come upon you? They are not at all befitting a man who knows the value of life and war. O son of Mohoma, do not yield to this degrading impotence. It does not belong to you. Give up such petty weakness of heart and arise, O chastiser of the enemy."

Mohoriti replied "O lord Krishna, you tell me for certain what is best for me. Now I am your disciple, and a soul surrendered onto you. Please instruct me. I can find no means to drive away this grief, which is drying up my senses. I will not be able to dispel it even if I win a prosperous or revenge."

Krishna replied him with explanation "While speaking of mourning words, you are mourning for what is not worthy of grief. Never was there an instance when I did not exist, neither you, nor all these kings; nor in the future shall any of us cease to be. As the embodied soul of our continuously passes, in this body, from boyhood to youth to old age, the soul similarly passes into another body at death. O son of Mohoma, the nonpermanent appearance of happiness and distress, and their disappearance in due course, are like the appearance and disappearance of various seasons. O Mohoriti, the person who is not disturbed by happiness and distress and is steady in both is certainly eligible for liberation. No one is able to destroy that imperishable soul within us. Our material body and eternal living entity is sure to come to an end; therefore, stand up, O descendant of Mohoma. For the soul, there is neither birth nor death at any time. It has not come into being, does not come into being, and will not come into being. It is unborn, eternal, ever existing and primeval. It is not slain when the body is slain. As our body puts on new garments, giving up old ones, the soul similarly accepts new body made of flesh and bone, giving up the old and useless ones. The soul can never be cut to pieces by any weapon, nor burnt by fire, nor moistened by water, nor withered by the wind. This individual soul is unbreakable and insoluble, and can be neither burned nor dried. It is everlasting, present everywhere, unchangeable, immovable and eternally the same forever and ever. Let me tell you that the soul is invisible, inconceivable and immutable. Knowing this, you should not grieve for the body. One who has taken his birth is sure to die, and after death one is sure to take birth again. Therefore, in the unavoidable discharge of your duty, you should not lament for your dear once. Therefore, you need not grieve for him. Considering your specific duty as a Kshatriya, you should know that there is no better engagement for you than be on warfield. If, however, you do not perform your religious duty of fighting or be on war land, then you will certainly incur sins for neglecting your duties and thus lose your reputation as a warrior. People will always speak of your weakness, and for a respectable person, dishonor is worse than death. The great generals who have highly esteemed your name and fame will think that you have left the battlefield out of fear only, and thus they will consider you insignificant. Your enemies will describe you in many unkind words and scorn your ability of being a warrior. What could be more painful for you? Therefore, get up with the determination and complete your duties. Your soul feels that work is still not complete. You wanted to leave all Kuru to ashes, may be your curse is over, leaving no interest in revenge but still perform your duty to rest your soul in peace. Be in Kurukshetra, if don't want to fight again, would not ask you to fight, destroy the bodies of soldiers and warriors to make them reach to heaven. Perform new job in war field, job of Antyesti (funeral rites for the dead in Hinduism), irrespective if dead body is of Kauravs or Pandavas, help them to rest in peace. You will be a person, collecting Chandan woods for Antyesti of each and every person martyred in this holy field of Kurukshetra. Your soul will rest in peace, once you complete your job to convert these bodies to ashes, that day would be your last day on this earth. Now stop mourning and stand up. Start your duty of Antyesti, O son of Mohoma."

Chapter-30
End of war

Mohoriti took words of Krishna and left for the jungles of Kurukshetra with an axe in his hand. He stopped speaking to anyone and started performing Antyesti ritual every night, collecting the dead bodies of soldiers and warriors, starting first with Tejaswa. He kept looking at his body to convert to ashes, with no tears in his eyes.

His feeling of revenge was moving upwards with smoke of every next body burning.

It was the fourth day of war and Bhima killed eight brothers of Duryodhana. Their bodies pooled in blood and slaughtered conditions kept for Antyesti, while Mohoriti was arranging woods for last rituals. There was no expression on his face, when he was completing his work. Bodies tied up in white shrouds, where visible as wind was blowing up shroud. Sound of the holy mantras enchanted by the sages present for last ritual could be heard till the camps of Kauravs and Pandavas, bells ringing at nearby lord Shiva temple, making everyone understand the concept of life and death.

Duryodhana and Karna stood mourning on the side of the bodies when Yudhishthira arrived with his other brothers. They moved towards the motionless bodies, bowed them, while Duryodhana looked them up in fury and anger.

Mohoriti, took help of Duryodhana, Karna and Nakul and picked up bodies one by one and placed them on eight arranged structures of Chandan woods. A sage performed mantras and last ritual and handed over firelight in hands of Duryodhana. His face was burning in anger, turning red as firelight left its reflection on him. Looking beyond fumes, Duryodhana showed his disrespect towards Pandavas.

Soon, all eight bodies were covered with fires, ready to turn to ashes soon. Yudhishthira then turned towards Mohoriti "O, great warrior Mohoriti, we are sorry for your loss and we miss one of the great warrior in our army."

Mohoriti linked his hands and replied with pain "Don't be sorry Maharaj, lord Krishna showed me the path. He showed the Kauravs too, but it depends who understands and who not. I am performing my last duties to get rid of sins which I have done in my whole life, may I then rest in peace."

Yudhishthira, then, blessed him and moved back to his camp along with his brothers. Mohoriti, stood there whole night, till every part of the body was turned to ashes and merged with soil.

Days after days passed in the war, he continued doing the same task of collecting woods and performed Antyesti of many warriors like Abhimanyu, Brihadbala, Jayadrath, Ghatotkacha, Drupad, Virata, Drona and many more.

He didn't sleep for days and was just cutting trees and performing last rituals and watched them turn to ashes, till last fumes in pyre. He decorated the pyres, the last chariot for each warrior of Kauravs and Pandavas.

Alas, destiny had, after all, supreme powers on side of Kurus. Duryodhana had gathered eleven akshauhini divisions of troops, and the Pandavas had gathered seven. Still the Pandavas had won in the great war of Kurukshetra.

Duryodhana was incapable of being slain by fair means. Certainly there was no warrior on this earth who could compete with Duryodhana in the use of the mace. Formerly, Duryodhana cheated Yudhishthira unfairly at a game of dice. He also caused Draupadi to be dragged into the king's assembly and ordered that she be undressed in front of all. He, then, showed her his thigh and asked her to be seated there. For that immoral behavior, Bhima vowed to break those thighs. Duryodhana reaped the fruits of his sinful activities. When Pandavas exiled in the forest, he was always planning some crooked scheme to put them into difficulty and make the exile reoccur, but he failed. Remembering all these atrocities, Bhima slain him and, thus, ended the deadly hostilities between Pandavas and Kauravs.

Mohoriti saw the great Maharathi and adhirathas lying on the field of battle of Kurukshetra. He saw their wives lamenting over their bodies. He could see King Duryodhana as well as his other brothers. He saw Karna, Bhishma, Drona, Salya, Jayadratha, Bhurishravas, as well as the Pandava's Generals, all slain in battle. As he saw the wives of those great warriors lamenting over the dead bodies, he felt great compassion.

Yudhishthira then spoke to Mohoriti, "It is now necessary to complete the last funeral rites of all these dead warriors. Mohoriti, then, took the necessary steps to see that all the warriors on the battlefield, numbering six hundred and forty million, be given a proper funeral. Their bodies, as well as their weapons and chariots, were piled in great mountains with wood, which Mohoriti kept of cutting and collecting for these days and burned to finally convert to ashes.

After this, the Pandavas and the Kauravs went to the banks of the Ganga to offer oblations to the dead relatives.

Krishna then asked Pandavas to proceed back to field of Kurukshetra and let immortal Bhishma rest in peace. Agreeing to the proposal of Lord Krishna, King Yudhishthira, Bhima, Arjuna, Nakula and Sahadeva ascended their chariots and made their way in procession to Kurukshetra, where Pitamah was stretched on a bed of arrows. At that time, the great grandsire Bhishma was surrounded by the foremost of the sages and rishis. By his side was Vyasa and Narada Muni. Stretched out on a bed of arrows, that tiger among men was in fascinated concentration on the spiritual form of the Lord. He was glorifying the Lord Krishna with a cheerful and strong voice "Now I can meditate with full concentration upon my Lord, Sri Krishna, now present before me."

Thus Bhishma deeply merged himself in concentration of the Lord Sri Krishna with his mind, speech, sight and actions, and thus he became silent, and his breathing stopped. Knowing that Bhishma had entered into the unlimited eternity of the lords, all present there became silent like birds at the end of the day. Thereafter, both men and gods sounded drums in honor, and the honest royal order commenced demonstrations of honor and respects and from the sky fell showers of flowers and holy water of river Ganga, mother of Bhishma.

King Yudhishthira performed the last funeral rites and was momentarily overwhelmed with grief. Mohoriti eyes were again in tears today, watching man whom he scorns his whole life, he was in tears realizing how wrong he was. He created special bed of Chandan woods, selected from special and sacred tree for him. While placing his restless, holy body on that bed, he touched his feet and asked forgiveness for his mistakes. On hearing this Krishna kept his hand on his shoulder and showed him forgiveness by his eyes.

Today, one of the immortals got converted to mortal because of his deeds and another immortal waiting for his chance to finally become restless and rest in peace.

Finally, King Yudhishthira gave fire to his body and lead him to spiritual realm in one of the Vaikuntam planets of the Lord.

Mohoriti knew his end was near, as Krishna told him that when everyone would burn to ashes by him, he will rest in peace.

He took permission of King Yudhishthira and lotus eyes lord Krishna for his leave to Himalayas, where he will find his way to peace and heaven. With permission and blessing, he moved to north of Himalayas.

Having offered holy water unto all the deceased friends and relatives of both Kauravs and Pandavas, the Pandavas continued to live on the banks of the Ganges for the period of one month. Many great sages and rishis came to see King Yudhishthira and offer him some consolation. Thousands of Brahmanas came to comfort the King who was mourning the death of so many kingsmen and his relatives.

King Yudhishthira then forgot all lamentation and ascended the royal chariot, which was drawn by sixteen spotless white horses. To the sounds of musical instruments and enchantment by the birds and minstrels, King Yudhishthira proceeded for Hastinapur, his kingdom. Bhima took the reins, taking position as charioteer, of the beautiful chariot, and Arjuna held the royal umbrella over him. Nakula and Sahadeva fanned the King with chamara whisks that were glorified with wires of gold and silver and as white as the rays of the moon. Behind the royal chariot rode the Lord with lotus eyes, Lord Krishna. At the head of the procession rode King Dhiritarashtra, along with his wife Gandhari. They were riding on a special royal palanquin. Also in that procession were the ladies such as Kunti, Subhadra and Draupadi. Behind the procession were a large number of chariots, elephants, horsemen and foot soldiers, following their new king, on his way to throne, which was won after lot of bloodshed.

While the procession was proceeding towards the city of Shantanu, the jubilant citizens were busy decorating the city to greet their King. The citizens were joyous and washed the streets with perfumed water, and flowers and festoons hung from the beautifully decorated houses.

At the time when the Pandavas entered kingdom of Shantanu, Hastinapur, thousands of citizens came out to behold the sight. The well adorned streets and squares decorated with garland of flowers were indeed beautiful. As the King passed in his procession, the ladies threw flowers and praised him accordingly. They exclaimed all glories to the great King Yudhishthira and his brothers. There was uproar of drums, kettledrums, conch shells and trumpets. The cheers of the citizens and the showers of flowers combined to present a wondrous scene. Even Gods could not stop themselves to not blink their eyes. Having passed through the streets of the city, Yudhishthira entered the palace of Kurus, which was decorated with every conceivable ornament and garland made of white flowers. The people, belonging to the city as well as other provinces, approached the palace uttering auspicious words and mantras. The King then descended from his chariot and entered the beautifully decorated palace. He offered obeisance to the deities and worshiped them accordingly. He then came out of the palace again and saw a large number of Brahmanas desiring to bless him with benedictions. When they surrounded him, it appeared as if sun was present with its many planets, surrounding him to appraise. The King then worshiped those Brahmanas. Then loud shouts saying, "this is a blessed day" filled the sky. The King heard those sounds as well as the sounds of drums and conch shells. This was all indicative of his triumph.

Chapter-31
His last Ritual

After completing his last ritual, Mohoriti traveled barefoot to Himalayas, struggling hard to end his life. He reached the base of Mount Kailash and resided in the forest.

He wanted to rest in peace but, somehow, he was not able to end his life. He could not sleep in nights remembering the saying of lotus eye, Lord Krishna that he will only rest in peace when all the requirements from Kuru will convert into ashes by him.

It was a cold, breezy night, with snow falling like cotton till wherever one could see; it was nature covered in white, the color of snow. He looked up at the sky, which was dark, and small snow particles fell in his eyes.

Since many days, silence was piercing his heart and soul. He always looked back while walking and felt as if being followed by many souls asking him questions. With every blink of an eye, he remembered the shrieks of the soldiers whom he had slaughtered to pieces, the bodies of Kauravs and Pandavas. Every time he looked back, it was only question echoing in the deep silence, 'why are you still alive, O Mohoriti?'

He kept on walking while snow particles kept covering his long white hairs. His strong feet were getting intruded deep in snow, leaving behind his footmarks. He was still carrying that one thought in his mind, "*why I am still alive?*"

Soon, after traveling for long, he reached close to a river passing by the lower areas of Mount Kailash. It was freezing water flowing fast, making a gushing sound and breaking the deep silence of Kailash.

"Oh Lord Shiva, I am at your feet to end my life. I hope I have completed all my duties as suggested by the lord of all, your avatar, Shri Krishna. Please take me into your shadow." After saying this, he looked around to locate the best rock on which he could place his foot and push his body to enter the river area. The water flow was fast and was making a perfect sound by splashing against the rocks. On other side of the river was a forest area covered with long grasses and tall trees.

He closed his eyes and saw every memory flashing in black and white in front of him. He could see himself walking holding the finger of his father, Mohoma, in the corridors of the palace of Hastinapur and could also see Mohoma smiling and talking with King Shantanu. He could see himself as a small child, playing around and as he ran towards them, saw them disappearing into ashes. He cried loud, but no one was there to hear him and in the next instance, he could see himself as a young man, standing in the arena practicing fighting with his sword with Satyavati smiling from a distance and his nineteen brothers giggling and playing around.

He, too, smiled and started running towards them. He jumped towards them, with his body covered with mud. He looked at Satyavati with his side eye and smiled at her but to his surprise, she, along with his brothers, started moving upwards converting into ashes. He cried loudly and tried to stop them. He even ran hard towards Satyavati but couldn't do anything.

His memories were playing games with him. He could recall his life as a brief story; he could see himself fighting a duel war with Bhishma, with swords in their hands and both of them smashing each other hard in order to kill. Bhishma was gripping his neck in his under his wide shoulders, while Mohoriti was on his knees, struggling to get rid of it. However, to his surprise, he could feel Bhishma convert to ashes and move towards the sky.

In the deep silence of Mount Kailash, Mohoriti understood

that his end is near and, thus, he could sense all his near and dear ones coming back in his memories. He closed his eyes again and found himself standing on a cloud along with Duru, Maaru, Indriya,Tejaswa and all his other family members. He was carrying a baby in his hands. He was smiling at everyone with a feeling of happiness and love. Tejaswa was jumping from one cloud to another. Mohoriti was very happy to see them all smiling and he smiled at them but to his surprise suddenly they all started turning into ashes; he tried to stop them, hold them and shouted loud opening his eyes and saw himself standing in front of the river ready to drown himself.

He started moving slowly inside the cold water of river. He was silent and had no fear of death. His eyes were open wide, trying to observe the creations for one last time and trying to remember the people, whom he had missed in his lifetime.

He linked his hands and started moving to the deep side of the river. With heavy flow of water, his feet slipped in the sand at the base but he continued walking. Soon, water reached his waist; he stopped and remembered Lord Krishna and, then, continued to walk where the water was deep. As he moved further, the water level started to increase with a high current. Further, his legs started losing grip from base and he started floating. He remembered Lord Krishna with his eyes closed as his body started flowing towards the large waterfall at some distance. He knew, he will move to heaven after he falls from the fall, so he continued recalling God, till the end.

Silence increased, animals stopped making sound and even the river was not happy to drown him to death. He continued recalling God and kept his hands linked, as he reached near the waterfall; a long, rope-like thing interrupted and pulled him up. He was pulled up and kept at the bank of river under big banyan tree.

He opened his eyes to see, who saved him and he saw he was pulled up from his waist by a strong tail circled to it. As he pulled himself out, the tail started moving back. He followed the tail and saw a big monkey sitting on the branch.

He immediately understood that he is none other than Lord Hanuman but still to confirm, he linked his hands and spoke, "Jai Shree Ram!"

The monkey sitting on the branch immediately smiled and

replied, "Bolo Jai Shree Ram!"

"Oh Lord Hanuman! Why did you save me? My job on this earth is over and I have to end my life now."

Hanuman gave him a pleasant smile and replied, "Oh, I am sorry Rajan, my tail is very naughty; sometimes it's not in my control. See, it saw you drowning and saved you. You don't worry and continue; it will not interrupt you again." and he closed his eyes and went to sleep again.

Mohoriti bowed before him and moved back to the river. With his eyes closed, he again moved inside the river to drown himself, but again as he reached the end of the fall, the tail of Hanuman picked him up and settled him below the banyan tree.

"Oh Rajan, I told you it is very naughty; you must not leave it if it troubles you next time."

Mohoriti tried again and the same thing happened. He tried multiple times and every time, the tail of Hanuman saved him from drowning and picked him up to banyan tree.

He understood by now that Hanuman would not let him commit suicide. He linked his hands and bowed, "Oh, Lord Hanuman, oh lord of strength, Ram Bhakta, Dada Durbar, please let me know why I am not allowed to leave my soul now. I hope I have completed the task given to me by Lord Krishna. Please help me to end my life and come out of pain."

Hanuman turned his face and smiled, "Everyone who took birth has to die one day, but no one will die before time of his death and your time has still not arrived. Think and search what is left over. Did you complete every job of your life?"

"But I still cannot remember what is missed, my lord." asked Mohoriti

"Go back to the forest. The coming days will show you path of missed duty and, then, you can convert yourself to ashes." replied Hanuman

Mohoriti was disheartened as he was not aware about the next chance he would get, after how many days, how many years or how many decades and he did not have any option other than waiting.

"Oh lord, how will I know that my end is now near and what is the task leftover?"

"Hmm..." Lord Hanuman smiled and said, "I think your task will come to you by itself and will ask you to complete it. Remember Lord Krishna and close your eyes when you feel it's your end. He will definitely guide you for the next step."

Lord Hanuman, then, smiled and jumped from one tree to another and disappeared in lush green forest, shouting Jai Shree Ram, Jai Shree Ram.

Mohoriti moved back to the southern side of the Himalaya mountains, which were the shelters of the great sages. The place was called Saptasrota because there the waters of the sacred Ganges were divided into seven tributaries. This was done for the satisfaction of the seven great rishis known as Sapta Rishi. On the banks of the Saptasrota, Mohoriti was now engaged in beginning astanga-yoga by bathing three times daily in the morning, noon and evening by performing the Agni-hotra sacrifice with fire and by drinking only water. By doing this, he could control his mind and the senses and freed himself completely from the thoughts of familial affection. Mohoriti was supposed to amalgamate his pure identity with intelligence and, then, merge into the supreme being with the knowledge of his qualitative oneness as a living entity with the Supreme Brahman. Being free from the blocked sky, he must rise to the spiritual sky. He must suspend all the actions of the senses, even from the outside, and must be impervious to interactions of the senses, which were influenced by the modes of material nature. After renouncing all material duties, he must become immovably established, beyond all sources of hindrances on the path of finally converting himself to ashes.

In Hastinapur, eternal time imperceptibly overcomes those who are too much attached to family affairs and are always engrossed in their thought. Mahatma Vidhura who returned after thirty seven years from pilgrimage, knew all this, and, therefore, he explained to Dhiritarashtra, "My dear king, please leave Hastinapur immediately. Do not delay or think of staying back. Just see how fear has overtaken you and your soul. My Lord, your father, brother, well wishers and sons are all dead and passed away. You yourself have expended the major portion of your life. Your body is now overtaken by invalidity and you are living in the home of another king. You have been blind from your very birth, and recently you have become hard of hearing, too.

Your memory is shortened and your intelligence is already disagreed by many. You have lost your teeth, your liver is defective, and you are coughing up regularly. Oh, how powerful are the hopes of a living being to continue his life. Somehow, you are living just like a household dog and are eating the remnants of food given by Bhima. There is no need to live a degraded life and subsist on the charity of those whom you tried to kill by arson and poisoning, along with your sons. You also insulted one of their wives and took away their kingdom and wealth. Despite your unwillingness to die and your desire to live even at the cost of honor and prestige, your miserly body will certainly dwindle and deteriorate like an old cloth. He is called undisturbed who goes to an unknown, remote place and, frees from all obligations, quits his material body when it has become useless. He is certainly the best human being who awakens and understands, either by himself or from others, the falsity and misery of this material world and, thus, leaves home and depends fully on the personality of Godhead residing within his heart. Please, therefore, leave for the Himalayas immediately, without letting your relatives know sooner that time will approach which will diminish the good qualities of human."

Hearing his eye-opening words, Maharaja Dhiritarashtra, the scion of the Kuru family, firmly convinced by his Gyan, broke at once the strong network of family affection by his soul determination. Thus, he immediately left palace to set out on the path of liberation, as directed by his younger brother, Vidhura, towards Himalayas. He left in the middle of the night, when everyone was asleep. The gentle Gandhari, who was the daughter of King Subala of Gandharva, followed her husband, seeing that he was going to the Himalaya Mountains. She insisted him that she remained blind throughout her life just because she loved him, now how could he leave her all alone on mercy of those, who killed their complete family.

Next morning, King Yudhishthira, known for his dharma, performed his daily morning duties by praying, offering fire sacrifice to the sun-god, and offering obeisance, grains, cows land and gold to the Brahmans. He, then, entered the palace to pay respects to the elderly of his kingdom. However, he could not find his mother Kunti, uncle Drithrastrya and Vidhura and aunt, Gandhari.

He felt alas, "where have they gone from here?"

While they kept walking bare foot, with Vidhura leading them, showing the way and the rest, Dhiritarashtra, Gandhari and Kunti, following him. On the other hand, in Hastinapur, Yudhishthira found Sage Narad as his guest and he explained him that the end time of his uncle, aunt and mother is near and he must not leave Hastinapur in their search. He explained him the truth of life and explained every soul on this earth appears as per wish of God and will leave to him back, after completing their duties.

Drithrastrya, along with others, moved to Saptasrota, with his eyes full of tears. As they reached there, they took shelter in a hut made up of hay and bamboos. Time changes everything, King of Hastinapur, who lived most lavish life, will be staying in a hut and would sleep on bed made up of grass.

Vidhura asked them to make themselves comfortable, while he would go out to get some fruits, woods and water to drink. As he moved out, Kunti came behind him and asked, "Vidhura, I can feel something strange in your behavior since you returned; is there something you are hiding or want to inform?"

Vidhura linked his hands and said, "Maharani Kunti, you are very intelligent and why not you are mother of most eligible warriors of the earth. I will not say lie to you as you have asked; I met lord Krishna before coming back to Hastinapur and he asked me to bring Dhiritarashtra to Saptasrota. He informed me this is a place, where his soul will move to world of gods. I did what was suggested to me by Lord Krishna and I expect, whatever he has suggested would be best for my brother."

Kunti linked his hands towards him with tears in her eyes, "Everyone on this earth is completing his duties; hope your duty is over, god bless you."

Vidhura linked his hands and without looking back in her eyes and moved out to get some woods.

He walked for some distance in forest and saw Mohoriti busy cutting wood for Havan, which was supposed to be performed by sages. Vidhura, who had never met him before, took him as a woodcutter.

"O, man, can u deliver some woods in hut, which is next to lake at the end of forest?" Vidhura asked him

Mohoriti, looked at him and recognized him as he had seen

him once during game of dice. Without second thought, he agreed to the same. Presence of Vidhura was some sort of direction, which he got in his life.

Vidhura knew what he needed to do next; on agreement of Mohoriti to deliver woods, Vidhura turned back and moved on his way, the way to never return. Then, he left that place for sacred pilgrimage. He didn't turn back in affections thereafter.

Mohoriti collected bale of woods and started walking towards the hut, unknowingly, to whom he would be meeting there.

As he reached outside the hut, he called someone to collect the wood but no one replied. He waited for some time but still no one replied.

Kunti and Gandhari were out in the forest to collect something to cook and look of the area, where they will be spending rest of their life.

Mohoriti opened the small door of hut to check if someone was there inside. He kept calling but no one was answering. As he moved in, he heard a voice. "Who is there? Please tell me your name?" asked Drithrastrya, who was sitting inside the hut, with tears in his eyes.

Mohoriti recognized him and immediately it was a total blackout in front of his eyes. His body temperature started rising; he started feeling a burning sensation in his body. He closed his eyes and saw complete hut burning, along with his son, Maaru, Duru, Indriya and Tejaswa. He could see Pandavas and Kauravs burning to fumes and converting to ashes. His eyes went red and he could feel the smell of burning bodies. He was sweating blood; he could feel the souls of the dead soldiers gathering in that hut. He was feeling the piled-up dead bodies and the body parts of the slaughtered soldiers, accumulating in that hut.

He was feeling scorned of himself. It felt like he was standing in a pool of blood and drowning slowly into it. He felt like he had entered hell and between all this dark picture, filled with fire, smoke and dead bodies, he saw a white light behind Shree Krishna standing in the middle.

Krishna smiled looking at him, "What are you waiting for Mohoriti? These dead people's soul and bodies are waiting for Antyesti; please help them convert to ashes. It's time for purification."

Mohoriti kept on looking that dark picture and could not hear the sound of external world, picked up woods which he was carrying on his back and started arranging around blind King Drithrastrya. He was not in his subconscious stage, he was doing like he was working on some different orders. Drithrastrya kept on asking "Who are you?" "What are you doing?" but Mohoriti continued arranging wood around him.

Drithrastrya shouted and shook him but he was not answering anything; his state of mind was not in his control. Drithrastrya shouted, "Stop, what are you doing? Kunti, Gandhari, Vidhura, where are you all, stop this man. Something is not correct here." He tried to hit Mohoriti, with wood log that came into his hands but could not stop him.

Mohoriti, then, pulled a firelight placed at the corner of the room, like he was performing Antyesti, Drithrastrya understood with the heat of firelight and started moving out fast, hitting himself with wood poles and wood logs placed all over. He fell on ground in the run, which he was trying to do. He stood up again and tried to run but this time Mohoriti held him. He seized Drithrastrya and squeezed him with all his strength and, thus, crushed it into his arms. While he placed firelight on the woods log he placed in the hut.

Soon, the complete hut started burning along with Mohoriti and Drithrastrya in his arms. Looking at fumes and smoke, Kunti, informed Gandhari and they both ran towards the hut. Gandhari started crying loud, recalling the name of her husband and shouting to save him. But fire spread very fast, taking up some parts of forest into it.

"Oh, my sister Kunti, please let me go in hut, I cannot live without my husband and would like to go sati with him." expressed Gandhari

"I respect your feelings, Gandhari, and know your love for your husband. Please go for it; you will be remembered in history." replied Kunti

Gandhari, then, started moving towards burning hut. As she entered, her sari caught fire first and started burning, taking over her complete body.

Kunti, who was standing out till now, found no reason to stay alive. She felt like destiny wanted her to move to skies and so she decides to move inside the hut. She started moving enchanting mantras into burning hut.

Gandhari's body was in fumes now, her blind fold started burning making her eyes open, she could see her husband Drithrastrya in hold of a man, with burning bodies. She tried moving to him, with fire in her legs and burning eye lashes. She fell before reaching even near to him and died in pain of fire. Soon her body converted to ashes.

Kunti kept in enchanting mantras remembering his five sons while her body took up fire all over and converted to ashes.

Mohoriti, still alive, kept hold of Drithrastrya who was dead by now. His body was full of fire. His right hand burned and dismantled from his body. Skin burned from his body leaving behind white liquid and blood flowing from his body. His eye lids were wide open with fire on them.

Mohoriti, whose body was also burnt by now, but was still alive, observed him convert to ashes. He then spoke in his mind "O, Krishna, my lord, I did my duty to convert Kuru' s to ashes, request you please forgive me for my sins and take away my soul from his earth" and then he closed his eyes.

His body burnt completely and converted to ashes, finishing story of Mohoriti.

The sons of Mohoma were eternal associates of the Lord. He, therefore, desired the association of the Lord of lotus eye, Lord Sri Krishna. Thus, by pure consciousness due to constant devotional remembrance, he attained the spiritual sky, which was ruled over by the Supreme Narayana, Lord Krishna.

The subject of the departure of the sons of Mohoma for the goal of life, back to Godhead, was fully auspicious and is perfectly pure. Therefore, anyone who heard this narration with devotional faith certainly gained the devotional service of the Lord, the highest perfection of life.

"Revenge could be taken in life, but remember, life never takes revenge."

Aftermath

Draupadi once plucked a low-hanging fruit from a tree in her palace in Hastinapur after the war of Kurukshetra had finished. As soon as she plucked it, the tree started speaking, "This fruit has been hanging for the last 12 years. It was being reserved for the *rishi* who had been performing meditation for the last hundred years and who was going to finally open his eyes later in the day today. He was supposed to eat this fruit, his first meal in the last hundred years, but now you have contaminated it. He will go hungry now and you will earn the demerit for this deed." Draupadi called out to her husbands and sought help but no one could fix the fruit back to the tree despite using all the celestial knowledge they had. This was when the tree stated to her that if she had the power of chastity, then she could have done it herself.

Draupadi was surprised and she replied that she is completely faithful to her five husbands and she loved them the most. The tree accused her of loving someone else and hiding it in her heart. Draupadi stated that she loved Krishna but only as a friend or a brother and never as a lover. The tree stated again that there is someone else. This is when Draupadi confessed, "I love Karna. I regret refusing his proposal on the account of his caste, but he was the one who possessed all the qualities which are distributed among my five husbands. If I had married him, I would not have been gambled away, publicly humiliated and called a whore." Having confessed, Draupadi was able to attach the fruit back to the tree.

Bhima and Arjuna found it difficult to accept the fact that Draupadi loved Karna, but then they recalled seeing Yudhishthira touch Draupadi' s feet one night. On being questioned, Yudhishthira took them to a banyan tree in the middle of the night. Under the tree, there were nine lakh deities who all invoked the Goddess. Draupadi presented herself before them. Arjuna and Bhima realized that Draupadi was not an ordinary woman but a form of Goddess herself.

About the Author

Chariot of Mahabharata is written by the author of the bestselling book, "*Recollecting the end*", Himanshu. He is a telecom professional, who is also passionate about storytelling. This book is a result of his research work on the progeny of Mahabharata and presents a fresh perspective of the people living in that era at the great war of Mahabharata.